MAKING SEAFOOD SUSTAINABLE

AMERICAN BUSINESS,
POLITICS, AND SOCIETY

Series Editors:
Richard R. John, Pamela Walker Laird, and Mark H. Rose

Books in the series American Business, Politics, and Society explore
the relationships over time between governmental institutions and
the creation and performance of markets, firms, and industries
large and small. The central theme of this series is that public
policy—understood broadly to embrace not only lawmaking but
also the structuring presence of governmental institutions—has
been fundamental to the evolution of American business from the
colonial era to the present. The series aims to explore, in particular,
developments that have enduring consequences.

A complete list of books in the series
is available from the publisher.

MAKING SEAFOOD
SUSTAINABLE

AMERICAN EXPERIENCES
IN GLOBAL PERSPECTIVE

MANSEL G. BLACKFORD

UNIVERSITY OF PENNSYLVANIA PRESS

PHILADELPHIA

Published by
University of Pennsylvania Press
Philadelphia, Pennsylvania 19104-4112
www.upenn.edu/pennpress

Printed in the United States of America on acid-free paper
10 9 8 7 6 5 4 3 2 1

Library of Congress Cataloging-in-Publication Data
Blackford, Mansel G., 1944–
    Making seafood sustainable : American experiences in global perspective /
Mansel G. Blackford. — 1st ed.
        p.   cm. — (American business, politics, and society)
    Includes bibliographical references and index.
ISBN 978-0-8122-4393-2 (hardcover : alk. paper)
    1. Sustainable aquaculture—United States. 2. Fishery policy—United States.
3. Fishery management—United States. I. Title. II. Series: American business,
politics, and society.
SH136.S88B53   2012
639.8—dc23   2011032477

For my wife, Victoria, and for my family,
including my grandsons Jasper, Liam, and Charlie

CONTENTS

PREFACE

Born in 1944, I remember clearly the excitement and relief that ran through members of my family on a cold, winter evening in 1952. Then a young boy growing up in a pre-Starbucks Seattle, I was delighted that my father, who pioneered in the development of Alaska's king-crab fishery as the captain of the *Deep Sea*, a combined catcher-processing vessel, was home for several weeks. That night he received a telephone call from a friend, who was the master of another fishing boat that had also just returned to Seattle from Alaskan seas. He told my father that water had entered one of his ship's cold-storage holds, partially flooding it and encasing the halibut there in ice. My father could have one of the fish, if he would come down to the vessel and chip it out. Times were tough, and my father was happy to do so. In the early morning, helped by a friend, he brought home a frozen 150-pound halibut. Fortunately, my family had a horizontal freezer large enough to receive the fish. For weeks, along with other family members, I ate halibut prepared in every conceivable manner—boiled, baked, fried, poached, broiled, and creamed. We also ate king crabs, for which a market was just being developed, from my father's vessel, until we could hardly face another dish of them. Meat was a rare treat, indeed, in those years. However, members of my family were unusual in their dining habits.

At the time, seafood such as king crabs and halibut did not reach the tables of most Americans, especially if they lived in inland cities. In many parts of the United States, seafood consisted of canned salmon and canned tuna fish. Processing seafood by freezing was in its infancy.[1] Fresh fish was sold in grocery stores and restaurants mainly in coastal cities such as Seattle, San Francisco, Boston, and New York. Today, technological advances, such as jet airplanes and new freezing techniques, have made it possible for processors and distributors to offer people throughout the United States and in other nations a wide variety of seafood. Fresh, wild salmon from Alaska nestle next to frozen, farm-raised tilapia from China in grocers' counters across America.

My book explains how this transformation occurred. To do so, I explore the interactions among fishers, executives of seafood-processing firms, governmental officials, scientists, and environmentalists in formulating policies that created the food chains connecting boats to consumers.[2] (Food chains consist of the many links involved in moving food from farms, ranches, and the seas to consumers. Thus, seafood chains are made up of fishers, processors, wholesalers, and retailers, along with the railroads, trucks, and airplanes used to move seafood from place to place.) In establishing seafood chains, Americans set up governmental regulatory regimes over about the past forty years designed to end over-fishing in their nation's waters, most successfully in Alaskan seas. (Regulatory regimes are composed of laws and rules, along with the government agencies which implement them.) Americans were trying to ensure steady flows of raw seafood through their food chains.[3]

Though many variables, from rising water temperatures to changes in marketing methods, have shaped the modern seafood industry in the United States and abroad, evolving governmental policies have been at the heart of the alterations. My book is, at its core, about governmental regulation of business and its ramifications. State and federal government oversight was the chosen path to make fishing sustainable. My study reveals that regulatory regimes for seafood have changed dramatically over the past four decades. My work analyzes especially how, during the past generation, new regulations and their implementation have created sustainable fishing for many types of seafood in the Northeast Pacific, a marked contrast to over-fishing, which has continued to devastate many of the world's commercial fisheries, including some in American waters, such as the New England cod fishery.

Congressional legislation has been crucial to this process. Passed in 1976, the Fishery Conservation and Management Act sought to protect American fishers from the onslaughts of their foreign counterparts by excluding foreigners from fishing within 200 miles of the American shores.[4] That same legislation made possible sustainable fishing by requiring that fishers harvest no more fish than could be replaced by natural reproduction each year. Leading seafood types of the Northeast Pacific—including salmon, king crab, and some bottom fish (such as Pacific cod, halibut, and pollock)—were at various times over-fished. However, new types of governmental regulation eventually limited the overall catches of many species and pulled them back from the brink of commercial extinction. My volume looks at how business leaders and government policy makers crafted and implemented this legislation.

Working on the topic of over-fishing has continued and expanded my long-term interest in the history of American politics and the nation's political economy. As I came of age in Seattle during the 1950s and early 1960s, I visited Alaska on several occasions. No doubt, my father's participation in king crabbing helped spur my interest in the history of fisheries. I attended college and graduate school on the Pacific Coast, in Seattle and Northern California during the 1960s and early 1970s. In the 1980s, I spent two years living with my family in southern Japan, where I taught in Fukuoka and Hiroshima as a Fulbright Lecturer. Travelling throughout Japan, I had many opportunities to talk with local fishers and was able to go out on the boats of several of them. Flying to and from Japan, I stopped over in the Hawaiian Islands. During the 1990s, moreover, I taught on Maui on several occasions for the University of Hawai`i, experiences that brought me into close contact with a broad range of Pacific Islanders, including fishers.

My professional work has allowed me to combine interests in business and environmental history, together with abiding concerns for the histories of the American West and the Pacific. Many of my books have explored intersections in these fields, as does this one. I have long been concerned in my research and teaching about connections among business changes, alterations in physical and social environments, and the development of government policy. My works have emphasized the complexity of political decision making and have stressed that most decisions have been compromises resulting from the inputs of numerous groups of stakeholders, ranging from politicians to business people to environmentalists and to indigenous peoples.[5] My study about fishing shows as well the complexities involved in reaching policy decisions, especially about natural resources. The nuances were many, varying by region, fish stock, and precise regulatory regime.[6] However, my research on the topic suggests that workable solutions to difficult problems were possible in open political systems in which members of different groups had at least some trust in each other and in which they shared basic assumptions about the parameters of feasible actions.

The shift in regulatory regimes leading to sustainability changed in important ways the very nature of fishing, thus altering the lives of thousands of fishers and people in their communities. Nor did changes stop at the shoreline. I analyze how companies serving the American seafood market as processors, wholesalers, and retailers underwent major changes in recent decades as they grappled with challenges stemming from over-fishing. The executives of leading American processors and wholesalers—such as the Red Chamber Company, headquartered in Los Angeles, Trident Seafoods, based in Seattle, and the Pacific Seafood Group, located in Portland, Oregon—altered their strategies and their corporate structures as a result of scarcities of some types of seafood. Vertical integration backward to control their companies' sources of their raw materials, their fish and crabs, was a common response. Similarly, the officers of large retailers—such as Wal-Mart, Kroger, and Target—reacted to over-fishing in a variety of ways, most importantly by encouraging fishers to harvest fish in sustainable manners. By handling only seafood caught in sustainable ways, retailers forced fishers to modify their fishing methods.

Most accounts of recent fishing and over-fishing issues have focused on negative developments, especially the collapse of many commercially harvested wild-fish stocks around the world. There have been many such tales to tell. Yet, as I illustrate, there have also been success stories. In 2008, the Marine Stewardship Council—a British organization, the globe's premier marine environmental organization—certified a scant two dozen fisheries around the world as being managed in sustainable ways. Impressively, this short list included most Alaskan salmon and bottom fish. The only other American fishery to achieve such status then was Oregon pink shrimp. In 2009, several other types of seafood joined the list, including Atlantic red crabs and West Coast Pacific whiting (hake), a type of bottom fish.

What can be learned from these successful experiences? Are they applicable elsewhere? Have there been downsides? How might problems be avoided? Beyond fishery matters, what do developments in America's seafood industry reveal about the intersections between environmental and business changes, especially with regard to the management and use of renewable resources? By way of a brief response to these questions, I would suggest that the attainment of sustainable fishing in the Northeast Pacific does have general lessons applicable elsewhere. Most obviously, it is extremely difficult, even when most parties are in rough agreement, to make fishing sustainable. Yet, sustainable fishing can be made to work under the kinds of circumstances spelled out in my study. The economic and social costs to achieve sustainable fishing, however, are significant, for not all fishers and processors can be allowed to operate at previous high levels. Some have to be excluded. Still, there were (and are) ways to mitigate the social and economic costs, as this study demonstrates.

INTRODUCTION

In 1981, Alaska's king crab catch collapsed, plummeting by about 80 percent. The harvest in that year came to 28 million pounds, much less than the 130 million pounds in 1980. Spike Walker, a leading fisher, rightly wrote about crabbing in 1981 as "scratchy (poor) fishing."[1] A bittersweet joke soon made the rounds in bars in Kodiak, Alaska: as a result of the crash in catches, Seattle banks owned so many repossessed crab boats that their officers would offer a free vessel to anyone opening a new account.[2] Alaska's king crab slump mirrored the collapse of the harvests of many types of wild seafood around the globe. In spring 2007, the introduction to three *National Geographic* essays about global fishing warned, "The oceans are in deep blue trouble. From the northernmost reaches of the Greenland Sea to the swirl of the Antarctic Circle, we are gutting our seas of fish. Since 1900, many species may have declined by nearly 90 percent, and it's getting worse. Nets scour reefs. Supertrawlers vacuum up shrimp. Nations flout laws."[3]

At the time, journalists may have overstated the globe's overfishing crisis, but not by much. There were legitimate grounds for concern. After increasing more than fourfold between 1950 and 1994, the global wild-fish catch reached a plateau and stagnated over the next decade and a half, despite an intensification of fishing efforts. As numerous scientific reports showed, many individual fish stocks around the world collapsed, creating a genuine global crisis. The United Nations Food and Agriculture Organization (UNFAO) concluded in a detailed report issued in 2008 that "the maximum wild capture potential from the world's oceans has probably been reached."[4] The loss of wild fish harvests was a serious problem for many people. By 1992, seafood supplied people worldwide with 14.9 percent of their animal protein. That proportion rose to 16 percent in 1996, but declined to 15.5 percent in 2003.[5] Studying changes in fishing has, then, worldwide significance for diets and lifestyles.

This volume investigates the ramifications of over-fishing for the United

Figure 1. A large king crab in the 1950s. Author's collection.

States seafood industry by analyzing how fishers, seafood processors-distributors, retailers, government officials, and others dealt with the looming crisis. I examine the ways they made changes in their business strategies and ok political steps to alleviate their difficulties, in the process making most fishing in Alaskan waters sustainable, the problems with king crabs in

1981 notwithstanding. To that end, and where possible, I look at people taking concrete actions. Individual fishers such as the king crabbers Andy and
Johnathan Hillstrand, "highliners" (high producers who caught lots of crabs)
operating in the Bering Sea, changed fishing methods on their boat *Time
Bandit*. Likewise, Chuck Bundrant, who headed Trident Seafoods, one of
the largest seafood processors in the United States, modified his firm's strategies and operations. Government officials serving on councils setting fishing
rules altered their approaches to regulation. My work thus illuminates important connections among environmental, political, and business changes.[6]
I show that public policies from the 1970s, resulting from meetings of those
in the fishing industry with government officials (and in the early 2000s with
environmentalists), largely determined how fish catches were limited and
allocated.

This book addresses two closely intertwined topics: how interactions between regulatory regimes and fishing methods affected supplies of seafood for
Americans and how, in turn, the availability of those supplies influenced the
nature of companies and the food chains they control. The shift from open-
access fishing with few limits on harvests to limited-entry fishing, in which
catches were restricted in the interest of making them sustainable, fundamentally altered harvesting and processing seafood and, more generally, modified
food chains for fish and crabs. The Fishery Conservation and Management
Act (FCMA), passed by Congress in 1976, largely ushered in those changes.
Many other issues have been related to these topics, including alterations in
the work and lives of fishers, and I look at them as well. For instance, I note
that fishing in Alaskan waters became safer once limited-entry regimes were
established. No one issue or theme has completely dominated fishing and the
development of seafood chains in all time periods; but government policies,
especially the switch to limited-entry fishing, were critical in the multifaceted
evolution of fishing as a form of modern capitalism.

*   *   *

This book addresses legal, economic, political, environmental, and social issues surrounding fishing and over-fishing, particularly as they unfolded in
recent decades in Pacific Northwestern and Alaskan waters. The year 1976
is a crucial date for my study, for it was then that Congress passed landmark
legislation, the Fishery Conservation and Management Act, banning most
foreign fishing within 200 miles of American shores. Building on United

Nations decisions and the earlier individual actions of nations, including the
United States, the FCMA made possible the conservation of fish stocks within
American waters. The year 2006 marks three decades of fishery conservation
efforts and is a logical point at which to conclude this study. It is legitimate
now to ask what has been accomplished, and at what costs. The seven chapters
examine three major, intertwined themes: the primacy of government regulations in establishing and altering fishing methods; the lived experiences of
fishers and others in seafood industries, especially as affected by government
regulations; and the changing nature of food chains for seafood, particularly
fish and crabs destined for American markets.

Part I outlines how the development of "industrial" fishing, with few limits on harvests, led to over-fishing; how over-fishing was "discovered" by scientists and others; and national and international efforts to regulate fishing in
attempts to make it sustainable. As early as 1945, President Harry Truman by
presidential proclamation put the United States in the forefront of efforts by
coastal states to control their continental shelves and the waters above them.
United Nations actions in the 1950s and 1960s set the stage for far-reaching
national legislation such as the FCMA, which was of prime importance for
American fishers. In this section, I also extend the story of U.S. regulation of
fishing by looking at elusive attempts to achieve sustainable fishing for cod
and blue-fin tuna in the Northwest Atlantic, shrimp in the Gulf of Mexico,
and salmon in California's waters.

Part II investigates efforts to regulate fishing for salmon, crabs, and bottom fish in Pacific Northwestern and Alaskan waters, and what these meant
for individuals and communities. Following extensive over-fishing in earlier
decades, fishers, executives of seafood-processing firms, and government officials created and implemented new regulatory regimes based on limited-
entry fishing. Between the mid-1970s and early 2000s, sustainable fishing
became the norm.

Fishers lived and labored in rapidly changing economic and environmental situations, indeed. Once able to pursue fish and crabs with few restrictions
on their actions, they found their labors circumscribed by government regulations limiting and allocating seafood catches. Steve Fink, a salmon fisher,
Derek Lawson, who took halibut, Cathy McCarthy and her daughter Peggy
Kohler, who engaged in crabbing, and William McCloskey, Jr., who pursued
salmon, crabs, and bottom fish—all of whom I interviewed in conducting
research for my study—were among the many fishers who found their work
and lives affected by regulatory changes. Most supported the growing scope

of regulations as necessary for the commercial survival of their fisheries, but many regretted what they thought was a loss of independence and individual freedom. Their exciting, adrenaline-driven "Wild West" vanished, more than one fisher lamented, as they found themselves banding together to take collective action to try to end over-fishing. Alaska's Bering Sea, a nostalgic king crabber wrote with regret, had been his "Lonesome Dove." Cherished ways of life, followed for decades past, changed, as fishers adhered to more and more detailed rules designating how they could act at sea.[7]

Part III examines how seafood reaches American consumers. As shoppers walk past seafood departments in markets few recognize connections between the fish under glass and the complex rules that govern the availability of seafood for purchase. However, scarcities of seafood and governmental regulations designed to end those scarcities affect processing and retailing seafood no less than harvesting it. I analyze the changes in the business of seafood processing for the American market. In recent years, large, publicly held, diversified processors such as ConAgra have left seafood processing and wholesaling—replaced by smaller, privately held family firms focused only on seafood. (In privately held firms, common stock is not available for sale to the general public; in publicly held firms, it is.) The officers of the big corporate firms lacked the detailed knowledge about seafood and the connections to sources of raw fish and crabs needed to succeed in the competitive business environment of seafood scarcity. Those in somewhat smaller family firms, such as Chuck Bundrant of Trident Seafoods, have had intimate knowledge of and control over seafood resources in Alaska and elsewhere.

I consider how fishery companies addressed processing, hygienic safety, and quality issues and how retailers in grocery stores and restaurants modified their seafood offerings and tried to mitigate the over-fishing crisis. Between 1994 and 2008, for example, many large retailers, such as Wal-Mart, pledged to sell only fish caught in a sustainable manner and became strong proponents of limited-entry fishing globally.

Many types of sources—government reports, first-hand accounts by fishers, newspaper stories, public testimony at governmental hearings, and oral-history interviews—undergird my narrative. I also look to fictional accounts of modern-day fishing, many written by fishers. When used with care, fictional accounts offer much about the details of fishing, insights into the characters of fishers and their understanding of the public policies and business relationships that governed their lives.

*   *   *

During the past two decades, scholars and popular writers have authored books and articles about the over-use of global oceanic resources, including many that look at over-fishing. The present volume contributes to that literature by advancing our knowledge of how American government leaders and fishers shaped regulations that made fishing sustainable in Alaskan waters, helping protect the marine environment there. At the same time, it highlights the trade-offs lawmakers approved to bring their regulatory regime into existence. For one thing, many fishers lost their jobs. Women and Alaskan Natives often found themselves excluded from commercial fishing. For another, lawmakers who regularly celebrated the primacy of markets found themselves replacing or supplementing markets with regulations. They established quotas for the numbers of fish that could be caught and sometimes set prices as well. Again, the changes varied in timing by fish stock and region, but, in general, increased government regulations starting in the 1970s followed over-fishing in earlier decades. New limited-entry fishing regimes were established, first for salmon, then for bottom fish, and finally for king crabs.

Historians and other scholars have recently made substantial contributions to our understanding of over-fishing.[8] Nonetheless, additional carefully argued historical accounts would be valuable at this point in time, for, as Poul Holm, Tim D. Smith, and David J. Starkey wrote, "Studies of fisheries have often been geared to the fisheries management needs of the day, and these often have narrow regional perspectives . . . Fisheries historians have so far made little impression. Theirs is an undeveloped field of enquiry."[9] While overstatements, these assertions are worthy of consideration.

There have been marked similarities in the regulation of fish stocks and some other renewable natural resources, particularly those governed by common-pool resource management regimes. Such resources are those held or worked in common, not by individual owners. They include some types of farm and grazing lands, many wild, oceanic fishery stocks, oil and water in underground basins with more than one owner. Multiple owners need to find ways to manage their resources in common, to have resources to exploit in the future. Doing so is difficult; nonetheless, it was done in many Alaskan fisheries, allowing common-pool resources to be utilized efficiently on a sustainable basis.[10]

Popular writers, scholars, and participants have produced a vast literature on the pros and cons of economic globalization for people around the world.[11] Critics have decried the outsourcing of air and water pollution as companies in advanced industrial nations built factories in less-developed nations. Japanese companies shifted industrial production to Southeast Asian nations like Cambodia, as did Silicon Valley's high-tech firms. Many multinational firms exploited workers in host nations, paying them less than they paid laborers in their home countries. Defenders of globalization have agreed that outsourcing pollution occurred and was an unfortunate way of running businesses. However, they have seen it as simply a temporary stage in doing business and have asserted that over time multinational companies usually introduced higher environmental standards to their host countries. They point out, too, that multinationals generally paid higher wages than the norm in host nations, raising living standards and economic expectations for workers. Above all, many defenders have stressed that multinationals very often transferred technologies and knowledge to host nations, spurring needed economic development.

A look at modern-day fishing contributes to an understanding of globalization. Commercial fishing in recent decades has involved seafood chains crossing national boundaries. In 2008, fully 37 percent of all seafood (by value) was traded across national boundaries. People in both the nations whose waters were sources of seafood and the consuming countries were affected, in both positive and negative ways. Physical, social, and cultural environments around the world were altered by global seafood chains. American companies in sourcing some of their crab meat from Southeast Asia introduced new technologies and scientific concepts to citizens in nations of that region. But foreign fishing fleets destroyed fish stocks off the coasts of some African nations, putting many local fishers out of work. By 2006, the net result of these modern food chains was still difficult to assess. Global fishing made animal protein available to people around the globe, but the social and economic costs were substantial.[12]

Finally, my volume helps broaden the historical study of political economy. Until very recently, most historians of business and politics have been slow to examine environmental issues. Focusing on the firm and its management, business historians have not usually probed deeply the externalities that have helped frame business actions.[13] Fisheries illuminate relatively understudied facets of capitalism, and the nature of relationships among communities, business groups, and governments worldwide. In addition, examining fisheries helps historians look with fresh eyes at topics with which they are already engaged: interplays between the development of global markets and the international regulation of business; connections between developments in science, technology, and industrialization; the commodification of food products; and intersections between capitalism and property rights. The story of fishing and over-fishing, and efforts to end over-fishing, is then a complex one, with relationships between the state and fishers at its center. The tale helps illuminate numerous aspects of the workings of the American and global political economies.

PART I

Government Regulation

1

Global Over-Fishing and New Regulatory Regimes

Writing in 1999, boat captain Linda Greenlaw claimed, "Fishermen using only hooks and harpoons could never wipe out any species of fish that reproduce by spawning, such as swordfish. And in seventeen years of swordfishing I have seen no evidence of depletion." Continuing, she asserted, "U.S. fishermen are not pirates. We are among the most regulated fishermen in the world, and penalties for non-compliance are stiff. Fishermen of my generation are conservation-minded. We are also frustrated that some of the public is being brainwashed with misinformation by a group of do-gooders." Greenlaw concluded, "If a problem with overfishing does develop, it is not the American fishermen who should be punished, but perhaps fishermen from countries that currently have no regulations in place. And continually exceed their allowable catch quotas. . . . Eat U.S. caught swordfish! It's legal!"[1] Greenlaw had a point, for not all fish species were over-fished.

And yet the numbers indicated a crisis. Between 1950 and 1960, the world's wild fish and shellfish catch nearly doubled, from 19 to 35 million metric tons (mmt; 1 metric ton = 1,000 kilograms or 2,204 pounds). Only a decade later, it almost doubled again, to 64 mmt, and rose to 86 mmt in 1990 and 94 mmt in 1995. There the catch stagnated, remaining 94 mmt in 2005.

Scientific findings lent credence to the numbers. In 1995, Carl Safina, founder of the National Audubon Society's Living Oceans Program, was one of the first to draw public attention to the issue, concluding that the worldwide extraction of wild fish had been in decline since the late 1980s due to "an explosion of fishing technologies during the 1950s and 1960s" combined with inappropriate government policies, such as subsidies, which kept fishers at sea long after fishing without subsidies would have been unprofitable.[2] Other reports advanced arguments similar to Safina's, attributing drops in

fish stocks to intensified and essentially unregulated fishing efforts.[3] In fall
2006, twelve Canadian, American, and European scientists led by Boris
Worm, a biologist at Dalhousie University in Halifax, Nova Scotia, published
a far-reaching article in *Science*. Like Safina a decade earlier, Worm and his
co-authors noted dramatic population and species losses in marine ecosystems and argued that "marine biodiversity loss is increasingly impairing the
ocean's capacity to provide food, maintain water quality, and recover from
perturbations." Benefiting from more oceanic research than had earlier existed, the authors brought increased specificity to their work. By 2003, they
contended, 29 percent of the world's fisheries were in a state of collapse. "This
trend," the scientists warned, "is of serious concern because it projects the
global collapse of all taxa currently fished by the mid-21st century."[4]

Though other marine biologists hotly contested Worm's report, even his
critics, such as Michael Wilberg and Thomas Miller at the University of Maryland's Chesapeake Biological Laboratory, agreed that over-fishing was a problem. Wilberg and Miller explained, "We believe people should be concerned
about conserving the world's marine resources, and we are not arguing that
some fisheries have not or are not collapsing."[5] Moreover, United Nations reports supported Worm's findings. A 2008 UNFAO report on global fisheries
concluded that the maximum harvest of wild fish had probably been reached
and that efforts to control over-fishing had been "unsuccessful in many parts
of the world."[6] Other reports reached the same basic conclusions. Officers for
Oceana, a global marine environmental body, observed in 2008 that more
than 80 percent of the world's ocean fisheries could not withstand increased
fishing pressure and only 17 percent of them were capable of any growth in
catches. "The world's fishing fleets can no longer expect to find new sources
of fish," claimed Courtney Sakai, a senior campaign director at Oceana. "If
the countries of the world want healthy and abundant fishery resources, they
must improve management and decrease the political and economic pressures that lead to overfishing."[7]

By the end of the twentieth century, then, over-fishing had become a complex global issue in which business interests, environmental concerns, and
policy proposals clashed. Before the 1970s, most fisheries were open-access.
Except for very narrow coastal strips of water, fishers such as Greenlaw and
her counterparts from every nation had access to fishing grounds around
the world. Beginning in the mid-1970s, however, governments increasingly
closed fisheries. In the United States and elsewhere, policymakers denied foreigners the right to fish within 200 miles of the nation's shores. Closing their

fisheries to outsiders in turn allowed coastal nations such as Japan and the United States to institute new regulations. Leaders of these nations sometimes developed conservation measures to make fishing in their waters sustainable. American policymakers hoped to fortify their nation's fishers and also to avoid a "tragedy of the commons," in which oceanic resources were over-used. Moving to sustainable fishing was neither easy nor automatic, and not all coastal nations took that step. As American experiences illustrate, doing so required agreement among fishers, fish-processors, government officials, and others, such as scientists and environmentalists, that over-fishing was in fact a major problem. It also called for agreement on how best to address the problem. Sometimes consensus could be reached, but not always.

The Industrialization of Fishing and the Problem of Over-Fishing

Over the course of the twentieth century, innovations in fishing and improvements in transportation helped fishers greatly boost their catches and sales of seafood. Industrial fishing began as early as the 1870s and 1880s, when fishers started to use steam-powered vessels in British and European waters, such as the North Sea. The move from sailing vessels to steam-powered trawlers increased fishing productivity at least fourfold. At about the same time, railroads connected fishing ports to interior towns, broadening markets for fish. Having depleted inshore and near-shore fishing grounds, by the 1920s and 1930s steam trawlers fished far from their home ports, dominating Canadian and American cod fisheries by these decades. Fast-freezing techniques, introduced to some fisheries in the 1920s and 1930s, further extended operations.[8]

During the decades after World War II, fishers undertook a tremendous expansion and intensification of global fishing. Looking specifically at the North Pacific, of which Pacific Northwestern and Alaskan waters are parts, a group of five fishery experts concluded in 1982, "Two main periods may be distinguished in the development of fisheries, which roughly correspond to the time before and after World War II." In the prewar years, fishers moved from "artisanal fisheries to organized commercial exploitation, including some distant-water operations, especially by Japan." The postwar period saw a "virtual explosion" in fishery development resulting from a "revolution" in the expansion of distant-water fisheries, technological improvements in fishing equipment, and increasing scale of operations."[9]

What happened in the North Pacific mirrored what was occurring globally. Many scientists and policy makers hoped that fish would provide people around the world with much-needed animal protein at reasonable costs. In the 1950s and 1960s, some scientists estimated that oceans and seas could sustain an annual seafood catch of 200–350 mmt, more than twice the highest level ever achieved.[10] Popular movies such as the 1954 production of Jules Verne's *20,000 Leagues Beneath the Sea* featured divers harvesting seemingly inexhaustible riches from the ocean. Americans in particular transferred ideas they had earlier harbored about the bounty of their nation's western frontiers to oceans and seas. Gary Kroll observed, "The ocean in the twentieth-century American imagination took on many of the characteristics that were typically associated with frontier territories: a trove of inexhaustible resources, an area to be conserved for industrial capitalism, a fragile ecosystem requiring stewardship and protection from 'civilizing' forces, a geography for sport, a space for recreation, and a seascape of imagination."[11] Clearly, the ocean meant different things to different people, but ideas of material abundance were dominant well after World War II. The tremendous optimism about oceanic resources was similar to that expressed around the same time about "clean" nuclear power and the bounties of resources in outer space. Americans embraced science and technology with open arms, giving little thought to possible downsides.

Responding to rising demand, the world's fishing vessels increased greatly in number, size, and effectiveness. Between 1970 and 1995, the number of commercial fishing vessels increased from 451,000 to 885,000, and their aggregate size from 11.6 million to 23 million gross registered tons. (A gross registered ton is a measure of storage space equal to one hundred cubic feet.) According to a comprehensive UN report, by 2004 there were probably a total of about 4 million fishing boats and ships, including those engaged in subsistence fishing. About 1.3 million were decked vessels, but 2.7 million were small open boats, two-thirds of them powered only by oars and sails.[12]

While their exact numbers are elusive, an increasing proportion of commercial fishing vessels were fast diesel and gasoline powered boats, which were much more efficient than earlier ones in catching fish. Many of the vessels used a broad array of sophisticated technological devices first developed for World War II naval ships, such as radar, sonar, and loran (a navigational aid) to locate fish. Global Positioning Systems came later. Describing getting her swordfishing ship *Hannah Borden* underway in the mid-1990s, captain Linda Greenlaw wrote, "I switched the two radars into their 'standby' position, turned on the GPS, the video plotter, two lorans, two single-side-band

[SSB] radios, and flipped the VHF radio to channel sixteen. Most of the other electronics would not be needed until later, so I left them tuned 'off' and returned to deck."[13]

Ships caught fish in a variety of ways. They took fish with long lines up to sixty-two miles in length having tens of thousands of hooks. They dragged huge trawl nets across the ocean floor, in effect "clear-cutting" the ocean bottom. Sometimes two vessels dragged one large net between them. By the 1990s, a single trawl net might be large enough to hold a fleet of twelve Boeing 747 jumbo jets. During the 1970s, trawlers dragged nets 1,000 feet below the ocean's surface; by the late 1990s the nets reached depths of 2,000 feet. Fishers also caught fish in gigantic gillnets and purse-seine nets made of light, strong synthetic fibers. Gillnets are stationary, hanging down from the surface, catching fish that swim into them by their gills. Purse-seine nets surround schools of fish and then are closed at the bottom (like a purse) and emptied on board fishing boats. Hydraulic power blocks, which came into use in the 1950s, assisted in pulling some nets on board the vessels. No longer did all the work in lifting nets have to be done by hand.[14] As a result of these innovations, one respected marine biologist wrote in 2007, "The twentieth century heralded an escalation in fishing intensity that is unprecedented in the history of the oceans, and modern fishing technologies leave fish no place to hide."[15]

World demand for animal protein drove the increase in fishing, with seafood becoming increasingly important as a source for that protein. Both plant and animal proteins have amino acids needed by people to produce body proteins, but animal proteins work better at this task than do plant proteins, which do not have the ideal ratio of the amino acids. Already in the mid-1960s, fish provided Canadians, Americans, Soviets, and Chinese with about 4 percent of their protein, South Koreans with 7 percent, and Japanese with 20 percent. By 1992, seafood supplied people worldwide with 14.9 percent of their animal protein. From 1909 to 1969, Americans ate about 11 pounds of seafood each year. They increased their per capita consumption of seafood considerably over the next three decades, while still trailing people in some other nations. In the early 2000s, Americans consumed 17 pounds of seafood per person annually, Britons 44 pounds, Canadians 52 pounds, Spaniards 97 pounds, and Japanese 128 pounds. By 2007, American per capita consumption had fallen slightly, but aggregate consumption was a hefty 4.9 billion pounds.[16] Over the second half of the twentieth century, the global per capita consumption of fish (including farmed fish) rose steadily, from 22 pounds in the 1960s, to 28 pounds in the 1980s, 32 pounds in the 1990s, and 36 pounds in 2005.[17]

Aquaculture—that is, fish farming—seemed to offer a way out of the over-fishing of wild fish. Indeed, growing varieties of fish were raised in large pens in the oceans. In 2000, fish-processing companies harvested nearly 30 million metric tons (mmt) of seafood from fish farms, including such species as prawn, carp, and salmon. By 2004, 45 mmt of seafood came from aquaculture operations, compared to 95 mmt of fish and shellfish caught in the wild. China accounted for about 70 percent of the global aquaculture output in that year. In 2006, farm-raised fish composed 47 percent of the world's supply of fish. However, aquaculture presented its own problems, especially for carnivorous species such as salmon, possibly limiting its future expansion. Herbivorous fish such as catfish and tilapia were farmed most successfully with less environmental damage. Aquaculture can lead to water pollution, spread diseases and parasites among fish, cause over-fishing of small wild fish needed to feed to captive fish, and spread genetic defects from farmed fish to wild fish through inadvertent fish escapes from pens and subsequent interbreeding of captive with wild fish. Responding to commercial fishers, as well as to perceived problems with aquaculture, in 1990 Alaskan legislators outlawed finfish farming (such as raising salmon).[18]

Negative views of fish farming reached into mass fiction with the publication by Clyde Cussler (with Paul Kemprecos) of the novel *White Death* in 2003. In this adventure-thriller, Cussler speculates about the possibility of genetically altered, farm-raised salmon escaping into the wild. "What would happen if these Frankenfish had some property that made them unfit for human consumption?" Cussler asks. "What if an unforeseen mutant strain resulted?" "What if the superfish offspring couldn't survive in the wild?" He answers, "You'd have neither the natural species nor the mutants," and "the ocean system would be thrown out of whack." The results would be disastrous: "Fishermen, processing people, and distributors would be idled around the world. This would disrupt whole societies that depend on fish protein for nourishment."[19] Fortunately, in the final pages of this piece of fiction Cussler's protagonist averts this dire possibility.

By the early 2000s, the commercial seafood industry was a significant economic force around the world. In 2006, fishing and aquaculture employed directly over 43 million people globally, with about 9 million of those engaged in aquaculture. Many were women. According to a far-reaching UNFAO report, "Millions of women in around the world, especially in developing countries, work in the fisheries sector." Women "participate as entrepreneurs and by providing labour before, during, and after the catch in both artisanal and commercial fisheries." Many of the industry went beyond the harvesting of fish. The UN report estimated that for every fishing job there were at least four positions in "secondary activities," such as cleaning and processing, for a total of more than 170 million jobs.[20]

In the early twenty-first century, then, the seafood industry was a thoroughly industrialized, globalized operation. About three-quarters of all seafood products were destined for direct human consumption. Most of the rest went into the making fish meal and fish oil. Of the seafood eaten by humans, 49 percent went to market fresh, but 51 percent was processed. About half of the processed seafood was frozen, with much of the remainder canned. A whopping 37 percent of this total production entered international trade.

Regulatory Efforts, from Ad Hoc to International

Before the 1950s, a mishmash of local and regional regulations governed fishing—to the extent that there was any regulation at all. The "management of the world ocean," several fishery experts have observed, was "characterized by a haphazard quilt of global, regional, bilateral, and national arrangements differentiated by activity and ocean, but without effective mechanisms for achieving coordination across either activities or ocean."[21] Agreements tended to be local in scope, limited to a single species of fish, and hard to enforce. In fact, most ocean fisheries were open access.[22] There existed few comprehensive arrangements, resulting in a system that failed to protect most fish species from over-fishing.

The Overfishing Convention, ratified by member nations in 1946 to govern fishing in the North Sea and coastal waters around Great Britain, was the international agreement that went farthest at the time to regulate the industry.[23] Dating back to a convention of representatives from European nations fronting on the North Sea held in London in 1937, the agreement sought to avoid the capture of young fish such as cod in trawl nets by requiring that the nets have wide enough meshes for juvenile fish to escape. The 1946 Convention led to the establishment of two important international commissions to regulate fishing in the Atlantic: the International Commission for Northwest Atlantic Fisheries, formed in 1949, of which the United States was a member, and the North East Atlantic Fisheries Commission, established in 1954. Both commissions sought to achieve maximum sustainable yields in the fisheries they governed. The agreement and resulting commissions did not, however, place any overall limits on fishing and so allowed over-fishing to continue.[24]

A similarly ad hoc regulatory situation prevailed in the Northeast Pacific. Only two bilateral agreements regulated fishing there before World War II. The International Pacific Halibut Commission, formed as a result of negotiations between representatives for the United States and Canada dating to 1925, regulated that fishery in the interests of achieving maximum sustainable yields. The International Pacific Salmon Fishery Commission, set up in 1930 by the United States and Canada, sought to preserve salmon runs in British Columbia's Fraser River system. Other agreements followed World War II. Starting in 1952, a multilateral agreement among the United States, Japan, and Canada limited high seas salmon fishing by the Japanese. Bilateral agreements between the United States and Japan in 1964 and between the United States and the Soviet Union a year later placed limits on Japanese and Soviet king-crab catches in the Bering Sea. Even so, in 1973 a leading fishery expert estimated that "in spite of the various specific agreements for fisheries in the North Pacific, well over 90% of the total catch comes from fisheries currently not subject to international regulation."[25] In that year, Japanese and Soviet ships took 4.6 billion and 2.2 billion pounds of seafood respectively from waters within 200 miles of United States coasts, while American fishers landed only 1.4 billion pounds.[26]

Agreements of the types reached in the North Atlantic and the Northeast Pacific set the stage for much more comprehensive regulatory efforts after the Second World War, as conflicts among nations over fishing rights mounted.[27] Open access fishing gave way to closed fishing, as coastal nations such as the United States reserved fishing grounds for their citizens. Under new closed-access fishing regimes, coastal nations could establish sustainable fishing, without fear that foreign fishers would enter their waters and subvert their conservation efforts. Moving from open to closed seas occurred in several steps.

American actions led the way. In 1945, President Harry Truman declared American ownership of its continental shelves, but not ownership of the fish in waters above them. Truman failed, however, to define the extent of the shelves; he was more concerned about asserting American control over oil found under the nation's continental shelves, as in the Gulf of Mexico, than with fishing. In 1964, Congress passed legislation declaring United States ownership of oil, minerals, and sedentary creatures (such as lobsters and crabs) on and under the nation's continental shelves to a depth of 200 meters.

Congress took this action over vehement protests from Japan, whose fishers had been harvesting crabs from shallow Alaskan off-shore waters for decades. Like many nations, the United States also extended its claims to near-shore waters and fish in them from three to twelve miles out to sea, doing so in 1966. At about the same time, many other countries joined the United States in claiming ownership of their continental shelves to a depth of 200 meters, but *not* ownership of fish in waters above them. A few nations—Argentina, Panama, Mexico, Peru, and Chile—went farther by asserting exclusive rights to their continental shelves *and* fish in their waters to a distance of 200 miles from shore.[28]

Despite Truman's actions, the U.S. extension of off-shore authority beyond the traditional three-mile (and from 1966, twelve-mile) limit has been accurately characterized as "long" and "tortuous."[29] In these Cold War years, American policy makers were often more concerned about maintaining free navigation for navy ships and commercial vessels in waters near other countries' coasts than with protecting American fisheries. Geopolitical issues trumped fishery matters in the minds of many in the State Department, for example. They were reluctant to extend American control over areas far from shore, lest other nations do the same, thus possibly excluding American ships from their waters. Then too, American fishers were divided. While some sought government protection from foreign fishers, not all did. United States' tuna fishers roamed seas far from American shores and did not want their access to foreign off-shore fisheries cut off, which they feared might occur if the United States excluded foreign fishers from its waters, prompting retaliation by other coastal nations.

Intersecting with unilateral national efforts were steps taken by the United Nations. In 1958 and 1960, the UN held two Law of the Sea Conferences to deal with oceanic matters, including fishing rights. Perhaps most important, the meetings recognized ownership rights of nations to their continental shelves (and sedentary creatures on them) to a depth of 200 meters. It was partially on the basis of UN actions that Congress passed its 1964 law, and it was a result of the terms of that law that Japanese and Soviet fishing for crabs in the eastern Bering Sea, part of Alaska's continental shelf, was cut back in 1964–65. Nonetheless, despite actions by the UN and many nations to extend control over continental shelves, relatively few fisheries were affected. None of the UN agreements, and few of the national proclamations, infringed on open access to fish swimming in the waters above continental shelves.[30] Anyone could fish there.

United States officials remained reluctant to accept limits on foreign fishing, so concerned were they about free navigation for American ships. Even in 1974, despite the passage of the1964 law by Congress, State Department emissaries argued at public hearings that lobsters jumped up and down when they got mad or excited and thus swam a few feet above the ocean floor. Lobsters, they claimed, were not sedentary creatures on the continental shelf and should not, therefore, be reserved for American fishers. They did not want to see any part of the ocean closed in any way. This stance enraged not just American lobster fishers, but also Alaskan king crabbers, who wanted to continue excluding foreign fishers from their shallow waters. State Department officials, however, did not want Congress to take unilateral actions dealing with off-shore fishing and favored waiting for definite decisions by the UN. Nevertheless, against State Department wishes, Congress passed legislation in 1974 declaring crabs and lobsters to be "creatures of the continental shelf" completely off-limit to non-American fishers.[31]

In the mid-1970s, major changes in the governance of global fishing occurred. Beginning in 1973, discussions at a third UN Law of the Sea Convention reconsidered continental shelf matters. At issue was the extension of coastal-state ownership of continental shelves 200 miles out to sea *and* coastal-state ownership of fish swimming in waters above those shelves. Presidents Richard M. Nixon, Gerald R. Ford, and Jimmy Carter sent American representatives, who were advised by scientists and officers from fish-processing companies. Lowell Wakefield, founder of Wakefield Seafoods, which pioneered king crabbing in Alaskan waters after World War II, was a prominent adviser to the American delegation. Walt Yonker, manager of the Association of Pacific Fisheries, representing seafood processors in Washington, Oregon, and Alaska, also played an important advisory role. After five sessions, the UN Law of the Sea Convention accepted the concept of 200-mile Exclusive Economic Zones, and coastal nations put them into practice. For the first time, the Zones included ownership of fish swimming in waters *above* the continental shelves—as compared to all earlier measures which gave coastal nations ownership of only sedentary creatures on the shelves.[32] This seemingly technical distinction was and remains critical to fishers, since most commercially sought fish live in relatively shallow waters above continental shelves, not in deeper seas farther offshore. Exclusive economic zones, which include most continental shelves, contain an estimated 75–90 percent of the world's commercial fish.[33]

Reflecting changes taking place in marine science, the UN Convention did not call for fishing at maximum sustainable yield levels. Instead, it specified a more flexible "optimal yield." There were two reasons for this decision. The maximum sustainable yields of fish stocks, a concept developed in the 1950s and 1960s, had in practice been very hard for scientists to determine with any accuracy. Beyond that issue, the broader concept of optimum yields could consider such matters as the impact of harvesting one fish stock on the viability of other fish stocks and the impacts of fishing restrictions on coastal communities.[34]

The goal of the UN Convention, it is worth stressing, was not to preserve oceans and seas in pristine states, but rather to fish them in sustainable ways. Alaskan fisheries expert Terry Johnson has called the establishment of exclusive economic zones "the most profound change in the world's commercial ocean fisheries."[35] He was correct. Even though the United States did not sign the UN Convention, American policy makers were directly affected by the basic premises of the Convention—the desirability of developing sustainable fishing in EEZs. In the North Pacific, the United States, Canada, Soviet Union, and North Korea declared 200-mile EEZs in 1976–77. Japan followed in 1996. Coastal nations for the first time enclosed some of the oceanic commons. Even so, foreign fishers were not immediately frozen out in every situation. The UN Convention, on which many of the national laws were based, called for the "optimum utilization of all living resources in the exclusive economic zone" and urged that foreign fishers be granted access to fisheries not fully utilized by coastal nations. The provision that foreign fishers be allowed into waters not fully fished by nationals was especially important in the Northeast Pacific during the 1970s and 1980s, for Americans harvested few bottom fish there until the 1980s and later.[36]

The Fishery Conservation and Management Act of 1976

Though not a signatory to the 1976 UN Convention, the United States codified its EEZ in 1976 with the passage by Congress of the Fishery Conservation and Management Act (FCMA), which was reenacted with some changes in 1996.[37] Many American fishers and fish processors entered the political arena to push for this 1976 legislation. Nearly all agreed that removing foreign fishers from American waters was a good idea. A knowledgeable participant, who was deeply involved in securing passage for the FCMA, noted, "For years U.S. fishermen—a disorganized lot of intense individuals who were slow to form coalitions as did other types of workmen—had dunned their congressmen for legislation that would give them a better chance against the foreign fleets at catching the seafood stocks in their own national waters."[38] C. Reid Rogers, president of the New England Fish Company, a large seafood-processing firm headquartered in Seattle, enthusiastically observed, "We have before us the opportunity to develop a major new U.S. food resource." He was referring especially to bottom fish like pollock found in Alaskan waters.[39] Many Alaskan fishers agreed. Denouncing foreign fishers in early 1976, high-producing fishers Bart Eaton and John Hall of Kodiak asserted, "Those fellows are ruining the fish stocks. And they are doing it so fast that the destruction may be irreversible within our lifetime."[40] New England cod fishers, fearing that what they considered their fishing grounds were beset by foreign fishers and processors, very strongly backed the measure. In spring 1976, posters plastered on buildings throughout the fishing port of New Bedford, Massachusetts, proclaimed: "The Soviet fishing fleet is twelve miles off our coast and sucking up everything that swims, crawls or hides in the sand; support the 200-mile limit."[41]

Still, not all American fishers or government officials favored the Fishery Conservation and Management Act. Tuna fishers based out of San Pedro, California, spoke out against it, fearing that other nations would retaliate and exclude them from their waters. As events later proved, they were correct. For instance, newly formed island nations in the South Pacific demanded and received substantial payments from American seafood companies to allow harvesting tuna within 200 miles of their shores.[42] Then too, some members of the United Fishermen's Marketing Association, composed of Alaskan fishers, decried the bill's initial wording, which, they thought, gave too much power to the State Department to allow foreign fishers to harvest under-utilized fish stocks in American waters—in exchange for agreements from those fishers' nations to lower tariff barriers on American manufactured goods. Amendments to the bill's wording reduced that possibility and satisfied the Alaskan fishers. Conversely, representatives of the State Department opposed unilateral American actions to regulate fisheries, fearing that "international chaos" might result. They favored waiting for UN actions. One opponent in the hearings on the FCMA explained, "The administration [of President Ford] argues that such unilateral action by the United States would jeopardize the touchy Law of the Sea negotiations, might open the door to future arbitrary seizures, like that of the *Mayaguez* 60 miles off the Cambodian coast, and might lead to confrontations with the Soviets and Japan similar to those in the ongoing cod war between Iceland and Great Britain."[43] For many members of the Ford administration, Cold War concerns still predominated.

Senators Warren Magnuson of Washington and Ted Stevens of Alaska, along with representatives Don Young of Alaska and Gerry Studds of Massachusetts, led the fight for legislation in Congress, with the 1976 law evolving from discussions dating back four or five years. One of those pushing for the legislation, former coastguardsman and at-the-time fisher William McCloskey, Jr., remembered, "We playfully used to call the bill on the House side the 'Young Studds' Act."[44] The FCMA passed the House by a vote of 346 to 52 and sailed through the Senate in a voice vote. President Ford signed it into law on 13 April 1976. Torn between economic and diplomatic needs, Ford was not particularly enthusiastic about the measure. As the bill was being written, he merely noted that he "would probably not veto" it, as long as the measure was implemented no earlier than 1977.[45] (House members initially desired implementation in July, 1976.) The FCMA went into effect on 1 March 1977.

Figure 2. Ketchikan was one of many Alaskan coastal towns dependent on fishing. With the permission of Richard Newman.

Adopting the idea of optimum yield from the UN Convention, the FCMA defined that concept broadly. The FMCA designated "optimum" as a harvest "which will provide greatest overall benefit to the Nation, with particular reference to food production and recreational activities . . . which is prescribed as such on the basis of maximum sustainable yield from such fishery, as modified by relevant economic, social, or ecological factor[s]."[46] That definition, we shall see, could cover a lot of ground. Foreign vessels could fish within the 200-mile zone only with American permission and only if American fishers did not take all the allowable catches of fish. As American fishers increased their harvesting and processing capabilities, foreign fishers were excluded from American waters. Looking back at the results of the FCMA in 2007, *Seafood Business*, a leading trade journal for the American seafood industry, observed approvingly, "The main impetus for its passage was to stop foreign factory trawlers from plundering U.S. fish stocks. In that regard, the bill has been a great success. Today virtually no foreign boats operate off the United States."[47]

Thus, even as the federal government lessened its regulation of many American industries, it increased its role in the seafood business. Starting in the 1970s, federal officials dramatically reduced the parts they played in the American economy through what is known as "deregulation." In an effort to foster economic growth by making industries ranging from banking to railroads more efficient and more responsive to market demands, federal oversight of them was decreased. In an era in which inflation often exceeded 10 percent a year, deregulation was expected to bring about a reduction in consumer prices.[48] Even though the FCMA moved in the opposite direction, advocates perceived similar goals of helping the American economy and saving American jobs. The U.S. economy in 1976–77 was just emerging from a deep recession, and the FCMA won noncontroversial congressional approval mainly as a jobs bill. Foreign fishers would be forced out of U.S. waters, opening opportunities for American fishers. Deregulation, while a powerful movement, did not conquer all in the political arena. Even as deregulation took hold, for example, farm subsidies continued. Farmers had strong supporters in Congress.[49] So did fishers—few were more powerful than senators Magnuson and Stevens—which explains in part the passage of the FCMA. Moreover, protection carried the appeal of bashing foreigners, often a popular political move.

At the same time the federal government moved toward deregulation, it greatly stepped up its role in environmental matters, such as clean air and clean water. In 1970, the Congress and President Richard M. Nixon created the Environmental Protection Agency. However, in 1976 the FCMA was not presented mainly as an environmental measure; again, proponents character-ized it largely as a jobs bill. Indeed, representatives of environmental organi-zations such as the Sierra Club did not flock to Washington to testify for the measure. They judged other issues as more important—clean air, clean water, creation of wilderness areas, and so forth. Invisible and seemingly plentiful fish came very low on their lists of priorities. To the extent that environmen-talists, such as those in the newly formed organization Greenpeace, consid-ered marine measures at all, they were concerned with ending what they perceived as the destruction of whales by commercial hunting. Only in the late 1990s and early 2000s did some environmentalists, now conversant with the scientific reports about over-fishing cited at the beginning of this chapter, become engaged to any substantial degree in the politics of regulating fishing.

The Tragedy of the Commons and the Use of Fishing Quotas

Governments administering exclusive economic zones frequently tried to place sustainable limits on fish catches, often by setting maximum catches called total allowable catches (TACs) each fishing season. Marine biologists and economists developed the basic concept of TACs in the 1960s, but it re-quired several decades for them to be implemented, for initially fishery ex-perts often had great difficulty in deciding at what levels TACs for each fish stock should be set to be sustainable.[50] Policy makers often divided the TACs among fishers by giving them individual transferable quotas (ITQs), virtu-ally vesting them with property rights in their fish stocks. The ITQs usually awarded fishers rights to a certain percentage of the annual catch of specified fish stocks, and ITQs were often salable.

The use of TACs and ITQs sought to avoid a "tragedy of the commons" in fisheries. In commonly held oceanic resources, there may be little motivation for conservation. If one fisher voluntarily refrains from taking as many fish as possible, other fishers, lacking legal restraints on their actions, might well harvest those fish, even if doing so means that a fish stock might be greatly reduced in size. TACs and ITQs were also intended to end "derby-style" fish-ing by commercial fishers. Ensuring the safety of fishers was involved. Before the creation of TACs and ITQs, governments typically sought to regulate fish-ing by setting time limits on commercial fishing seasons. Eager to catch as many fish as possible while short seasons were open, fishers rushed to fishing grounds and fished them relentlessly around the clock, as in a fishing contest or derby, often in dangerous conditions such as stormy Alaskan waters. Injuries, accidents, and boat sinkings resulted.[51] Derby fishing also encouraged "capital stuffing," loading fishing vessels with large amounts of the most highly advanced, expensive gear to allow them to catch as many fish as possible in short time periods—decried by many as an economically wasteful form of fishing.[52]

Yet state policies, especially government policies designed to promote fisheries in the interest of creating jobs, along with the actions of fishers and processors, had often contributed to over-fishing. Governments made inexpensive boat loans to fishers to try to provide jobs for people in coastal towns, people with few economic options other than fishing. For instance, the 1980 Fisheries Promotion Act, pushed by fishers and seafood processors, provided low-cost financing and tax breaks for the construction of American fishing vessels. Thus, direct and indirect government assistance for fisheries came at the very moment that the administration of Jimmy Carter was pushing deregulation in many other industries. Over-fishing usually resulted from many interconnected factors, each acting on the others.[53]

Even the most successful application of total allowable catches and individual transferable quotas spawned many environmental justice issues. America's environmental justice movement was a campaign begun in the 1970s and 1980s to address the placing of garbage dumps, hazardous waste sites, power plants, and other nuisances in neighborhoods populated mainly by poor people of color. It spread in later decades to embrace many other issues.[54] The key question in fishing was and is, Who should receive fishing quotas? Usually, they went only to well-established fishers, excluding newcomers, including most women and many indigenous peoples, unless they purchased ITQs, often at very high prices. Older fishers were grandfathered into the industry, making it very expensive for new people to enter. Conflicts over ITQs pitted subsistence or "artisanal" fishers against commercial fishers, sports fishers against commercial fishers, and indigenous peoples against others.[55]

Both government officials and fishers recognized some of the problems the quota systems engendered. One fisheries expert has aptly written that in setting catch limits and quotas, "Concepts of justice and fairness often conflicted with concepts of efficiency."[56] Cathy McCarthy, who fished with her daughters out of Kodiak in the 1980s and 1990s, and who benefited from holding fishing quotas, nonetheless realized that Alaska's quotas were discriminatory. She and her daughters observed that fishing quotas generally "benefited people who had a lot of money." They thought of fish as a public resource and felt that, "There was no reason for a few people to make a lot of money" from fishing at the expense of those excluded.[57]

The basic problem in many fisheries globally was, of course, overcapacity. The industrialization of fishing begun in the late nineteenth century accelerated after World War II. Commercial fish stocks became overstressed as too many fishers chased too few fish. As a former member of the U.S. coast guard explained in 1998, "The hard fact is that not enough seafood lies in the world's productive waters to fill the nets and hooks of all of the world's fishing vessels. Some lose."[58] This situation put pressure on national governments and international fishery commissions to allow catches to continue at unsustainable levels, for few political leaders wanted unemployed fishers in their countries. Fishers vote. Moreover, the situation led fishers to ignore conservation measures in their competition to land every available fish. These circumstances could, in turn, lead to additional rounds of over-fishing, a downward spiral.

However, as UN actions and the steps taken by some nations, including the United States, showed, there were ways out of this dilemma. By enclosing the commons and by instituting new regulatory regimes, nations could make harvesting seafood sustainable. The Fishery Conservation and Management Act did just that for some major American fisheries. Over time, foreigners were excluded, and sustainable fishing practices were instituted. Doing so was far from easy. Sustainable fishing was difficult to establish and entailed social costs. Not all fishers could remain in the fisheries. For fisheries to thrive and for fishers to prosper, total allowable catches and individual transferable quotas had to be limited. In many American waters, sustainable fishing proved elusive, but in Alaskan waters it was largely achieved. Nuances in the histories of fish stocks, regions, and fishers accounted for the differences. And, above all, politics was in the diver's seat.

2

Successes and Failures
in the Regulation of American Fisheries

Carl Safina has been by far most influential of the writers who have since the 1990s decried over-fishing. After earning a doctorate in ecology from Rutgers University, Safina founded the Living Oceans Program of the National Audubon Society in 1990, serving for the next decade as its vice president for ocean conservation.[1] In 2003 he co-founded the Blue Ocean Institute, an organization that uses science, art, and literature to try to inspire closer relationships between people and the sea. Profiled by the *New York Times* and featured on the ABC television program *Nightline*, Safina was named one of the "100 Notable Conservationists of the Twentieth Century" by *Audubon Magazine*. He lobbied hard in the 1990s for the implementation of the United Nations Convention on the Law of the Sea to try to end over-fishing. While dealing with global developments, Safina focused on those occurring in American waters.

Based on personal observations, interviews with fishers, policymakers, and environmentalists, and a thorough immersion in fishery reports, Safina's *Song for the Blue Ocean*, published in 1997, explained in almost lyrical prose the extent and causes of over-fishing. Safina's book built on his 1993 article in the *Scientific American* to reach a large audience. Called "the *Silent Spring* of our time" by the *Los Angeles Times Book Review*, the study was labeled, "A haunting melody. A howl. A lament," by the *Seattle Post-Intelligencer*. Well-known environmental writer Peter Matthiessen observed that the work was "a wide-ranging, well-written, and profoundly disturbing book."[2]

Safina's personal background sparked his interest in fisheries. "When I was a boy," he wrote, "on warm spring evenings in the rich light before sunset my father would often take me down to the pebbly shore of Long Island

Sound to hunt striped bass . . . the world seemed unspeakably beautiful." Then came change: "The arrival of bulldozers on our shoreline was an unfathomable tragedy. . . . Loss of my beach amounted to expatriation." Safina's environmental education continued through college and graduate studies. "In graduate school," Safina later observed, he "arranged to do field work on the ecological relationships between seabirds and fishes," which allowed him "to spend many hours out in the coastal ocean habitats that had opened my heart on my boyhood shores." In the course of his studies, Safina noticed that, "The oceans were being depopulated; that creatures were not just being used—they were being used up. Watching them disappear, I felt helpless." In researching *Song for the Blue Ocean*, Safina believed that he was undertaking "a journey of discovery beyond the blue horizon."[3]

Safina devoted much of his study to the over-fishing of blue-fin tuna and other billed fishes, such as marlin and swordfish, in the Northwest Atlantic. From the Atlantic, Safina turned to the Pacific Northwest's salmon fishery. There, he pointed out, challenges to the sustainability of the fish stock were especially complex, for habitat destruction and over-fishing combined to decimate salmon stocks.[4] Safina indicted ocean fishery management, concluding that, "Catches in the Atlantic, Pacific, Mediterranean, and Antarctic have all fallen from highs reached in the 1970s and 1980s, in some cases by 30 to 50 percent." Instead of "stewarding living, renewable resources for continuity, long-term wealth, and well-being," fishers, he thought, had "approached fishing more like mining."[5]

Recent fishing trends in most American waters have been similar to those in many other regions. Between 1970 and 1995, the number of fishing vessels, foreign and domestic, plying North American waters jumped from 17,700 to 42,500, while total American fish landings rose from about 2.5 million metric tons (mmt) in 1950 to a peak of 5.6 mmt in 1987. But by 2004, landings came to just 5 mmt.[6] Only a tremendous expansion of fisheries in Alaskan waters allowed overall catches in American waters to remain as high as they did. As seafood harvests slumped in many other waters of the United States, catches from the North nearly compensated for the decline elsewhere.

Over-Fishing in the Northwest Atlantic

Centered on Georges Bank off Maine and the Grand Banks off Nova Scotia, the Northwest Atlantic cod fishery was a particularly disastrous example of treating the ocean as a nearly unregulated commons for too long,.[7] The cod were initially so abundant in this area that in 1497, according to British explorer John Cabot, his men caught the fish by simply lowering weighted baskets into dense schools of them, using used no lines or nets.[8] Soon, ocean-going schooners employed skiffs called dories manned by individual fishers to catch the cod on their lines. Near-shore fishers took the fish on hand lines from dories. Rudyard Kipling's novel *Captains Courageous: A Story of the Grand Banks*, published in 1897, offers a close look at the dory cod fishery.[9] Commercially exploited from the 1500s, the fishery yielded about 250,000 metric tons of fish annually in the seventeenth through the nineteenth centuries, causing some local depletion. Cod were, locals recognized, a source of relatively inexpensive animal protein. By the 1700s, much of the New England catch went in sun-dried ("flaked") or salted form to British and French islands in the Caribbean. There plantation masters raising sugar cane fed the cod to their slaves. In return, molasses derived from the cane journeyed north to New England where it was distilled into rum. Cod also found markets in Europe, especially the Iberian Peninsula.[10]

By the twentieth century, cod came under greatly increased pressure with the advent of long-distance trawling and processing vessels. As early as the 1880s, British fishers had begun using otter trawls, which tremendously increased the efficiency of trawling. According to one marine writer at the time, "The otter trawl, now the standard bottom trawl, consists of a large bag-shaped net that is towed through the water with its mouth held open by various ropes, weights, and floats in conjunction with angled 'otter boards' (also known as 'doors'), which draw apart the net as it is pulled over the seabed. Its depth and distance from the bottom can be controlled by floats. The narrow, tapered end of the net, into which the trapped fish gather, is known as the 'cod end.'"[11] Cod and other bottom fish were harvested in otter-trawling operations off New England shores by 1905, largely replacing the less efficient schooners and dories.

After World War II, fishing for cod in the Northwest Atlantic soared when British companies sent new vessels to the area. The British ship *Fairtry* introduced full-scale industrial fishing methods to the region. Some 245 feet in length, the *Fairtry* caught and processed cod in unprecedented numbers. Featuring a stern ramp up which the trawl net could be dragged to be emptied, the ship was the epitome of efficiency in her day. Below decks, machines removed the heads from the cod and automatically skinned, filleted, and quick-froze the fish. The ship also had its own cod-liver oil plant.[12] Nothing was wasted. The *Fairtry*'s operations were quickly copied by East German and Soviet vessels. One observer at the time commented of these large vessels, "They're fishing with ocean liners." By 1965, the Soviet Union alone had 106 large factory trawlers and 425 smaller trawlers supplying 30 mother ships (processing vessels) in these waters. The total reported Soviet catch in the Northwest Atlantic came to 886,000 metric tons that year, including 278,000 metric tons of cod and haddock, another bottom fish. Nine years later, 1,076 Soviet and Communist-bloc vessels extracted 2,716,00 metric tons of fish from the banks, ten times the catch taken by American fishers and three times that of Canadian fishers. In the late 1960s and early 1970s, cod accounted for about 23 percent by value of all the fish caught commercially around the world.[13]

After the passage of the Fishery Conservation and Management Act in 1976 and the enactment of similar legislation by Canada's Parliament, Georges Bank and most of the Grand Banks were off-limits to the British and Spanish, who had long frequented these grounds, as well as to newcomers

Figure 3. Soviet fishing vessels off Long Island in 1976. Courtesy of William B. McCloskey, Jr.

such as Soviet and East German fishers. The legislation alone, however, did not lead to sustainable fishing. Much depended on how government agencies established to administer national laws operated, especially the choices their members made about catch sizes.

Particularly important for American fishers were eight regional councils, mandated by the FCMA and established in 1977, to manage fishery resources within 200 miles of the U.S. coast. Composed of state and federal officials, along with fishers and officers of fish-processing companies, these councils set catch limits and devised the details by which fishing was done. Two of the eight councils are most important for this study: the New England Fishery Management Council (NEFMC) and the North Pacific Fishery Management Council (NPFMC). The FCMA charged the councils with sometimes contradictory goals: to promote American fishing by, among other actions, excluding foreign fishers, and to regulate the sizes of catches in the interest of achieving sustainable fishing. Sustainability came to mean limiting overall catch totals of different species and allocating those catches among individual fishers. Those fishers allowed to pursue seafood prospered; those excluded did not. Usually, only those who had fished commercially for four or five consecutive years were permitted to continue. Often dominated in their early years by fishers and representatives of seafood processing companies, in later years the councils embraced a wider range of stakeholders, including environmentalists.

Urged on by the federal government, which made low-interest loans available for construction of new fishing vessels, American fishers working through the NEFMC replaced foreign fishers in over-fishing cod and other bottom fish. So did Canadian fishers, aided by a national fishery agency. In fact, American and Canadian fishers and fish processors drove an intensification of fishing. Government agencies lowered the allowable overall harvest of cod a bit, but not nearly enough, given the perilous state into which the catch had already fallen. Henry Lyman, an early chair of the NEFMC, observed in 1979 that, "When the 200-mile limit came in, everybody said, 'Oh Boy, the lid's off.' What they forgot was that the stocks were already far down from overfishing."[14] Two reasons explained the continuing deterioration. First, scientific knowledge of cod was rudimentary, making it difficult to establish accurate sustainable catch limits. Second, fishers and fish processors, thinking only of short-term gains, successfully lobbied the NEFMC to establish catch limits higher than those that could be sustained.

With NEFMC and Canadian catch limits set too high, fishing pressure continued, causing a crash of cod fisheries in both the American and the Canadian exclusive economic zones. The loss was tremendous. Summing up the consequences of several decades of over-fishing, the editor of *Seafood Business* observed, "After the U.S. fleet eventually geared up, it took up where the foreign fleets had left off, especially in the Northeast." By the mid-1990s, catches of bedrock species like Atlantic cod had plummeted from more than 40,000 metric tons to about 10,000 metric tons," making cod "a cause célèbre."[15] In 2002, northern cod populations off Newfoundland were less than 0.5 percent of what they had been as late as the 1960s. Despite closures of Georges Bank and the Grand Banks to cod fishing in the early and mid-1990s, cod did not rebound in population.[16]

As its operations evolved, by the 1990s and early 2000s the NEFMC came to have eighteen voting members, who were probably too attentive to the wishes of fishers. Members included the principal officers in charge of fishery matters for the states of Maine, Rhode Island, Massachusetts, Connecticut, and New Hampshire. Twelve additional voting members were nominated by the governors of the New England coastal states and appointed by the U.S. secretary of commerce. They were usually representatives of fishing and fish-processing organizations, such as the Cape Cod Commercial Hook Fisherman's Association and Atlantic Trawlers Fishing. The NEFMC bylaws stated: "Council members may have an interest in any fishery-related harvesting, processing, lobbying, advocacy or marketing activity as long as they disclose the extent of this interest to the public."[17] This statement ensured that knowledgeable fishing industry members could serve on the Council. Members recused themselves from votes where there might be conflicts of interest. The Council also included as nonvoting members representatives of the Coast Guard, U.S. Fish and Wildlife Service, Department of State, and Atlantic States Marine Fisheries Commission. Oversight committees composed of members of the Council met several times each year to develop fishery management plans for individual fish stocks. In doing so, they received advice from panels made up of members from the commercial fishing industry, scientists, and (from the early 2000s) environmental advocates. The committees sent their plans to the full Council for further discussion, public hearings, and adoption.

Despite the Council's efforts, cod suffered an additional 25 percent drop in population between 2001 and 2005. In 1973, cod, haddock, and similar bottom fish composed 70 percent of the fish stocks on the Georges Bank. By the late 1980s, they made up only 15 percent. In the same period the shares of skate (a less commercially desirable bottom fish) and dogfish (a type of shark) rose from 22 to 74 percent of the total catch. There were unexpected consequences. No longer eaten by cod, which had nearly vanished, snow crabs exploded in population.[18]

A few Gloucester cod fishers survived, indeed thrived, by marketing hand-lined cod, which they labeled "Chatham" cod, successfully differentiating it from the few cod still caught by trawling. They argued that cod taken in trawling operations were often bruised, while cod harvested by hand lines were not. Thus, through creative marketing cod, once the food of slaves, was transformed into an upscale product sold at high prices. Chatham cod became an expensive, boutique item.[19]

E. Annie Proulx captures what the loss of cod meant to fishers and their communities in the Northwest Atlantic in her novel *The Shipping News*, published in 1993. Set in a small town on the Newfoundland coast, the story revolves around the efforts of a thirty-six-year-old "third-rate newspaperman" named Quoyle, who had "stumbled" through his twenties and thirties, to rebuild his life after a failed marriage and lost job.[20] Working as a reporter in charge of the shipping pages for the newspaper the *Gammy Bird* in the fictional town of Killick-Claw, Quoyle observes the changes in fishing firsthand. A day or two into his new position, he is told by his editor, "It used to be a good living, fishing. It was all inshore fishing when I was young. You'd have your skiff, your nets. . . . It was a hard life, but you had the satisfaction." However, over the decades this way of life disappeared: "And the fishing's went down, down, down, forty years sliding away to nothing, the goddamn Canada government giving fishing rights to every country on the face of the earth, but regulating us out of existence. The damn foreign trawlers. That's where all the fish is went." As Quoyle talks with the harbormaster for Killick-Claw a bit later, the two are interrupted, when the harbormaster receives a call saying that the coast guard has seized a Russian trawler fishing within Canada's 200-mile limit without a license.[21]

Instead of cod-fishing vessels, cruise ships increasingly visit Killick-Claw, sixteen during Quoyle's first year there. So do refrigerated ships taking sea-urchin roe and fish to Japanese markets.[22] Proulx highlights the altered nature of the port and the changing lives of its inhabitants throughout her novel. The elegant beauty and "menacing strength" of a yacht in the harbor serves as a telling contrast to the more work-a-day appearances of the few remaining fishing boats.[23] In the novel's dramatic climax, a drunken mob of men, many of them unemployed fishers, destroy a yacht that had displaced fishing vessels from their accustomed moorage: "The black-haired man lifted his axe and

Figure 4. Gloucester cod on a small American trawler in 1976. Courtesy of William B. McCloskey, Jr.

brought it down on the deck with all his strength. A chain saw bit into the mast. Tremendous pummeling and wrenching noises, splashes as pieces of the *Borogove* went into the water."[24] *The Shipping News* concludes with mixed messages. Though Quoyle succeeds in fitting into his community, and even learning how to handle a small boat, there is little hope for the community, as fishing continues to decline and fish-processing plants close.

Only in 2009 did the NEFMC move toward sustainable fishing by establishing an effective system of total allowable catches and individual fishing quotas. By then, the amount of cod left in the sea was, according to federal government officials, only 12 percent of the stock needed to produce a sustainable harvest (up, however, from just 7 percent in 2005). As one official put it, "The era of lawless rule-breaking and Wild West mentality has put us between the rock and the hard place we are in today."[25]

Yet, even the establishment of quotas caused problems. Not everyone could acquire them; only well-established fishers qualified. The individual quotas were salable, leading to an increase in prices as a market developed for them. Lee Schatvet, a twenty-one-year-old fisher in Rye Harbor, New Hampshire, wanted to run his own boat in 2010, but could not. He figured that he needed about $500,000 to purchase a small cod-fishing boat, the permit (quota), and fishing gear. He failed to raise the money and lamented, "It's basically impossible to get into the industry nowadays." Not surprisingly, the median age of commercial fishing permit holders in Massachusetts rose from forty-six in 2000 to fifty-one in 2009.[26]

The collapse of the cod fisheries of the Northwest Atlantic imposed tremendous damage on people and their towns. In 2009, only 600 fishing boats remained active in the New England fleet, half the number that went to sea in 2001. About 30,000 of Newfoundland's total 570,000 residents, a figure that includes all women and children, were unemployed in 1997, even after 3 percent of the province's people had left between 1991 and 1996 alone.[27] Among young adult males who stayed in their home ports the unemployment rate soared. A way of life was at the edge of extinction.

Problems with cod extended to northern European waters, with overfishing again the main problem. In the 1970s, there were an estimated 250,000 metric tons of wild cod in the North Sea, the eastern English Channel, and Scandinavia's Skagerrak Strait. However, illegal fishing combined with setting legal catch quotas too high led to over-fishing. By the early 2000s, the cod stock had been reduced to an estimated 50,000 metric tons. In fall 2009, Jose Rodriguez, a marine biologist with the marine conservation organization

Oceana, lamented, "We are not far away from a complete collapse." The European Commission, which regulated the harvesting of wild cod in European Union waters, called for reductions in harvest quotas of 25 percent.[28] Despite experiencing all the problems typical of oceanic aquaculture discussed in Chapter 1, Norwegians sought in the early 2000s to raise farmed cod to ensure having that white fish on their dinner tables. Norwegian scientists experimented with feeding the cod meals composed of soybeans, corn, rapeseed, sunflower seeds, and other sources of vegetable protein.[29]

The story of decline was similar for blue-fin tuna and other types of billed fish, such as marlin and swordfish, in the North Atlantic. The breeding population of blue-fin tuna dropped by about 90 percent in the 1980s and 1990s as a result of intensive fishing with the most modern equipment, including boats that were guided to schools of fish by spotter airplanes. Stephen Sloan, a sports fisherman critical of fishing by commercial fishers, described commercial harvesting: "The method of purse-seining is simple. A spotter plane finds a school of fish, contacts the purse seine vessel, relays the type of fish in a school and its size in metric tons; bluefin or yellowfin tunas, mackerel or herring. The vessel then encircles the school with a large net pulled around the school by a smaller boat, usually thirty feet in length, that is dispatched from the larger purse seine vessel. . . . A hydraulic power head off a block and tackle mounted on a boom of the large seiner pulls helps haul in the net and its contents. The size of the entrapped school could be a hundred metric tons and [is] handled easily by the ship's equipment."[30]

Critics like Sloan lambasted the management practices of the international body set up to regulate tuna fishing, the International Commission for the Conservation of Atlantic Tunas (ICCAT)—with good reason. The ICCAT was established in 1969 to regulate catches of blue-fin tuna and other billed fish to achieve the maximum sustainable yield for each fish stock. By 2000, the Commission consisted of representatives from thirty-one nations on both sides of the Atlantic plus Japan, Korea, and Russia. The ICCAT failed dismally, especially with regard to blue-fin tuna. The Commission perennially set catch quotas that were much too high to be sustained, against the advice of its own marine scientists, who reported each year to ICCAT's Standing Committee on Research and Statistics. Most of the work at the Commission was conducted by four panels, one each for swordfish, blue-fin tuna, other tunas (such as yellow-fin tuna and albacore), and other billed fishes and sharks. Yet the national representatives comprising those panels ignored the advice of members of the Standing Committee and kept quotas at unsustainable levels.[31]

One reason for this worrisome situation was that the representatives were often fishers. In 1991, for example, Carmen Blondin was the U.S. government representative, appointed by president George H. W. Bush. He was closely advised by two commissioners from the private sector: Lee Weddig, head of the National Fishery Institute, a lobbying organization of fishers and fish processors, and Mike Montgomery, a California lawyer and fundraiser for Ronald Reagan and George W. Bush.[32] This approach to the regulation of business was typical of the administrations of Ronald Reagan and the two Bushs. Those three presidents gave businesspeople the power to regulate themselves and in general lessened federal government oversight of many industries.

Particularly notorious examples of harmful blue-fin management occurred in 1991. American sports fishers found their share of the Western Atlantic catch of blue-fin tuna cut to just 15 percent of the total. They argued that, given the economic importance of sports fishing, their allocation should be much higher. Sloan testified: "Of all the United States finfish landings, recreational anglers accounted for only 3 percent of that total measured in pounds of fish landed. But, in landing that 3 percent, recreational anglers spent over $20 billion. Meanwhile the other 97 percent of finfish landings by commercial fishing operations are valued at just $1.6 billion."[33] Sloan's figures were correct, although they did not include secondary and tertiary economic impacts of commercial fishing. More important, however, was the issue of the total allowable catch. Swedish representatives called on other members to recognize that blue-fin tuna were "endangered" and in need of protection from over-fishing. The Swedes put forward a motion to that effect, and it initially won some support. However, it was ultimately defeated, when American and Japanese representatives, the countries with the strongest interests in catching tuna, rallied others in ICCAT to vote against it. (Japanese ate 36 percent of the world's tuna, Americans 31 percent.)[34] Such decisions led Richard Ellis, author of the most thoroughgoing study on tuna, to conclude, "Under pressure from powerful commercial fishing interests, ICCAT has consistently supported fishers at the expense of the fish."[35]

In short, political decisions led to a tragedy of the commons, as decisions to permit unsustainable fishing to continue cut into harvests. The result was declining catches. The blue-fin tuna harvest in the western Atlantic fell from 20,000 tons in 1964 to just 6,100 tons in 1978. Further losses took place in later years. From the mid-1980s to the early 2000s, the blue-fin stock dropped an additional 50 percent in the western Atlantic and an astonishing 80 percent in the eastern Atlantic.[36]

Not even this fall in numbers led to adoption of effective conservation measures for blue-fin tuna, for their scarcity increased their value, leading to even more over-fishing, a vicious cycle. On 5 January 2001, in Tokyo's Tsukiji market, the world's largest fish market, one blue-fin tuna sold for $392 per pound wholesale, for a total price of $173,600,. In late 2008, the American delegation to the ICCAT, now finally alarmed by declines in their fishers' catches, urged that the quota for the coming year's Atlantic catch be reduced from 29,000 to 15,000 metric tons. And yet members set the catch at 22,000 mt. In early 2009, scientists for the World Wildlife Fund environmental group reported that the entire breeding population of Atlantic blue-fin tuna was likely to be eliminated within three years unless catches were very sharply reduced.[37] Nonetheless, members established a catch limit of 13,500 tons for 2010.While considerably lower than before, this limit was much higher than the 8,500 tons recommended by marine conservation groups such the British organization Seafish. They were not alone. Officers of the Atlantis Group, an Icelandic seafood company, proposed lowering the catch limit "in accordance with scientific advice." In reporting ICCAT's decision, the conservative British journal the *Economist* observed that "the results can scarcely be described as good" and that the Commission was "notorious for ignoring the advice of its own scientists."[38]

Nor did matters improve for blue-fin tuna in 2010. Early in the year, an American proposal that the Convention on International Trade in Endangered Species, a United Nations body, ban all trade in blue-fin tuna was defeated, largely as a result of Japanese opposition.[39] Oil from the BP Gulf of Mexico off-shore well disaster in spring and summer 2010 further endangered blue-fin tuna by threatening one of their major breeding grounds.[40] As 2010 came to a close, ICCAT delegates reduced the catch for the coming fishing season only slightly, from 13,500 tons to 12,900 tons. Environmentalists flayed this action as much too small a decrease. "This is business as usual," declared a spokesperson for Greenpeace. The director of international policy for the Pew Environmental Group was more outspoken: "It is now clear that the entire management system of high-seas fisheries is flawed and inadequate."[41]

A major response of fishers to the declining catches of wild blue-fin tuna was to raise them in "ranches." In Mediterranean and Australian waters, juvenile blue-fin tuna were captured in massive purse-seining operations. From the nets they were transferred alive to large cages and then towed in the cages, sometimes for hundreds of miles, to huge permanent pens off shore ports. (Ranching fish is usually differentiated from fish farming. In farming, fish are raised from eggs.) In the pens, the tuna were "fattened," by being fed on sardines and other small fish. By the early 2000s, about 150 pens, each containing twenty to fifty tons of tuna, dotted the coast off southern Australia. Every nation fronting on the Mediterranean was engaged in tuna farming by 2000.[42]

When the tuna were ready for market about seven months later, "wranglers" jumped into the pens and wrestled the fish on board nearby vessels, where they were killed. Modern-day seagoing cowboys dressed in wetsuits rather than Stetsons and chaps, the wranglers were usually well-muscled young men. Worldwide totals for ranched tuna are elusive, but in 2003 Australian tuna ranchers produced 8,308 tons of blue-fin tuna. Much of the global catch was airlifted to Japan.[43]

Self-serving regulation, which responded to the short-term demands of fishers to keep harvests at artificially high levels combined with a scarcity of scientific knowledge (in some instances) to decimate Atlantic cod and blue-fin tuna stocks. National and international regulatory agencies pressured by fishers, and politicians who did not want to have to deal with complaints from fishers, too often set catch quotas at unsustainable levels. At first in the 1970s it was unclear, given the state of the knowledge by marine biologists about cod, just what sustainable harvests were; but even later, when it was abundantly clear that over-fishing was occurring, NEFMC failed to reduce the quotas quickly enough. Similarly, ICCAT considered the blue-fin tuna populations of the eastern and western Atlantic two separate groups, even when scientific tagging and tracking of tuna showed that many tuna swam back and forth across the Atlantic each year. Confusion on this basic point made effective regulation difficult. Then too, the ICCAT was dominated by fishers, to the extent that in the 1990s many environmentalists derided the Commission as the "International Conspiracy to Catch All the Tunas."

Problems in the Gulf of Mexico

Habitat destruction rather than over-fishing plagued shrimpers and other fishers in the Gulf of Mexico. Particularly worrisome were industrial toxins flowing downstream into the Gulf from plants along a ninety-mile stretch of the lower Mississippi River known as "Cancer Alley." In 2000, this section of the Mississippi between New Orleans and Baton Rouge included 136 petro-chemical plants, seven oil refineries, and a number of paper mills fronting on it. All dumped poisons into the river, which delivered them to the sea. Fertilizer and pesticide run-off from farms also hurt fishing. Along with the Ohio and Missouri Rivers, the Mississippi River drains thirty-one states and two Canadian provinces. Nutrient pollution from fertilizer run-off increased greatly after World War II, when synthetic chemicals like nitrogen came into common use in fertilizers. The United States Geological Survey has estimated that 70 percent of the nitrogen carried into the Gulf from the Mississippi River originated north of that river's confluence with the Ohio just below St. Louis. Iowa has recently been the source for 250,000 tons of nitrate-nitrogen entering the Gulf each year. The Survey also estimated that 90 percent of the nitrogen reaching the Gulf comes from "non-point" sources. Agricultural run-off has been by far the most important component; others include industrial effluent, such as that from Cancer Alley, and municipal sewage.[44]

The nitrogen run-off in particular fed large algae blooms in the Gulf of Mexico. Almost every summer, part of the Gulf turned green as a result. These algae blooms robbed the sea of oxygen, and sea water without oxygen cannot support fish life. In effect, a "dead zone" was created, extending out to sea from the mouth of the Mississippi River and down the coasts of Louisiana and Texas. When this dead zone was first mapped in 1985, it covered 3,500 square miles. It extended from the seafloor upward to include 10 to 80 percent of the total depth of the water in different places. By the mid-1990s, the zone had doubled in size to 7,000 square miles; by 2010 it spread over at least 8,000 square miles. It formed every spring and summer, fed by nitrogen run-off from the Mississippi River, and dissolved only in the fall, broken up when hurricanes stirred the water and nitrogen run-off lessened. Within the dead zone "no fish could be seen at all" and only occasionally were there "a few stray mantis shrimp."[45]

The federal government, even though pushed by the environmental organization Greenpeace, mounted a lackluster response, funding a very small demonstration project to show how run-off might be decreased. Faced with the enormity of cleaning up the entire drainage of the Mississippi River and its tributaries to eliminate the dead zone, federal officials proceeded slowly.[46]

Economic problems stemming directly from globalization added to environmental ones, as fishers netted shrimp in areas beyond the dead zone. Despite environmental challenges, Louisiana shrimpers harvested 90 million pounds of shrimp worth $135 million in 2008. However, they faced increasing competition. Shrimp brought into the United States from other nations—Thailand, Indonesia, and Ecuador, especially—totaled 1.6 billion pounds in 2007, twice the amount as in 1998. Imports depressed prices. Large domestic shrimp that had sold for $6 per pound brought only $1 per pound. The number of shrimpers operating from Louisiana ports fell from 16,500 in 1989 to just 4,700 in 2008. In 2009, the governor of Louisiana called upon his nation's International Trade Commission to halt (or at least slow) the import of shrimp to help his state's fishers, arguing that "Louisiana shrimp fishermen have never had greater need for protection from unfair trade practices that threaten their livelihood."[47]

Politicians and politics did not "interfere" with efforts to halt over-fishing. Instead, from the outset they were closely linked. It proved, for example, very difficult politically to mandate new farming methods that might have lessened fertilizer run-off to the Gulf of Mexico. There were many more farmers in the Midwest than there were shrimpers in Gulf states, and the farmers packed more political clout. Although political actions sought to control run-off in the early 2000s—state legislation sometimes encouraged or required farmers to stop plowing and planting right to the edges of streams—run-off continued to contribute to the annual formation of a dead zone in the Gulf of Mexico.[48]

Difficulties in California Waters

Challenges for salmon fishers in California's waters, like those for Gulf shrimpers, came mainly from habitat destruction; and, once again, politics were deeply involved in fishery matters. Because salmon spend part of their lives in freshwater streams and rivers and only part of them in offshore oceanic waters, they are regulated mainly by state, not federal officials. Generally speaking, federal officials set the rules for taking fish that spend their lives in offshore waters beyond state boundaries—that is, three miles (or from 1966 twelve miles) out to sea. State officials usually regulate fisheries in their state's lakes and streams and in oceanic waters close to shore.

William Hume pioneered in developing a canned-salmon industry on California's Sacramento River. In 1852, Hume trekked as a gold prospector to California from Augusta, Maine, on the Kennebec River. He had little success in the diggings. However, he carried with him a gill net, and soon put it to use pulling salmon from the Sacramento River. He established a commercial fishery with several classmates from the East. Family members and their friends joined him in the 1860s, and they were soon packing their catches in red, hand-soldered cans.[49] From these scant beginnings, the salmon fishery became one of California's leading industries in the late nineteenth century, with the Sacramento and San Joaquin Rivers (and their many tributaries), which empty into San Francisco Bay, supporting major runs at various times of year.

The degradation of salmon habitats began early. Starting in the 1800s, logging hurt salmon streams flowing directly into the Pacific Ocean. Debris blocked the streams, making it hard for salmon to swim upstream to spawn, and the removal of trees from stream banks reduced the shade needed to cool water for young salmon. In the nineteenth century, as well, hydraulic mining for gold washed enormous amounts of dirt and gravel down the Sacramento River, harming fishing and farming alike. Despite these problems, salmon runs up the Sacramento and San Joaquin Rivers generally remained strong into the 1920s and 1930s.[50]

Even more deterioration in salmon runs took place after World War II, as they became victims of increased habitat degradation. Together, the San Joaquin and Sacramento Rivers drain California's Central Valley, a region that became the premier U.S. growing locale for fruits and vegetables. Central Valley farms required enormous amounts of fresh water for irrigation. Thirsty urbanites in southern California also needed prodigious supplies of water. Two mammoth projects—one built by the federal government in the 1930s, the other by the state of California in the 1960s—tapped the two rivers and their tributaries for the needed water. Literally dozens of dams went up on salmon streams, a system of large pumps was put in place, and miles of irrigation canals were built. Salmon habitat was destroyed in the process. The Friant Dam, constructed on the San Joaquin River in 1944, closed much of that stream to migrating salmon, and the six-hundred-foot Shasta Dam, built a bit later, blocked the Upper Sacramento River. Many more dams blocked rivers over the next four decades, until 6,000 miles of California's salmon-spawning habitat was reduced to just 300 miles.[51]

Like farming, fishing in California became a creature of the state, with few consumers of food fully recognizing the reach of governmental decisions. Salmon fishing suffered from those decisions. Between 1980 and 1995, the number of boats fishing for salmon in Californian waters dropped from over 6,000 to just over 2,000. The number of people employed in the state's salmon fisheries plummeted from 50,000 to 10,000. The demands of farms and cities for water decimated the Golden State's salmon fisheries. Decreasing salmon runs and catches led state officials to periodically close some salmon fisheries and greatly decrease the length of time fishers could work other ones. These actions, however, simply led fishers to intensify their efforts, aided by the most advanced technologies available, during the days when fisheries remained open—a good example of the dangers of "derby fishing" and "technology stuffing." Fishers went out in all types of nasty weather and used expensive electronic aids to catch salmon, whenever state and federal authorities permitted fishing. It was a "zero-sum" game in which over-fishing added to problems with habitat destruction. Safina has described the resulting situation well: "The 1.5 million fish that hit the decks of seagoing boats in 1988 became a skeletonized catch of 150,000 in 1992; down 90 percent. But these were vast numbers compared to the tatters that were making it upstream."[52]

In his novel *The Fisherman's Son*, published in 1998, Michael Koepf, a fisher for nineteen years, captures the changing nature of salmon fishing on the Pacific Coast. Set in northern California in the mid- and late twentieth century, the book contains such vivid descriptions that readers can almost smell the kelp rotting on the beach. Koepf's account focuses on two generations of fishers, a father and his son Neil, both of whom captain small boats pursuing salmon from Half Moon Bay, just south of San Francisco. There is little wasted time or effort on the father's troller: "His father worked without pause: operating the gurdies [small winches handing the fishing lines], playing fish, steering the boat, checking the compass, running the lines, watching the poles, adjusting the depths of the cables, keeping an eye to the sea all around. His father was a symphonic conductor of fishing."[53] Koepf understands the character of fishers: "Fishermen lived apart from other men. They belonged to no organizations or clubs in town. They never went to school on parents' night. . . . The fishermen were strange and different. Not the 'Ozzie and Harriet' men he had seen on television, not the 'I love Lucy' men, the kind fool men, the men in suits who drove Chevrolets home to rows of perfect homes in perfect towns with wives who turned them into jokes."[54]

Koepf describes a dawning realization on the part of fishers of the problems salmon faced and the growing scarcity of fish. In a speech made to other fishers, Neil declares, "Now those rivers are all dammed up so that big-time farmers can have lots of water to grow things the government pays them to plow under. The few fish that still make it up the San Joaquin [River] search for spawning gravel that's already been scooped up and hauled away to make highways. They die before they spawn in dirty pools of silt."[55] Neither father nor son can earn an adequate living from fishing alone. The father supplements his earnings by smuggling liquor from off-shore mother ships during Prohibition, and the son smuggles drugs and illegal immigrants from China (called "yellowfish"). At one point, Neil and his father "tried to imagine the sea without salmon boats. A sea empty of men." However, not for long: "If Neil's father and his friends worried about the future, it was quickly put away. Their life was now."[56] That lack of concern was a mistake. Near the end of his novel, Koepf describes how fishing had changed: "Cabins bristled with electronics. The fish couldn't hide. New boats were made of steel. The new men were made of deals and debt. They went longer and farther for less and less. Competition increased. The fish declined."[57]

Problems for California's salmon fisheries continued in the 1990s and early 2000s. In 1992, Congress passed the Central Valley Improvement Act, a measure that allocated half the water of the Sacramento River to fish (most of the rest went to agriculture), with the objective of doubling the number of salmon on the river.[58] However, this move proved inadequate. Salmon suffered from multiple challenges. The severity of the problems became apparent in 2006, when salmon runs on the Klamath River in northern California collapsed. Historically, the Klamath had produced the third-largest salmon runs in the West, after only those on the Sacramento and Columbia. But "dams, diversions and recent drought" combined to push "the spawning salmon population in the Klamath well below the 35,000-fish threshold deemed necessary for the river to maintain a sustainable salmon population." Federal officials greatly restricted fishing off 700 miles of coastline in northern California and southern Oregon.[59] In early 2010, California's governor Arnold Schwarzenegger announced a plan to remove four dams from the Klamath River, a move that, however, would require considerable time and substantial funding.[60]

Problems on the Klamath River spread to salmon runs on the Sacramento River in 2008 and 2009. No one, not even marine biologists, knew why the already depleted salmon runs plummeted still more. The best guess (for it was only a guess) was that the dearth of salmon resulted from some combination of "ocean conditions, habitat destruction, dam operations or agricultural pollution."[61] Widespread drought, which lessened water supplies in western rivers, also hurt salmon runs.[62] In fall 2008, the fewest numbers of Chinook salmon ever recorded made their way up the Sacramento and San Joaquin Rivers. Between 1993 and 2006, Chinook salmon runs on the Sacramento had been above 200,000 fish each year. In 2007, they fell to 90,000 and in 2008 to just 59,000. "There are just no fish," lamented Zeke Grader, leader of a fishers' association, in 2008.[63]

In an unprecedented move, federal officials banned nearly all commercial and sport salmon fishing off the Oregon and California coasts in 2008 and again in 2009.[64] State officials concurred in these decisions. Although they received some federal disaster relief, fishers were upset by the closures. Greg Ambiel, who operated a forty-eight-foot salmon troller out of Half Moon Bay, the same area Michael Koepf described in his fiction, voiced the dismay many fishers felt, when he observed in summer 2008: "I love this business. You just can't get this kind of adrenaline high anywhere else. But, I can't fish salmon this summer, and it really feels weird."[65]

In fall 2009, members of the California state legislature considered new measures to restore fisheries. They were prompted by a 2007 federal court decision. Designed to protect delta smelt, a small fish living in the deltas of the Sacramento and San Joaquin Rivers where they enter San Francisco Bay, that decision ordered the huge pumping stations there to reduce by one-third the fresh water they sent south via the federal and state aqueducts to farmers and urbanites. The pumps were killing numerous quantities of smelt, an endangered species, and many salmon each year. Both agriculturalists and people living in Los Angeles soon felt the blows of lessened water supplies. Their outcries led the state legislature to take up water matters. Proposed legislation would treat fish, farms, and cities as "coequals" in their calls on fresh water. Exactly what that legislation might eventually entail was unclear, but it likely would include additional water conservation measures and some reallocation of water away from farms and cities.[66] In California, salmon suffered from numerous obstacles, but especially from habitat destruction and over-fishing. Just as the problems facing salmon were multiple, so solutions needed to be multifaceted.[67]

Commercial Fishing in the North Pacific

Compared to other American waters, fishing was better in much of the North Pacific, especially that part of the ocean that washed American and Canadian shores. Here large portions of the commercial fishing industry became sustainable. While different in results, for reasons we shall examine, political decision-making lay at the heart of fishing in the North Pacific, as in other American waters.

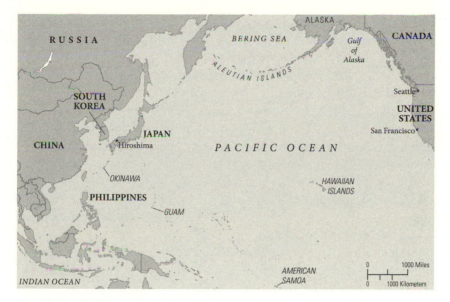

Figure 5. The Pacific.

Most of the fish taken in the North Pacific in the late 1970s came from the Northwest Pacific—the waters off the Soviet Union, China, Korea, and Japan—totaling 18.6 mmt annually, compared to 1.8 mmt from the waters of the Northeast Pacific, that is, Alaskan, Canadian, and Pacific Northwest waters. Japanese vessels harvested about 47 percent of the total catch in the North Pacific, Soviet 15 percent, Chinese 11 percent, South Korean 10 percent, North Korean 8 percent, American 2 percent, and Canadian 1 percent. Most fisheries in Alaskan waters were simply not as fully developed in the 1970s as those of Asian nations.[68] This situation changed dramatically in the 1980s and 1990s. As Americans developed their fishing capabilities under the terms of the FCMA, nearly all foreign fishers were excluded from U.S. waters. By the early 2000s, the Northeast Pacific had largely become a U.S. and Canadian lake.

As with the NEFMC for New England's fishers, the North Pacific Fishery Management Council (NPFMC) regulated much of the fishing in the Northeast Pacific. Like its sister agency, the NPFMC was a creation of 1976 federal legislation and was composed mainly of state and federal officials, along with fishers and representatives of fish-processing companies. While individual fishers and boat owners often made the front pages of newspapers in Alaska and the Pacific Northwest—their stories exhibited dramatic local color, especially when accidents struck their vessels—the decisions of the NPFMC increasingly determined how fishing was conducted.

Leaders of the North Pacific Council made decisions that, over several decades, excluded foreign fishers from nearly all the fisheries of the Northeast Pacific. In 1977, the Council set the allowable foreign catch at 1.74 mmt of a total optimum yield for the region of 1.8 mmt. Of that allowable catch, Japanese fishers received an allocation of 1.15mmt, Soviet fishers 412,000 mt, and South Korean fishers 91,000 mt. Smaller amounts went to fishers from Taiwan and Mexico. The total foreign catch was worth $200 million, for which foreign fishers paid the United States $8 million in license and poundage fees.[69] By 1986, however, American catches in the Gulf of Alaska and the Bering Sea exceeded those of foreign fishers.

The speed with which Americans came to dominate different fisheries in the Northeast Pacific varied tremendously. Even before the passage of the FCMA, foreign fishers had been ejected from nearly all Alaska's crab fisheries. Nor by the 1970s were they very active in catching salmon in American waters. Indeed, only Japanese fishers took high-seas salmon in the Northeast Pacific, and then only in the western Bering Sea, as specified in a multilateral treaty with the United States and Canada. Americans were much slower to go after most bottom fish, which were less valuable than salmon or crabs, but in the 1980s and 1990s American fishers increased their harvests. Accordingly, the NPFMC reduced allocations of bottom fish for foreign fishers until the fishers disappeared. In 2009, foreign fishers were even forbidden to catch krill—small, shrimplike animals that many types of fish eat as food—within 200 miles of American shores.[70] The Council had ample powers to enforce its rules. Before they were totally excluded, foreign vessels were often required to carry American observers on board at their expense, and American officials could board to inspect catches. The Council fined foreign vessels for breaking regulations and sometimes banished them from American waters.[71]

International politics comprised an additional factor in setting fishing allocations. The NPFMC cut the Soviet Union's allocation of fish in Alaskan waters from 25 percent of the total foreign harvest in 1979 to just 3.8 percent a year later, as a result of that nation's invasion of Afghanistan. A fictional character explained the situation in William McCloskey's novel *Breakers* about fishing in Alaskan waters. "There's a game in progress," he observed, "Russia's invested in JVs [joint ventures with American fishers], but since they invaded

Afghanistan, Carter's trying to freeze any fish quotas they've counted on from us. It's easy politics."[72]

The North Pacific Fishery Management Council

The NPFMC developed over time, but in the 1990s and early 2000s had fifteen members, eleven voting and four nonvoting. Seven of the voting members were appointed by the secretary of commerce (acting for the president) on the recommendation of the governors of Alaska and Washington. The governors submitted three names for each vacancy occurring on the Council, indicating preferred choices. The governor of Alaska nominated candidates for five voting seats, and the governor of Washington for two. Typically, the governors nominated fishers and representatives of major seafood companies. Each member served a three-year term and could be reappointed for three consecutive terms. There were four mandatory voting members: the leading fisheries officials from Alaska, Washington, and Oregon along with the Alaska regional director for the National Marine Fisheries Service. From the voting membership, Council members elected a chairman and vice-chairman to serve one-year terms. The four nonvoting members were the executive director of the Pacific States Marine Fisheries Commission, the area director for the U.S. Fish and Wildlife Service, the commander of the 17th Coast Guard District, and a representative from the U.S. State Department.[73] The goal was to combine practical with scientific knowledge in the membership of the Council to achieve sustainable fishing.

Representatives of major seafood-processing companies were always important as voting members of the Council. At times, they called most of the shots, such as fixing fishing quotas. Executives of Trident Seafoods, one of the major American processing firms served on the NPFMC from its inception—going back to Bart Eaton, one of Trident's founders and an original member of the Council. In 2008, David Benson—an executive of LFS, Inc., a subsidiary of Trident in Bellingham, Washington—was a member of the Council, becoming its chair a year later. Joseph Plesha, who joined Trident in 1988 and became the firm's chief legal officer in 2009, was very active in lobbying the Council. Representatives of three other seafood companies were voting Council members in 2008: John Bundy of the Glacier Fish Company of Seattle, Gerry Merrigan of Prowler Fisheries of St. Petersburg, Alaska, and Eric Olsen of Kwikpak Fisheries of Anchorage.[74] Fishers who were voting

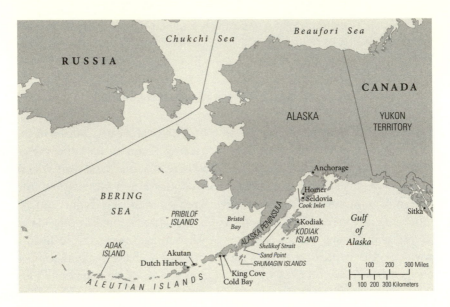

Figure 6. Alaskan waters.

members included men (but no women) from the Alaskan communities of
Eagle River and Anchor Point.[75]

Domination of the Council by large commercial fishers and processors
meant that small-scale independent commercial fishers found it harder and
harder to be heard. As well, sports fishers had little representation. In his
novel *Raiders* McCloskey describes how matters evolved from the late 1970s
to the early 1980s. "Council meetings had changed greatly in the five years
since they had been established under the national act that claimed for Americans the fish within two hundred miles of their coasts," he observed. "At first,
fishermen came in clean boat clothes to state their cases, and the few lawyers
and many fishery bureaucrats who listened all tried to dress like fishermen."
Not so, by 1983. "Now the lawyers had multiplied enough to dominate the
scene, so that the bureaucrats dressed like lawyers, and fishermen felt they
needed to dress the same to be heard."[76]

As a practical matter, this system favored well-established fishers and seafood processors, who had the time and funds to attend meetings. Council
Meetings typically lasted for several days, but sometimes for a week or longer.
The executive director of the body explained in 2006, "There are three major
meetings that make up a typical North Pacific Fishery Management Council

meeting. The Scientific and Statistical Committee and the Advisory Panel take up the same agenda as the Council does—they just begin two days in advance so they can provide their recommendations to the Council." Scientists and economists composed the Committee; the Advisory Panel included a broad range of people from the fishing industry and conservation groups. Public testimony was permitted before the Committee, the Panel, and the Council but was limited to three minutes for individuals and six minutes for representatives of groups. Within a week of each meeting, Council staff put together a summary of all decisions and made it available to the public. The Council held five or six major meetings each year. After public hearings, which might result in modifications to scientific recommendations, the Council adopted regulations for the fishing seasons.[77]

Their near exclusion from the NPFMC encouraged a language of independence and anti-federalism on the part of sports fishers. In early 2008, the North Pacific Fishery Management Coalition, composed of Alaskan sports-charter fishers, condemned the Council as "a US Government organization that has 'TOTAL' control of most of Alaska's Groundfish *and* is managed by the Large Seattle Based Commercial Fishing Industry itself." Sports fishers, the group contended, "have '*NO*' say as to policy making."[78] Then too, as we shall see in more detail in later chapters, members of environmental organizations such as Greenpeace and Oceana criticized Council decisions in debates over the appropriate sizes of bottom-fish harvests in the early 2000s.

In all, the results of the work of the North Pacific Fishery Management Council were generally what major fishers and processors desired: the exclusion of foreigners from their fisheries and an end to most over-fishing. Importantly, the NPFMC actions helped stabilize fisheries. Council members and the other fishery-management councils sent their recommendations to the secretary of commerce in Washington, D.C. Representatives of the secretary then consulted with the secretary of state about the fishing plans to determine possible effects on diplomatic relations with other nations and also met with representatives of the coast guard about enforcement plans. In any disagreement, the secretary of commerce, not the secretary of state, had the final say, just as American fishers wanted.[79] In practice, the decisions of the councils were rarely modified. In effect, policy making about fishing devolved from the national to the regional level. The secretary of commerce could not, for example, impose any type of limited-entry fishing regime on fishers unless the regional fishery management council agreed to the plan.

The secretary never took such an action. The plans moved from the councils to the secretary, not in the reverse direction.

The principal task of the NPFMC, like that of the other fishery management councils, was to produce management plans "with respect to each fishery within its geographic area." According to the Fishery Conservation and Management Act, the plans needed to be based on the best available science, had to try to prevent over-fishing, and had to be nondiscriminatory among American fishers. The plans were also to use the concept of optimum rather than maximum sustainable yield. At the start of each fishing season, scientists with the NPFMC recommended a maximum sustainable yield for each fish stock in distinct regions off the Pacific Coast and Alaska. These became the basis for determining allowable biological catches and optimum yields. Allowable biological catches were deviations, plus or minus, from maximum sustainable yields, made mainly for biological reasons.[80]

Then came what was often the most difficult task, setting optimum yields. These had to take into account industry and community concerns. Optimum yields could differ from maximum sustainable yields for a broad range of social, economic, and ecological reasons. For instance, how changes in an allowable fish catch affected employment in a community could factor into the determination of an optimum yield. As we shall see, for example, in 2005 the NPFMC decided to try to make king crabbing sustainable by limiting the overall crab harvest and allocating shares to certain well-established crabbers in a limited number of communities. Many fishers and some entire communities were excluded from king crabbing. After public protests the council modified its rulings to include fishers from some of the previously excluded towns and villages.[81]

The achievement of sustainable fishing in Alaskan waters greatly increased the importance of seafood from the North to Americans. As fishing declined in many other American waters, Alaskan and Pacific Northwestern waters grew in relative importance.

In 2000, William McCloskey, the former coastguardsman and fisher turned writer, eloquently described the fecundity of Alaskan waters: "Sea life boils throughout the water column off Alaska, on the sea floor crawl thick king crabs with sluggish claws, spidery tanner crabs, both in search of baby halibut, cod, and other bottomfish." Continuing, McCloskey observed, "Meanwhile, mature bottomfish search for baby crabs. Deeper still, in trenches below the seafloor, mill fat black sablefish." Supporting these large fish and crab were smaller creatures: "In the center of the water column swarm cloudy masses of minute plankton—simple-celled animals and vegetables the size of pinheads—which are gobbled by pollack, herring, capelin, and all manner of other fish and crustaceans." These tiny creatures supported a complex food web. "Halibut lie half buried in the mud with only watchful eyes exposed, then flash upward at the sight of prey. Cod also hover near the bottom." Above all, were salmon. "Swimming near the surface are schools of plankton-feeding salmon and other anadromous fish that hatch in fresh water, migrate to salt water, then return to fresh water to spawn."[82]

Increasingly preserved by limited-entry fishery regimes, natural abundance translated into large catches compared to those in other American waters. By the early 2000s, Alaskan waters alone accounted for about half the seafood caught in the United States, with the annual dockside value of the state's seafood harvest coming to about $1.4 billion. In 2001, the ex-vessel value (the amount paid directly to fishers) of Alaska's salmon catch came to $345 million, and the ex-vessel value of the bottom-fish catch to $510 million.[83] In 2005, seafood catches in Alaskan waters included 220 million salmon, 40,000 mt of herring, more than 1.5 mmt of pollock (making Alaskan pollock the world's largest fishery), about 250,000 mt of Pacific cod, more than 40,000 mt of halibut and sablefish (black cod), about 10,000 mt of king crabs, and about 20,000 mt of tanner crabs.[84]

Most of those catches came from waters above Alaska's continental shelves. As was the case worldwide, most commercial fishing took place within a few hundred miles of shore. In Alaska, continental shelves cover 550,000 square miles, nearly double the 300,000 square miles off the remainder of the United States, and much more than the 70,000 square miles of the Grand Banks off Newfoundland or the 12,000 square miles of Georges Bank off New England. Particularly important were the shallow, nutrient-rich waters of the Bering Sea, north of the Aleutian Islands, with 300,000 square miles. From the Bering Sea's waters came 3 percent of the world's wild fish catch.[85]

Toward Sustainable Fishing

First approved by Congress in 1976 and renewed in 1996, the Fishery Conservation and Management Act required that the eight United States fishery-management councils devise ten-year plans to rebuild depleted fisheries in American waters. A survey of 300 major fish species completed in 1998 by the United States Marine Fisheries Service showed that 90 were over-fished,

10 were approaching that condition, and 200 were healthy. A survey in 2006 suggested that the situation had worsened: 82 percent of major fished stocks in American waters suffered from over-fishing. Of the 67 commercial fish stocks with ten-year rebuilding plans, only three were completely restored, with nine more recovering.[86] The failure of many plans, according to the report, lay in a combination of continued over-fishing in defiance of plans, high fish mortality rates resulting from inadequate monitoring, and an unwillingness of some councils to revise faulty plans. Late in 2006, Congress passed legislation requiring an end to over-fishing in American waters by 2011, and in mid-2008 the Marine Fisheries Service proposed rules to put this law into practice. Yet, according to members of some environmental groups, "critical loopholes remain in the legislation, requiring additional Congressional actions."[87]

Particularly disastrous had been over-fishing and its consequences in the Northwest Atlantic. Faulty regulation allowed catches to continue at high, unsustainable levels, and over-fishing led to the near-disappearance of cod and blue-fin tuna. Composed in large part of fishers and fish processors, the agencies established to regulate fishing for cod and blue-fin tuna took very short-term approaches that encouraged over-fishing. Nor were fish stocks exempt from problems elsewhere in American waters. Combinations of over-fishing, habitat destruction, and misguided regulatory practices decimated stocks in the Gulf of Mexico and the waters off California.

On the other hand, largely sustainable fishing was eventually established in Alaskan waters. Most important in the establishment of sustainable fishing in the North was regulation by the NPFMC, which adopted a longer-term perspective than its counterparts in many other American agencies regulating fisheries. Recovery from over-fishing came when participants agreed on the need for new types of regulatory regimes and put them in place. Alaskans in particular adopted sustainable fishing methods. They benefited from fishing in newer areas with less habitat destruction than their brethren in in the lower forty-eight states. Then too, Alaskans were helped by the findings of more advanced marine science. Finally, Alaskans were alarmed by the negative examples of the decimation of fisheries like the Atlantic cod and blue-fin tuna. The movement to sustainable fishing was difficult and involved human costs, but it conserved fish stocks for future fishers. Pacific cod did not go the way of its Atlantic cousin.

A changing political economy lay at the heart of the development of sustainable seafood harvesting. At the core of all the developments was political decision-making, in which fishers and processors were deeply involved. Once fisheries passed from virgin, boom-time industries to more mature ones, a process that varied by fish stock and region, those in the fisheries often turned to government for help. To the extent that it existed at all, "laissez-faire" free enterprise had a relatively brief existence in most modern American fisheries. To the contrary, government bodies, such as the NPFMC, often partly staffed by fishers and processors, greatly influenced fishing practices, total catches, and even who fished. As in so many American industries, state and federal governmental policies for development and regulation loomed large in the evolution of fisheries.

PART II

The Industry

3

Salmon Fishing: From Open Access
to Limited Entry

In 2008, Alaskan salmon fisher Bert Bender looked back over his thirty years of gillnetting in Cook Inlet, near Anchorage. He noted that "the thought of any commercial fishing in the twenty-first century arouses our fears for the endangered seas." However, he further observed that, "thanks to our marine biologists and management programs that have existed for many years in Alaska, the wild sockeye has not been and probably will not be driven to extinction by the commercial fishery." In fact, he concluded, "Most fishermen know quite well that we must be restrained."[1] Bender was correct. Moving from open-access to limited-entry fishing in the mid-1970s saved the Alaskan salmon fishery from possible self-destruction by over-fishing. Governmental agencies—driven by fishers and representatives of fish-processing companies, who feared that their natural resource might disappear—set sustainable limits on the total catches of salmon and allocated those catches among well-established fishers, especially in Alaskan waters. This shift fundamentally altered the nature of the salmon industry. No longer could anyone who wanted to pursue salmon enter the fishery. No longer was unsustainable harvesting allowed. Salmon's fate in Alaskan waters was consequently very different from that of cod and blue-fin tuna in the Northwest Atlantic.

Salmon was long the premier fishery in the waters of the Pacific Northwest and Alaska.[2] In 1974, fisheries expert Robert Browning labeled salmon "the single most valuable fish of the North Pacific."[3] Canned salmon had become especially popular as a relatively inexpensive source of protein for working-class Americans (and was recognized as such at that time), especially after many soldiers were introduced to the fish as part of their rations in World

War I. Salmon later lost its leading designation to pollock, a bottom fish that emerged as a new type of mass-consumption food processed in the forms of surimi (fish paste), fish cakes, and fish sticks in the 1980s and 1990s. Even so, salmon remained important for fishers, processors, and consumers. Salmon was repositioned in markets as a "prestige" dish in the 1970s and later, as new technologies allowed an increasing proportion of the catch to reach consumers fresh and frozen. Between 2000 and 2010 or so, some salmon, such as "Copper River" salmon, even achieved branded, boutique status, and sold fresh at retail for as much as $38 per pound.

In this chapter I focus on the development of new state regulatory regimes for salmon by looking at two closely related issues. As in the following chapters on king crab and bottom-fish harvesting, I examine especially the development of limited-entry regimes for fishing, analyzing how fishers pursuing salmon achieved sustainable fishing through this new form of government regulation. Limited-entry fishing was, I argue, essential to the continuing health of the salmon fishery. I also investigate how changes in regulatory regimes affected the day-to-day work and lives of fishers and people in their communities.

My investigation of salmon fishing proceeds in two steps. I begin by examining salmon fishing in the Pacific Northwest, where, as in California, sustainable fishing proved elusive. Next, I turn to Alaskan waters. A boom-time fishery in the late nineteenth and early twentieth centuries, Alaskan salmon fishing suffered acutely from over-fishing by the 1950s and 1960s. The failure of the federal government to adequately regulate Alaska's salmon fishery before the territory became a state in 1959 contributed greatly to the growing scarcity of fish. Conversely, state laws establishing a limited-entry regime for salmon in Alaskan waters in the mid-1970s made the fishery sustainable. No one person or small group of people drove these changes. Rather, substantial numbers of fishers and fish-processors, alarmed about the future of their businesses and with the negative example of the Northwest Atlantic cod fishery on their minds, pushed the formation of a new, sustainable salmon-fishery regime. Among salmon fishers who found their work altered by the movement to limited-entry fishing were Francis Caldwell, Bob Durr, Joe Upton, and Steve Fink, whose life stories I tell in this chapter. Like those denied the chance to become taxi drivers in New York by that city's medallion system, sustainable fishing entailed social costs, I conclude, as many women and Alaskan Natives were excluded from the fishery.

Salmon Fishing in Pacific Northwest Waters

The commercial salmon industry of the Pacific Northwest began in the 1820s and 1830s, when the Hudson's Bay Company and a few American firms began shipping salted salmon in barrels from the Columbia River. It is the oldest commercial fishery of the Northeast Pacific. The salted salmon went to Hawai'i, Australia, China, England, California, and the U.S. East Coast. Just a bit later, fishers on Puget Sound and the Fraser River in British Columbia followed suit. From the first, the salmon industry of the Pacific Northwest was global in scope.[4] As we shall see, the same was true of salmon taken from Alaskan waters. Reaching international markets, salmon fisheries were important engines of economic growth for their regions, especially once canning began. Canned salmon put up in Alaska between 1880 and 1937 was more valuable than all the minerals mined in the territory in the same years. In Oregon and Washington before World War II, only timber and wheat were more valuable products than canned salmon.[5]

William Hume, who pioneered in developing the canned-salmon industry on California's Sacramento River, did the same a few years later on the Columbia River, which forms much of the border between Oregon and Washington. By 1866, Hume, along with friends, was already looking north to new fishing grounds. In the summer of that year, their firm of Hapgood, Hume, and Company began canning operations on the Columbia, the first enterprise to do so. A major market developed when British merchants sold canned salmon as a cheap source of protein to industrial workers. Pacific salmon soon reached worldwide markets—Britain and its colonies, but also Latin American and the Far East. Other entrepreneurs quickly followed Hume and his partners north, until in 1881 thirty-five canneries lined the Columbia, with the Hume founders involved in about half of them.[6] A federal government report observed that on the Columbia "the canning of salmon . . . grew rapidly at first . . . by 1883, the number [of canneries] reached a peak of 39. The combined pack of these 39 canneries in 1889 was 629,000 cases . . . by 1890, the number of canneries had declined to 21. . . . The reduction was due to a number of factors, including an apparent decline in the abundance of Chinook salmon."[7]

The growth of the canned-salmon industry was explosive. In 1875, fourteen canneries packed 25 million pounds of salmon on the Columbia River; by 1884 thirty-seven canneries put up 42 million pounds. In 1889, some 1,226 gillnets, 40 seine nets, 164 fish traps, and 49 fish wheels fished the Columbia.

Fifteen years later, there were nearly 2,600 gillnets, almost 400 fish traps, 92 seine nets, and 49 fish wheels. Catches fell by half between 1884 and 1889, bounced back briefly in the 1890s, and then dropped again in the twentieth century. It was not simply over-fishing that hurt salmon. Natural events were also important. Climactic developments disrupted the life cycles of salmon at various times during these years, as heavy rains and snowmelts led to flooding in 1861, 1878, 1879, 1881, and 1890. An El Niño event occurred in the late 1870s, contributing to floods.[8]

Native American fishing put considerable pressure on salmon stocks, but did not lead to their depletion. On the Columbia River, Native Americans annually harvested 4.5–6.3 million salmon from runs totaling 11–16 million, about the same number as was taken by commercial fishers in their heyday in 1883–1919. However, Natives fished all over the Columbia River basin, while Euro-American commercial fishers focused on just the lower Columbia, about a forty-mile stretch. Then too, the timing of Native fishing fit better with the life cycles of salmon than did the efforts of commercial fishers. Natives also sought to propitiate nature. They returned salmon bones to rivers with respectful ceremonies, first salmon rites, to try to ensure that salmon would come back in the future.[9]

The reduction of salmon in the Columbia resulted from a combination of over-fishing, degradation of salmon habitat, and natural phenomena such as the El Niño events. The historical roots of the decline of salmon on the Columbia in the late nineteenth and twentieth centuries were complex and interrelated.[10] Much the same can be said for other salmon runs throughout the Pacific Northwest. Along the coasts and up the rivers of Oregon and Washington in the 1900s, challenges to the sustainability of salmon catches were complicated.[11] Habitat destruction, over-fishing by Americans, and inept management by government bodies combined with natural events to greatly reduce salmon runs and catches, especially after World War II.[12]

While there were many causes for the decline of salmon catches, misguided public policies were especially important. As in Californian waters, habitat destruction in the Pacific Northwest took many forms. Dams blocked rivers, making it difficult for young salmon to reach the ocean and mature salmon to return to spawning grounds. This development was especially harmful as "high" dams such as the Grand Coulee were completed on the Columbia and its tributaries in the 1940s and later. Salmon were, in effect, traded by policymakers for electricity needed for new defense industries such as aluminum and irrigation water for farmers. Deforestation resulting from cattle grazing and logging removed brush and trees from stream banks, eliminating shade needed to keep streams cool. Farm fertilizer run-off degraded water quality. In addition, salmon were accidentally diverted from rivers into irrigation ditches serving farms in eastern Washington, eastern Oregon, and western Idaho. Mining destroyed gravel streambeds needed for spawning. In short, nearly all other industries won favor ahead of fishing, whenever they collided. Large lumber companies, ranches, and agribusinesses wielded more political clout than the usually atomized fishers. National security concerns also mattered. Federal officials favored locating new aluminum plants in the West, where they would be far from potential attack by European nations.

Friction among fishers according to ethnicities and gear types combined with divisions among fishers, loggers, ranchers, farmers, and urban boosters to make agreements on how to reduce fish losses difficult, especially as Pacific Coast cities like Seattle and Portland boomed during and after World War II. One of the very few items most Northwesterners could agree on in the early and mid-twentieth century was the use of fish hatcheries. In fact, efforts to make up for salmon losses led scientists and Pacific Northwest politicians to embrace hatcheries as a panacea well into the postwar years—a step that only made a bad situation worse. While in line with Progressive-era beliefs in the importance of science and man's hegemony over nature, artificial propagation did not bring back large runs of salmon. Many technical problems plagued the hatcheries, and groups of fishers and others did not readily agree on how to implement them. Moreover, by diverting attention from the growing number and severity of the problems wild salmon faced, the hatcheries hurt the cause of conservation. They were a false hope.[13]

The decline of salmon continued throughout the Pacific Northwest. Fisheries expert Browning observed in 1974, "Man, reshaping and polluting his environment, has remade and poisoned that of salmon, too." The drop in salmon catches resulted from many factors, he thought, "the major of them the despoliation of spawning grounds by human activities, abetted by stream pollution from domestic and industrial sources."[14] Twenty-three years later, the situation had worsened. Carl Safina found in 1997 that over 100 salmon populations, each unique to a specific river, had been extinguished in Washington, Oregon, California, and Idaho, with another 300 "at moderate to high risk of extinction." Only 16 percent of the runs, he concluded, were free of danger. The dock value of the Pacific Northwest's salmon catch plummeted by 93 percent between 1980 and 1993; Safina wrote that in many of the region's fishing towns, "A day on the docks is like a walk through a hospital where all the doors are open, exposing the suffering patients."[15]

There were occasional exceptions to this dismal state of affairs. Sockeye salmon were, for example, reestablished in the Cedar River near Seattle. In the mid-1970s, fisheries experts hoped that a million-salmon-per-year fishery could be made permanent. By 1971 a fairly large-scale salmon fishery exploited by 550 commercial fishers was in operation on the east side of Puget Sound just north of Seattle.[16] Success in restoring salmon runs, however, was more the exception than the rule.[17] Difficulties for salmon persisted into the early 2000s, a situation that had unexpected consequences. The drop in the number of Chinook salmon decimated the killer whale (orca) population in Puget Sound. Chinook salmon is their major source of food, so with salmon in short supply, the number of killer whales fell. Seven were missing and presumed dead in fall 2008, from just the previous year. The total number of killer whales in Puget Sound dropped from ninety-seven in 1996 to eighty-three in 2008. Two Pacific Northwest icons, Chinook salmon and killer whales, were endangered.[18]

Native American Fishing Rights

Salmon destruction profoundly affected Native Americans in the Pacific Northwest. For many of them, salmon were what the buffalo had once been for nomadic Plains Indians—a source of sustenance, but also a spiritual symbol of their very existence. The decline of salmon harvests thus affected Pacific Northwest Indians in a multitude of ways beyond simply economic ones.

From the 1960s, a growing number of Native Americans across the United States asserted a need for self-determination and sovereignty; indeed, these were major goals of the Red Power movement of that decade.[19] Native American actions, combined with important congressional legislation and Supreme Court decisions, made these goals reality—nowhere more clearly than in the case of fishing rights in the Pacific Northwest.[20] Broadly speaking, the struggles of Native Americans to regain fishing rights may best be seen as part of an environmental-justice movement in the United States, an effort to redress social and environmental injustices foisted on poor people and people of color, such as locating trash dumps, power plants, and nuclear waste sites in their neighborhoods.

In the 1960s and later, self-determination and sovereignty meant that

Native Americans did not need permission from the federal government for what they did. Tribes were now able to to run their own governments and legal systems, land bases, and natural resources, and Indians on and off reservations could engage in cultural renewal. These developments represent a reversal of much Indian history for over a century, for from the time they were defeated and put on reservations Native Americans faced a multipronged attack on their culture by the federal government.

The year 1975 stands out as the beginning of national recognition of self-determination for Indians. In that year, Congress passed the Indian Self-Determination and Education Assistance Act. President Nixon, pushed by Native American leaders, had for several years earlier supported such legislation, saying that Congress should empower tribes to take control of federal programs whenever Indians wanted to. This stance fit in with Nixon's general desire to favor local rights over the powers of the federal government. The legislation, passed during the presidency of Nixon's successor, Gerald Ford, required the federal agencies responsible for Native American programs, such as the Bureau of Indian Affairs and the Indian Health Service, to contract with tribes for the planning and administration of programs, and to do what the tribes wanted. Essential for Indians desiring self-determination has been ownership of natural resources, in effect control over their own economic futures. Those resources included fish, particularly in the Great Lakes and the Pacific Northwest. In fact, most stunning have been the rights Indians have regained about fishing, acquired through protests and court cases.

Bruce Wilkie and Hank Adams, two young Native Americans, led the fight for fishing rights in the Pacific Northwest. Wilkie was the treasurer-manager of the Makah tribal council (the Makah lived on a reservation on the far northwestern tip of the state of Washington). He joined the National Indian Youth Council (NIYC) in 1963 and was soon serving as its secretary. Adams was an Assiniboine from Montana, who had grown up on the Quinault reservation, just down the Washington coast from where the Makah lived. He, too, was a member of the NIYC (and became a leader of the Native American seizure of Alcatraz Island in San Francisco Bay in 1969). Organized by a group of college-educated Indians in 1960, the NIYC pushed for a wide range of sovereignty issues for Native Americans, not least fishing rights. Wilkie and Adams argued that Native Americans had never relinquished fishing rights in Pacific Northwest waters and were, therefore, entitled to pursue salmon and other fish according to tribal customs, without regard to state laws and regulations. To dramatize their stance, they staged a series of "fish-ins," modeled on African American sit-ins, beginning in March 1964, which attracted thousands of participants from across the United States. "It was a major source of encouragement and hope to have a Ponca from Oklahoma, a Paiute from Nevada, a Tuscarora from New York, a Flathead from Montana, a Navajo from New Mexico, a Mohawk from Michigan, a Pottawatomie from Ford Motors, among others offering to fight for their cause," Adams observed shortly after the first fish-in.[21] Arrests and court cases followed.

The Indians' attorneys successfully defended those charged with illegal fishing by arguing that even though their tribes had ceded lands to the federal government in the mid-1850s, they had never given up their fishing rights, which were guaranteed by treaties. In a landmark decision handed down in 1974, *United States v. Washington*, Judge George H. Boldt of the U.S. district court concluded that the tribes were entitled to half the harvestable salmon and other fish caught in Washington's waters, and his decision was upheld on appeal to the Supreme Court five years later. A similar decision at about the same time upheld Chippewa fishing rights in the Great Lakes region.

In the wake of the decision, politicians starting with president Ronald Reagan returned authority over fishing to Native Americans. As Indians assumed control of fishing and hunting on and (sometimes) beyond their reservations, they became increasingly involved in fish and game management. Tribes worked together, and eventually with state government officials, in the interests of sustainable yields, which many Indians came to see much as did their Euro American counterparts. For some Native Americans spiritual matters were also important, as members of many tribes in the coastal region of the Pacific Northwest continued to believe in "Salmon Boy," a mythical figure who gave life to their peoples. Cooperation between Native American and Euro American fishery managers became known as "co-management." During the 1980s and 1990s, for example, dozens of tribal fisheries scientists worked with Washington state officials to try to ensure a future for salmon.

In his fictional account, *River Song: A Novel*, Craig Lesley describes the meaning of salmon for Native Americans in the Pacific Northwest and their struggles to regain fishing rights on the Columbia River.[22] The story revolves around the efforts of Danny Kachiah and his son Jack, Nez Perce Indians, to deal with the complexities of Native life in Oregon, especially as seen in the lives of Native fishers along the Columbia River in the 1970s and 1980s. Lesley contrasts the lifestyles of Natives and non-Natives by juxtaposing dramatic scenes: Native Americans fighting a forest fire on reservation lands, while non-Natives enjoy golf and swimming in a pool at a nearby resort;

Natives fishing on the Columbia River with hand-pulled seine nets, while non-Natives sailboard close by, sometimes ripping up the nets in their recreational pursuits. *River Song* reaches a climax in depicting violence between commercial Native fishers and non-Native sports fishers over fishing rights, culminating in the destruction of a Native fishing community. Yet, the novel ends on an optimistic note, with the description of a Native Washat service—a traditional ceremony of reconciliation featuring feasting, dancing and drumming, and gifting.

To some degree, Native American victories in the courts by which they won back fishing rights proved to be Pyrrhic. Native Americans achieved success in winning rights to part of the commercial salmon catch. By that time, however, catches were already in freefall. Not even co-management regimes proved capable of reversing the decline brought about by over-fishing and habitat destruction. Although often blamed by non-Native fishers for the decline in salmon catches, Native Americans in fact suffered from all the over-fishing and habitat destruction that had previously occurred.

Salmon Fishing in Alaskan Waters Before World War II

As fish catches, especially for salmon, dropped in the Pacific Northwest, Alaskan fisheries grew in relative importance. Moving their operations north, salmon companies set up their first canneries in Alaska during the 1870s and 1880s. In 1878, the North Pacific Trading and Packing Company established a small cannery in southeastern Alaska, the first in the territory. Others soon followed—on Cook Inlet in 1882, Kodiak Island a year later, and Bristol Bay in 1884.[23] In 1889, thirty-seven canneries packed 714,000 cases of salmon (34,272,000 pounds). Capitalized at $4 million, they employed about 6,000 people. By the 1890s, Alaska's salmon pack dwarfed that of the Pacific Northwest: Sacramento River runs of salmon peaked in 1882 and then declined, Columbia River runs in 1895, Klamath River runs in 1912, and runs on Puget Sound streams around 1915. However, few Alaskan residents derived much benefit at first from the growth of their territory's salmon fishery. Most workers were brought from outside Alaska for summer and fall canning seasons, and few local residents initially found employment in the canneries. Nor at first did residents benefit much by catching fish, for the canneries relied mainly on their own fish traps and nets set at the mouths of rivers up which the salmon swam to spawn. By 1910, the Alaskan salmon pack came to 2.5

million cases. About 6.7 million cases were packed in 1918, as the U.S. army bought canned salmon for its troops. Output fell to fewer than 3 million cases in 1921, but recovered to more than 8 million cases in 1936, a high point.[24]

Efforts to regulate Alaska's salmon industry pitted "outside" salmon canneries against local Alaskan fishers, and federal officials against territorial residents. As early as 1889, an inspector for the U.S. Fish Commission, worried that the fish traps were depleting Alaska's salmon runs, recommended conservation measures. The packers disagreed on what to do and accomplished little. Instead, as in the Pacific Northwest, the federal government and packers turned to artificial propagation in fish hatcheries, which did little to help. Alarmed by failures at conservation, in 1922 secretary of commerce Herbert Hoover convinced president Warren G. Harding to establish a salmon-fishing reservation (a no-fishing zone) in southwestern Alaska. Hoover often involved the federal government in trying to organize and regulate smaller firms in such industries as lumber, aviation, and motion pictures—by, for example, holding government-sponsored conferences for them in Washington, D.C. At these conferences, he sought to have company officers reach agreements to make their industry operations more efficient.[25]

However, there were no such conferences for salmon fishers or processors. Local fishers opposed this action as unfairly limiting their activities. Legislation following Harding's executive order, the 1924 White Act (named after Rep. Wallace H. White of Maine who introduced it in the House) was ineffective. Its two most controversial sections—prohibiting fish traps, as desired by Alaskan residents, and establishing more fishing reservations, as sought by the packers—were deleted before passage. The White Act gave the secretary of commerce the power to limit fishing in parts of Alaskan waters and to designate the types of fishing gear that could be deployed, but not the authority to limit the amount of fishing gear, a crucial omission. The legislation also decreed that half the salmon be allowed to swim upstream to spawn, but this last requirement was only rarely enforced.[26] Little more was accomplished over the next two decades.

Fishing for Salmon in Alaska, 1950s–1970s

Significant alterations came to Alaskan salmon fishing in the 1950s, first from international negotiations and a bit later from domestic political changes, especially Alaska statehood.

International negotiations came in response to Japanese actions. Japanese fishers had instituted salmon fishing in the eastern Bering Sea in the 1930s, only to be vigorously opposed by American counterparts already well established there. World War II temporarily ended the Japanese fishing, and for several years after the conflict Japanese fishers stayed close to their home islands, within the "MacArthur Line" imposed by the victorious allied nations. However, with the return of full independence to Japan in 1952, that nation's fishers again looked to the high seas, including Alaskan waters. The Japanese government shifted some fishing vessels from the China Sea to the region. To counter renewed Japanese salmon fishing, U.S. and Canadian officials—pushed by fishers from their nations, with only grudging Japanese participation—spearheaded the formation of the International North Pacific Fisheries Commission (INPFC) in 1952.[27]

The objective of INPFC was "to ensure the maximum sustained productivity of resources of the North Pacific Ocean," a seemingly broad mandate. In practice, the commission had only a limited number of staff scientists, who encouraged and coordinated studies on fish stocks by others, such as university biologists. INPFC limited its efforts to salmon, halibut, and herring, with most of the work involving salmon. Very importantly, INPFC could decide whether the status of any of the fish stocks called for an abstention from fishing. The work of the body had particularly important consequences for salmon stocks. The organization excluded the Japanese from harvesting salmon in the eastern Bering Sea, specifically the large region east of 175 degrees west longitude. American and Canadian fishers feared that without such an agreement Japanese fishers would take salmon bound for their coastlines and their hooks and nets. Fisheries experts have generally judged the work of the INPFC in the 1950s and 1960s to have been successful in limiting conflicts with Japanese fishers and stimulating biological research on salmon.[28]

Later changes occurred in international salmon-fishing agreements for the Northeast Pacific. Shortly after Congress passed the Fishery Conservation and Management Act in 1976, the United States renegotiated the issue of high-seas salmon fishing with Japan: continued prohibition of Japanese fishing in the eastern Bering Sea and new restrictions on fishing in some other areas within the U.S. 200-mile exclusive economic zone. Finally, in 1992, INPFC rulings were subsumed into the UN Convention for the Conservation of Anadromous Stocks in the North Pacific, which forbade taking any salmon on the high seas.[29] Although ordinary Americans were rarely aware of these policy changes, the net result was more American-caught salmon on their dinner plates.

While these significant international developments were taking place, Alaska became a state in 1959, leading to additional changes in the regulation of salmon fishing. Some authority over fisheries devolved from the federal to the state level, for example, control of inshore fisheries within three miles of the shore, or within twelve miles from 1966. One of the first actions of the new Alaskan state legislature was to outlaw fish traps, hated symbols of non-resident canneries and fishers. (A provisional measure had forbidden the use of fish traps three years earlier.)

Fishing technologies gradually advanced. Into the early 1950s, salmon canneries provided double-ended sailboats for two-person crews to use in catching salmon—especially in shallow Bristol Bay, one of Alaska's most productive salmon-fishing grounds. Fishers delivered their salmon to the cannery that supplied their boats, at prices decreed by the cannery. Motor-propelled salmon-fishing vessels were legalized for Bristol Bay only in 1951. Most canneries continued to be owned by non-Alaskan fishery companies headquartered in Seattle, intensifying Alaskan dislike of "outsiders."[30]

Fishing was a tough business on a day-to-day basis. Rudy Anich, who owned the seiner *Naknek Made*, with which he worked Pacific Northwestern and Alaskan waters, recalled what landing nets was like: "Well, from all the gripping and pulling web with your hands, your fingers would be locked tight each morning. Couldn't open them, couldn't hold a thing. We learned from the old-timers to urinate on our hands, and that would start them moving."[31] Then too, fishing by sail could be dangerous. On 5 July 1948, twenty-six fishers died when their boats were caught in a gale and pounded to pieces on Deadman Sands in Bristol Bay.

This system eroded in the early 1950s and disappeared in later decades. Fishers came to possess their own boats, now larger, gasoline- or diesel-powered, and featuring hydraulic power blocks, which operated like winches to haul in nets. The power block was invented in 1955, perfected by 1958, and put to common use within a few more years. Coastguardsman and fisher William McCloskey has concluded that the hydraulic power block "might be the single most important development in fishing since the contrivance of the first net many years B.C., freeing fishermen from being beasts of burden just as the tractor freed farmers."[32]

Salmon boats' design and lack of maintenance added to dangers. McCloskey recalled, "In the early 1950s, before the advent of the great Alaska money

Figure 7. Purse seining for salmon in Alaska in the mid-1970s. Note the power block suspended from the boom pulling in the net. With the permission of Richard Newman.

fisheries, fishing boats were often wooden, gasoline-driven craft maintained by the seat-of-the-pants. Often, when engines patched with wires failed near rocks or when gassy bilges caught fire, our ship [the coast guard cutter *Sweet-brier*] was summoned to the rescue." In Bristol Bay, gillnet boats were limited to thirty-two feet in length and were characterized by McCloskey as "able work machines" that looked like "bathtubs with stovepipes for masts."[33]

The examples of two fishers—Francis E. Caldwell, a troller, and Joe Upton, a gillnetter—illlustrate that salmon fishing involved in southeastern Alaskan waters was a lifestyle choice, as well as a way to make money.[34] The personal memoir of Bob Durr, who fished in Bristol Bay, provides a look at purse sein- ing and gillnetting for salmon north of the Aleutians.

Caldwell was typical of fishers who trolled for salmon along the Pacific Coast north into southeastern Alaskan waters, as far as the Fairweather grounds, off Cape Fairweather, just west of Skagway. By 1978, when he pub- lished his first-hand account, Caldwell had been fishing commercially for two decades. Beginning with a small eighteen-foot skiff capable of fishing only in sheltered waters, he had moved up to the ownership of a fifty-four-foot steel troller suitable for offshore work, the *Donna C.*

For Caldwell, fishing was "a gambling business," with the fisher betting his/her strength and knowledge against the elements. Money was part of the motivation, and at the start of each season fishers, Caldwell observed, had "thoughts of fresh money in the bank." However, there was more involved in fishing than the profit motive. Fishers were above all, independent people—a refrain coming through time and again in first-hand accounts. "The com- mercial fisherman," Caldwell wrote, "has contempt and pity for anyone who works at a regular job." In this feeling fishers resembled some commercial truckers, who yearned for the open road. Caldwell also observed, "The fish- erman will struggle to keep his feet on a slimy, rolling deck 20 hours a day in freezing wind and rain and consider himself the salt of the earth." Fish- ers were, he concluded, "true romantics." At the end of a long day of fishing in stormy conditions, Caldwell asked rhetorically, "For what reason would a man lead such a miserable life? Riches? Certainly not. Glory? What Glory? Love? How could anyone love a bitch such as the sea? Why then? I pondered the question."[35]

Difficulties punctuated Caldwell's personal story of trolling. Bad weather was part of his everyday life, with "gloomy rain," "mountainous seas," "sudden gales," and "bitter cold" his constant companions. Williwaws, fierce winds roaring off nearby lands at 100 mph, commanded instant respect. In one case a "storm front struck like a falling brick." The first gust laid Caldwell's boat "over on her side and held her there," and water soon "sloshed back and forth."[36]

Hard work was a fact of life for Caldwell, when fishing: catching the salmon and icing them in his boat's holds. Even more difficult, however, was the loneliness, boredom, and tedium of his work. Constructed in 1954, the *Donna C* was a one-man boat, much smaller than many of the larger vessels used in king crabbing and bottom fishing. Caldwell fished alone most of the time. His radio, and later a CB, was his lifeline to the outside world, for "a commercial fisherman is isolated without his radio." Having a sense of humor helped. It was, Caldwell thought, "His defense against boredom." In his journal, he related a radio conversation he heard. When asked why the captain of one boat had reduced the number of crew members from three to one, the captain replied, "We always used to have four [including the captain], but that was back when we played bridge and needed 'em. Nowadays we play cribbage. So we need only two."[37]

As the joke he told suggested, Caldwell found a fishing lifestyle appealing. Except when actually trolling for and landing salmon, there was time for relaxation: cups of coffee, napping, even sightseeing. After finishing "dreary chores" one evening, Caldwell observed, "Some of the wildest and most beautiful scenery in America spun slowly by the windows as my boat turned on the anchor." On another occasion, he wrote of a sunrise in poetic terms: "Suddenly, I'm enveloped in a world of molten gold as Veta Bay becomes livid with reflections. Out on the edge, the sea and sky remain mated together in inky nothingness. I watch spellbound as the gold turns to copper." He liked the seasonal pattern of his work: getting his boat ready in the winter and early spring in Port Angeles on Puget Sound, his home port, cruising north through the Inside Passage to the Alaskan fishing grounds in the late spring and early summer, fishing in the summer and early fall, and then returning south to his home. In this activity, Caldwell asserted, "My boat and I are a team."[38]

Joe Upton also worked as a fisher. Captain and owner of a thirty-two-foot fiberglass workboat, the *Doreen*, he fished for thirteen years with his wife and a large dog named Sam. Upton got his start in 1965 by operating a tender boat buying salmon from fishers for a processing company and leasing "a tired and rotting 30-foot gill-netter" five years later. In 1972, he purchased the *Doreen*, which he rigged for both trolling and gillnetting. "Trolling pays a lot of our bills," he noted, "but this gill-netting—that's where we make our season."

Diesel-powered and with a power reel on the stern to handle the gillnet, the *Doreen* was also well equipped with hydraulic gurdies (small winches) to haul in fish lines on the trolling poles. The boat boasted a toilet (many boats did not and were known colloquially as "stern-shitters"), galley (kitchen), marine radio, CB, and radar.[39]

In many ways, Upton's account of fishing is similar to Caldwell's. Seattle was his home port, but Alaska was where he fished. Dirty weather was a constant companion in Upton's search for salmon in southeastern Alaska. Even in mid-May, his journal recorded a "nasty day with half a gale" and noted, "We were blown in today, the weather was too tough even for fishing on the inside" (in the Inside Passage, away from the open seas). The weather improved some in the summer, but by fall it was again "stormy" with many "squalls blotting out everything at times." On 28 October, near Ketchikan, Upton wrote: "A southeast gale sweeps up the channel," and on the next day he observed, "the gale continues."[40] Fog, rain, and wind were common throughout the summer and fall fishing seasons. Accidents and breakdowns in equipment occurred, and in the isolated conditions of Alaska it sometimes took weeks to have replacement parts flown in at considerable expense.[41] Fishing was "always in spurts." The result, Upton thought, was "often very aggressive and competitive fishing, as many boats crowd into an area with room for a few and jockey to be at the right spot at the right stage of the tide." When salmon were located, Upton worked nonstop. Hauling in the net, even with a power drum, was physically demanding, as the salmon had to be hand-picked from the mesh as the net came on board. Icing down and storing the salmon also took time and effort.[42]

Even so, Upton liked fishing. After discussing his many hardships, he concluded, "Still it can be an enjoyable way to fish, and for most fishermen, running your own boat and being your own boss is hard to beat." Like Caldwell, Upton embraced the independence of his work and life. Except when the salmon were running, he and his wife found plenty of time for coffee get-togethers, dinners with friends (mainly other fishers), shore excursions, and even gardening (his wife maintained a small cabin and garden onshore).[43] Making high profits was not Upton's major motivation, and he thought his income was satisfactory. His diary records his daily catch and the prices he received for his salmon. "The money is good up here," he wrote on one occasion.[44] More important, though, was Upton's feeling of satisfaction. As he explained, "This is our world, and how it satisfies, at the end of the day, to sell a few fish and to sit at the cabin watching the evening sky and the water." Three months later at the close of the fishing season, he made a similar observation, "We are tired now from the trip and the season, but still, it's sad to have it end. Our work is sometimes hard, and these trips tedious." But "Still, life fills up in a way it won't ashore."[45]

For Bob Durr, fishing for salmon in Bristol Bay north of the Aleutian Islands was a somewhat different experience from those of Caldwell and Upton in southeastern Alaska. Beginning in the 1960s, Bristol Bay replaced southeastern Alaska as the state's prime fishing area for salmon. A number of interacting factors accounted for this shift: Japanese and Soviet high-seas interception of salmon bound for southeastern streams, careless logging practices that harmed spawning grounds, over-fishing by sport and commercial fishers, and destructive freezes at crucial times.[46]

When he first took up fishing, Durr was forty-three years old, had a wife and four children, and was a tenured faculty member in English at Syracuse University. At first, he fished only during summers, returning to New York to teach during the academic year. However, mixed desires for imagined freedom and a need to "earn some dollars" soon led him to abandon academic life for fishing, and he moved to Alaska with his family. Durr harbored a romantic view of Alaska. "I dreamed of wilderness," he later remembered. For him Alaska was like "a Winslow Homer watercolor."[47]

Fishing in the 1960s as a crew member, boat captain, and boat owner at various times, Durr had a less-structured life than Upton or Caldwell. Durr fished in more of a boom-time atmosphere. On first reaching Bristol Bay in 1964, he later recalled, there was "excitement in the air." The next year, 1965, was "a big one in Bristol Bay," with the average boat earning a net profit of $20,000. "Everyone's nets [were] smoking," and the fishing grounds were "vibrating with excitement." In 1967, Durr thought, "Fishing was like war . . . the fish suddenly showing, the hustle and fever of the catch, the element of danger in the heavy seas, and then the shutdown of closed periods and the spillover restlessness."[48] The work was—just as Caldwell, Upton, and many other fishers described it—hard, monotonous, backbreaking labor, even with power blocks for purse seine nets and power drums for gillnets. The salmon were all that mattered. As Durr later remembered, graffiti scrawled in "big Magic Marker letters" on one bar's toilet wall summed up the importance of the salmon: "The Fish!"[49]

Money was important, but was not the only reason to fish. The lifestyle was equally significant. Looking back in 1999, Durr lamented, "To most fishermen today the fish means only money. They see dollar bills coming over the roller" (the stern drum over which a gillnet passes as it comes aboard a boat).[50] Many fishers I interviewed made this point. To some degree they may have been remembering a nonexistent, mythical golden age. However, as we shall see, fishing did change in the 1970s and 1980s, with much more emphasis on immediate monetary returns.

In this situation, partying seemed essential to Durr, a much more riotous form of social recreation than the coffee get-togethers and dinners described by Caldwell and Upton. Relaxing meant, above all, drinking hard liquor. "If you don't drink, you're no good," Durr wrote. "This was the real Alaska," he continued, "the frontier. Men drank." Dillingham, the major settlement fronting on Bristol Bay, seemed at times to be like a town of the Wild West, with numerous bars and little else except canneries. The "toughest" men in Dillingham were known as "tigers."[51] Durr devoted a significant part of his memoirs to an end-of-the-season party that lasted for days on an inland lake, with alcohol flowing copiously. "Back on the beach," he observed of participants on the third evening, "bonfires blaze, and it looks like a witches' Sabbath, silhouetted figures leaping and dancing. Pope [a fisher] is banging the guitar and singing in his booming voice about the sloop *John B*, but nobody yet looks so broke they want to go home."[52]

Not all those pursuing salmon made fishing their career. Many were temporary workers, as was Steve Fink, one of the young men (and occasionally women) who went north to take part in Alaska's summer salmon fisheries. Fink grew up in Minneapolis-St. Paul.[53] He received a B.A. from the University of California, Berkeley in 1974, an M.A. in English from Columbia University in 1975, and a Ph.D. in English from the University of Washington, and became a faculty member at The Ohio State University. However, he worked as a fisher in Alaska in summer 1975. Fishing appealed to Fink for several reasons. He was looking for a break; he "wanted to do something very different from graduate school." He was seeking adventure, "a good time," "physical work," and a chance to make money before beginning doctoral studies. In retrospect, Fink noted that "I didn't come home with money in my pockets." However, he did cover his expenses, and he had "a terrific experience."

Fink learned about salmon fishing in Alaska from a high-school friend who had fished out of Ketchikan the previous summer. With that friend, he drove to Seattle and "got a ride up" on a boat to Ketchikan. Fink did not have a job lined up. "I was up there cold," he recalled. In Ketchikan, he "cruised the docks . . . asking if they [boat captains] needed crew," and fortunately was hired onto a salmon boat as a green hand, working on a share basis. Fink's boat was a fifty-eight-foot purse seiner, the *Jose Maria*. Electronics on the vessel, Fink later recalled, were "pretty minimal. . . . It was definitely a very basic boat." The boat had radar, but other electronics like loran were absent. The boat did use a power block to bring in the net and lift it out of the sea. The *Jose Maria* had a raft but, like most fishing boats then, did not have survival suits or other emergency gear.

Once at sea, Fink and the other five crew members looked for "jumpers," salmon leaping out of the water, to find schools of fish. The captain, an Alaskan Native, relied on his experience to seek out good salmon-fishing grounds. "The skipper went to places he was familiar with," Fink remembered; it was "all off-shore fishing." The crew worked as a team. Each person had one distinct task. The captain and the skiff driver—a skiff took the net from the *Jose Maria* to encircle a school of salmon—were "locals and experienced," but the rest of the crew were "green or had only fished for one season." Once the purse-seine net was hauled on board and opened to spill out the salmon, all worked to get the salmon into the holds with ice. They tried to avoid touching jellyfish in the net, for they could sting hands and arms badly. Usually, the *Jose Maria* took the fish back to Ketchikan for sale. Sometimes, however, the boat sold its fish to tenders, which used brails (basket-like devices) to offload the salmon.

Fink remembered his fishing experiences as "good." "Overall," he concluded, "it was easy fishing." He worked sixteen-hour days, but even so there was time for sleep. The work "was demanding, but it was not constant"; there was "downtime." There was the usual need to fix items of gear that broke. "Things went wrong when we were fishing." There was the problem of fog and rain, but the fog usually burned off in the afternoons. There were plus sides to the fishing life. Fink remembered nature—the mountains, the ocean, and animals (killer whales, porpoises, and bald eagles)—as "spectacular." There was ample free time in Ketchikan. Fink enjoyed hiking on Deer Mountain behind the city. There were numerous bars: "There were bars, and the bars were open all of the time." In them, ringing a bell meant treating everyone to free drinks. Fink also remembered playing cribbage, listening to music, and simply loafing. After his one summer, Fink never went back to commercial fishing, despite thinking about doing so from time to time. "It's one of those things I regret," he observed.

William McCloskey, the coastguardsman and fisher, caught the character and motivation of Alaskan fishers of the 1960s and 1970s. They came, he noted, "from several backgrounds and interests." Many wanted to "make

Figure 8. The *Jose Maria* near Ketchikan in the mid-1970s. With the permission of Richard Newman.

their money and then return south with it to enjoy the comforts of more urbanized area." However, "the pattern has begun to change, . . . despite the wretched Alaskan winters." By the 1970s, "most men fishing from Ketchikan and about half of those in Kodiak are now residents, having been attracted to the open life of Alaska from all parts of the U.S. and from that traditional land of northern seafarers, Scandinavia." Not all were temporaries like Steve Fink. On the other hand, Dutch Harbor, in the western Aleutian Islands, the center for crab and bottom-fish operations, was "called home by few except native villagers." One common element for all Alaskan fishers was danger: "the life of a fisherman is rougher and more dangerous than that of any other seafarer."[54]

The Changing Regulatory Regime: Limited-Entry Fishing

In the early years of statehood, regulating Alaskan salmon fishing was accomplished mainly by setting the number of hours and days during which boats could fish the many different runs of salmon in various Alaskan waters.[55] These times were called "openings." Once fishery officials thought that enough salmon had returned from the ocean and swum up their rivers to guarantee an adequate spawning generation—a process they called "escapement"—they opened the waters to fishing. In the early years, estimates by fishery biologists of escapement requirements were crude, based on sightings of salmon runs from boats and airplanes and test fishing. Later on, estimates became more exact as electronic devices were placed at rivers' mouths to count individual salmon as they entered streams. Even so, judging necessary escapements remained an inexact affair.

What resulted was "derby" fishing, or, as it was sometimes called, "Olympic" fishing. Fishers rushed to sea in all kinds of weather, anxious to take as many salmon as possible before fishery officials closed the opening. Economically inefficient and sometimes dangerous, derby fishing resulted from the regulatory system then in place.

Fishers often criticized derby fishing. Upton noted in his journal at one point, "This gill-netting is getting to be too crazy for me with these 24-hour periods."[56] Fisher and journalist Brad Matsen described salmon fishing in Bristol Bay as "a cross between a Brazilian soccer riot and a summer camp where counselors pass out hundred-dollar bills instead of marshmallows." He observed, "The whole show lasts just six weeks in June and July and attracts an international crowd of 20,000 men and women to catch, butcher, and haul . . . salmon."[57] Another participant made much the same point, looking at the opening of salmon fishing near the town of Naknek on Bristol Bay: "Boats gun to be free of each other, tossing off lines as wet cold wind lashes hands and faces. The river turns as crowded as a freeway at rush hour. Nobody has time to lose. . . . The water has become a floating city, a battlefield swaying to wind-driven waves."[58]

The haste with which fishers worked during the limited fishing openings sometimes resulted in accidents. McCloskey related watching a purse seiner overturn during one opening.[59] Sig Hansen described opening day as simply "chaos."[60] Some of the excitement continued into the early 2000s. Pete Andrews, who fished for salmon in Bristol Bay, explained preparations in summer 2009: "We'll get the nets ready and get them patched. We'll pull the [engine] hatches open, change the belts, if we need to, the hydraulic hoses. . . . It's like getting a race car ready."[61]

Since officials placed few limits on the number of fishing vessels or the amount of gear they could place in the water, over-fishing sometimes resulted, especially since estimates of the necessary salmon escapes up streams

Figure 9. Opening day for salmon fishing on Bristol Bay in 1995. Courtesy of William B. McCloskey, Jr.

often proved to be inaccurate. In 1967, 62 companies operated 71 canneries in Alaska but put up only 1.4 million cases of salmon, down from 2 million in 1960 and the smallest pack since the 1880s. From that low point, Alaska's salmon catch more than tripled by 1970, only to fall back to its 1967 level in 1974.[62] Between 1960 and 1972, as historian and former fisher David Arnold pointed out, "Canneries rapidly expanded their fleets, bringing even more competition into the fishery and increasing the amount of gear in the salmon fisheries by 74 percent."[63] The result was even more over-fishing.

New "limited-entry" methods regulated Alaska's salmon catch from the mid-1970s on and brought about sustainable fishing. Fishers, fish processors, and politicians—concerned about declining salmon catches—spearheaded a drive that convinced Alaska's voters to approve an amendment to the state constitution allowing limiting entry into their state's fisheries. Next, the state legislature passed the Limited Entry Act of 1973. That legislation set up a three-member Alaska Commercial Fisheries Entry Commission, empowered to restrict entry into commercial fishing in the state's waters, those seas within twelve miles of shore. The commissioners were required to be people with broad professional experiences in fishing, but without current interests in commercial salmon fishing or processing. The goals of the act were to "promote the conservation and sustained yield management of those fisheries and the economic health and stability of commercial fishing."[64]

In 1974, the Commission began limiting the number of permits given to salmon fisheries. Within a year, nineteen of Alaska's major salmon fisheries were under limited-entry management. With help from the Alaska Department of Fish and Game, the commission also established what types of fishing gear could be used in different state waters and set fishing openings, which, as before, were allowed only after adequate escapement periods. For the first time, limits were placed on the number of boats and amounts of gear that could fish for salmon. Permits went to boat owners and fishers with previous records in commercial fishing, as established fishers were grandfathered into the new regime. Issued on the basis of a point system that rewarded earlier fishing efforts in Alaskan waters, the permits could be transferred by gift, inheritance, or sale.

Open access to the fishery was closed, and sustainable salmon fishing became possible. Arnold summarized what the move to limited-entry fishing meant: "Salmon managers now embraced a property-right system that restricted use. . . . For salmon it meant—theoretically at least—less gear to navigate on their way to the spawning grounds. For conservation officials it

meant more direct control about fishing intensity. For industrialists it meant
a more reliable, stable, professional, and efficient fleet, but one that would be
increasingly 'independent' and liberated from cannery control." There were,
Arnold thought, downsides to the change in fishing, for "limited entry made
it harder for younger men to obtain permits and carry on family fishing traditions." Instead, "Commercial fishing permits began to make their way into
the hands of a new breed of fisherman: highly capitalized independent entrepreneurs without historic ties to the fishery."[65]

In establishing a limited-entry regime for salmon fishing within state
boundaries, Alaskan officials moved in a direction opposite from that being
taken by federal officials with regard to many industries. As noted earlier,
Presidents Ford and Carter sought to deregulate the airline and trucking industries, opening—not restricting—entry. However, fishers and Alaskans in
general saw Alaska salmon fishing as needing closer regulation. Fishers and
fish processors feared that without limited entry, their fishery might disappear and their livelihoods vanish. Even intensely individualistic fishers came
to see the attractions of state intervention, when that intervention might benefit them. Such behavior was not surprising. Individualistic business leaders often turned to government when doing so helped them. For instance,
nineteenth-century steel baron Andrew Carnegie, a staunch individualist,
backed tariffs to exclude British steel from American markets and supported
government construction of the Sault Ste. Marie locks between Lakes Michigan and Huron to enable ships carrying iron ore to reach his steel mills.
During the nineteenth and twentieth centuries, business leaders welcomed
government efforts to foster economic expansion—for example, aid to canals,
railroads, trucking firms, and airlines. Up to the 1970s, factory managers expected the government to regulate rates charged by airlines, railroads, and
truckers.

In Alaska, limited-entry fishing regimes soon controlled most commercial fishing. In 2007, the chairman of the Commercial Fisheries Entry Commission offered a statistical overview of how the permit system had worked
from its inception in 1974. Through 2005, the state had issued 16,264 limited-
entry permits in sixty-five Alaskan fisheries. About 80 percent of the permits had initially been granted to Alaskan residents, the other 20 percent to
non-Alaskans. Some 14,536 permits remained in effect at the close of 2005,
with 1,728 having been canceled. About 23 percent of those permits still in
effect were held by nonresidents, 38 percent by rural Alaskans living in their
permit areas, 6 percent by rural Alaskans living outside their permit areas,

24 percent by urban Alaskans living in their permit areas, and 9 percent by urban Alaskans living outside their permit areas. While acknowledging that "total permit holdings by nonresidents has risen since initial issuance," the chairman claimed, "Over time there has been little change in the communities holding the highest number of entry permits." These were Ketchikan, Anchorage, Cordova, Kodiak, Sitka, Wrangell, Togiak, and Dillingham—all major centers for salmon fishing.[66]

Nonetheless, an unintended effect was that limited-entry fishing also excluded some women from fisheries, for they generally had a more difficult time than men in securing the credit need to buy permits. By 1994, for example, the price of a Bristol Bay gill netting permit was $202,000.[67] Some Alaskan Natives were also excluded, as salmon fishing, and fishing in general, became more capital intensive. Boats became larger, powered by bigger engines, and equipped with more and more sophisticated technological devices designed to find, catch, and haul salmon. The increasing prices of boats exacerbated the problems caused by the escalating prices of permits. Bert Bender, the Cook Inlet fisher, observed, "In order to remain competitive, fishermen began to invest in bigger and faster boats . . . and wooden boats, in general, began to give way to more efficient vessels made of aluminum or fiberglass and powered by larger gasoline and diesel engines."[68]

Eric Rosvold, a longtime fisher in Petersburg, presented a careful accounting of his expenses and income for the previous year in a public hearing in 2007. Like many fishers in southeastern Alaska, he used his boat to seine for salmon. However, again like many fishers, Rosvold also went after tanner crabs (smaller cousins of king crabs), sablefish (black cod), and halibut. He placed the value of his 58-foot "limit" seiner at $575,000, his seining equipment at $75,000, his long-lining equipment for halibut and sablefish at $75,000, and his crabbing equipment at $60,000. Rosvold valued his limited-entry permit for salmon seining at $40,000. His limited-entry permit for tanner crabs cost $150,000, his rights to pursue sablefish $3,010,000, and his permits to harvest halibut $1,315,000. These fishing rights were mainly multiyear permits. Thus, the value of his vessel, gear, and fishing permits came to about $5,300,000. His annual fishing income amounted to about $1,220,000, before expenses for fuel, groceries, insurance, repairs, and moorage. He estimated that his annual return on equity before taxes was about 5.5 percent, but that after taxes he lost $162,000.[69] This accounting was probably pretty typical for a small-scale family fisher. Fishing was expensive and not always profitable.

Despite some exclusion from fisheries due to limited-entry requirements, starting in the 1980s women composed about 5 percent of the commercial fishers in Alaska. While women were present in all the region's major fisheries—crabbing, shrimping, and bottom fishing, as well as salmon fishing—they were most active in going after salmon. The costs of entry were lowest in salmon fishing. Women could start as family members operating beach-seine nets, or as deckhands on purse seiners or gillnetters, which cost less than king-crab or bottom-fish vessels. Some women fishers progressed to become boat captains and owners, sometimes operating with all-female, sometimes with mixed-gender, crews. Like men, women went into commercial fishing for a variety of motives—money, excitement, competition, independence of lifestyle, and love of the physical act of fishing. Like many men, they used the analogy of war. "You're either bored to death or scared to death," concluded one woman about her experiences fishing for salmon near Cordova, Alaska.[70]

Women faced the same challenges as male fishers, along with some that were specific to their gender. Fishing was physically demanding and often dangerous. Many found, however, that endurance, mental as well as physical, was more necessary than brute strength, a circumstance which, they thought, gave them opportunities to succeed. Like men, they worked round-the-clock when "on the fish or crab." "When you're on a boat, you don't have a life, you don't have any physical space, you don't have any time to yourself," remembered a woman who captained a purse seiner operating out of Kodiak: "It's all the boat, the fishing, for four months straight."[71] Dangers were ever-present, just as for men, especially bad weather conditions, resulting in injuries incurred when handling salmon nets or crab pots.

For some women, sexual harassment was an assumed fact of life on board the vessels. "The conflict takes many forms," explained one woman salmon fisher, "from the 'two for one syndrome' when a skipper hires a woman as a cook and expects her to double as bunkmate, though she may not know it, to obscenities and verbal barrages attacking competency to life-threatening attacks." Most commonly, women observed that they had to prove that they were "twice as good as men" at their tasks to succeed in commercial fishing's "macho" environment.[72]

Although most women fishers, like most men, came to recognize that limited-entry fishing was needed, they believed it hurt women unduly. Sarah Palin, Alaska's governor for several years in the early 2000s, recalled in 2009 how important family fishing had been for her: "My experience fishing commercially has been a joy as I join my husband at a set net site in Bristol Bay that his family has fished for generations. We have since passed this tradition on to our children, spending our summers harvesting the magnificent red salmon that return to Bristol Bay year after year."[73]

Such experiences became more difficult under the limited-entry fishing regime. One woman salmon fisher explained in the 1970s: "As fishing became more lucrative, everything changed. People sold their permits because suddenly the permits were worth so much more. It became more difficult for women to get into the fishery at that point. You couldn't be an auxiliary to your husband's operation: you either were fishing 100 percent or you weren't fishing at all. Then in '74 when fishing changed with the limited entry system, it made it more difficult for women to get in because you had to have cash up front."[74]

Alaskan Natives also faced increasing limitations. For decades, they had combined subsistence and commercial salmon fishing, moving in and out of each type of fishery as their needs for food and cash dictated. The advent of limited-entry fishing threatened that arrangement. Historian and fisher David Arnold observed in a detailed look at salmon fishing in southeastern Alaska that, "The move to limited entry was an especially bitter pill for Native communities." Alaskan Natives often did not have the funds to buy the permits and boats needed for commercial fishing. Arnold found that the lack of capital in Native communities had two important consequences. On the one hand, Natives who received commercial fishing permits were likely to sell them to get cash. By 1980 about 30 percent of the permits initially issued to rural fishers (Native and non-Native alike) were owned by nonresident outsiders. On the other hand, Alaskan Natives who did not receive permits were excluded altogether from commercial fishing, one of their few avenues for earning cash. Declining participation in commercial fishing also led to declining participation in subsistence fishing for Alaskan Natives. A way of life was vanishing. Arnold observed, "For Native communities limited entry did not just constitute an economic loss, but a cultural one."[75]

Regulation brought still other consequences to Alaskan residents. Excluded from fishing in Alaskan waters, Japanese responded by entering into joint ventures with Americans to build new, state-of-the-art salmon-processing plants on shore and on barges at sea. The large, efficient processing barges were nicknamed "death barges" by American competitors—a play of words on the "Star War" movies of the time, which featured a "death star." Japanese purchases, combined with technological advances, fundamentally altered salmon fishing. Desiring only very high quality salmon, Japanese processors shipped fresh or fast-frozen salmon to Japan. Salmon could no longer be roughly pitchforked off boats to waiting tenders. Doing so injured the flesh of the fish too much. "Salmon suddenly became much more valuable," Bender observed, "and the Japanese taught us how to take care of it, demanding that we treat this valuable food with more respect than we ever had." He noted, "We had once unloaded our fish by jabbing each one with the single tine of a peugh and throwing it aboard a tender; now we learned how to pick up each fish, not by the tail, but by the body, using both hands and carefully throwing it into a bin."[76]

Canning salmon became less common than in the past, as fresh and frozen salmon increasingly made their ways to restaurants and stores, an alteration made possible by fast-freezing techniques and jet aircraft. Spurred by demand, the wholesale price of sockeye salmon jumped from $0.50 to $2.10 per pound in 1980 alone.[77] In McCloskey's fictional *Breakers* a salmon-cannery superintendent laments in mid-1978, "The rules I learned came from a different time. Thank God people still put salmon in cans. I do that very well. But Japanese—he lowered his voice—Jap money's paying so much for frozen reds this year I'm not sure we can compete on prices and still make canned reds pay. . . . Up here we didn't win World War II." Just four years later, a fictional fisher explains the shift to another: "Everything's changed, Vito. Since the Japanese started buying to freeze in '79. That's what I'm trying to drive home. Canning used to be the only show. . . . Now freezing's a different monkey with a different market."[78]

In fact, the large freezer barges ended the hegemony onshore plants once maintained over salmon processing. Fisher and writer Brad Matsen observed in 1998, without much exaggeration, "Eventually, Japanese buyers would completely control red salmon from Bristol Bay and buy most of the production capacity in Alaska," to the extent that in 1996 Alaskan fishers filed a class action suit against the Japanese processors claiming price fixing.[79] If not all of the changes occurring under the new limited-entry salmon-fishing regime could be anticipated, the hope that salmon catches would recover was born out.

Sustainable Salmon Fishing in Alaska

Catches of Alaskan salmon did indeed rise dramatically under the limited-entry regime. Restricting the number of boats and the amount of gear that could fish for salmon, along with limiting overall catches by species, brought about resurgence in Alaskan salmon. Signs of improving harvests occurred very soon after limited-entry fishing began. As early as 1976, one prominent observer noted, "Salmon pack figures for 1976 show just enough improvement over 1975, the worst year ever, to justify in some small measure this belief (or perhaps just hope) that things will indeed get better."[80]

From fewer than 25 million salmon in the mid-1970s, the annual Alaskan catch soared to a record high of 217 million in 1997, at about which level it remained, with fluctuations, into the early 2000s. The catch stood at 213 million fish in 2007, fourth-largest since statehood. It fell to 146 million in 2008, still the sixteenth-largest since statehood, due mainly to a decline in the harvest of pink salmon. The resurgence of salmon catches firmly established Alaska as the leading source of wild salmon in the North Pacific, which in turn was the major source of wild salmon for the world. In 2008, Alaskan waters produced 43 percent of the North Pacific's wild salmon, Russian waters 31 percent, Japanese waters 21 percent, Canadian waters 4 percent, and the waters of Washington, Oregon, and California a scant 1 percent.[81]

Environmental changes, as well as the issuance of limited-entry regulations, may have been involved in the surge of Alaskan salmon harvests, although scientists debate this possibility. For reasons still not clear, the Bering Sea, of which Bristol Bay is a part, experienced a rise in temperature of about 2 degrees Celsius in 1977. Salmon were better able to accommodate this increase than some other fish species and thrived. In fact, in 1996 the *Wall Street Journal* reported that "Alaska is awash in salmon." The increasing Alaskan catches, along with the development of fish farming for salmon in some nations, glutted world markets. In 1980, farm-raised salmon accounted for 1 percent of the global supply; by 2002 they composed 60 percent. In the same years, wild Alaska salmon fell from over 40 percent to less than 20 percent of the global supply. Between 1989 and 2004, consumption of farmed salmon increased more than fourfold in Europe and the United States. Prices for wild salmon plummeted, leading Alaskan officials to conclude that the state's salmon industry was on the ropes.[82]

Such thoughts proved overly alarmist. Despite ups and downs in catches and prices, salmon fishing in Alaska was sustainable and usually profitable, despite Eric Rosvold's experiences fishing out of Ketchikan in 2006. A leading Alaskan fisheries expert explained, "Near cataclysmic declines in salmon stocks between World War II and the mid-1970s were mostly due to human action—overharvest. Likewise, the subsequent recovery of salmon primarily was due to human action—ban of fish traps, limited entry to the fisheries, enhancement of wild stocks via salmon ranching, and habitat rehabilitation."[83] Alaskan fishers and processors also had considerable success in the early 2000s in differentiating their wild salmon from salmon farmed elsewhere. In 2008, the Beech-Nut Corporation even launched a wild Alaska salmon baby food.[84]

Salmon farming had its own problems. In mid-2007, an outbreak of the infectious salmon anemia virus forced Chile's salmon-farming industry to shut down many facilities. In October 2008, the industry group SalmonChile warned that the country's salmon production might fall to just 275,000 mt in 2009, down from 400,000 mt in 2007, due to continuing problems. American imports of Chilean salmon fillets were down 6 percent in fall 2009, compared to the previous year. Some 7,000 workers were laid off in Chile as a result of the difficulties with farmed salmon.[85]

Some Alaskan fishers turned their salmon into specialty, "branded" products for niche markets. Once working-class fare, salmon moved upscale. This "new" salmon was not the canned salmon of the late nineteenth and early twentieth centuries, but premium fresh salmon marketed at high prices. In 2008, fresh Copper River salmon from the Gulf of Alaska commanded premier prices in stores and restaurants, sometimes higher than $30 per pound—just like Chatham cod in New England.[86] It may be, as one scholar has observed, that "people want to taste the fish's untamed life" and that "they'll pay a premium to partake of the energy and strength that helped it survive." Copper River salmon particularly appealed to those who were health-conscious, for it had extra-strong, extra-rich fat, brimming with Omega-3 fatty acids, which were good for human vascular systems. In the early 1980s, thirty-five Cordova fishers formed the Copper River Fishermen's Cooperative. As Matsen has explained, they "deliver within twelve hours to a tender or plant with refrigeration, eliminating what was once the most destructive period in the gillnet-to-table journey of a salmon." Most Cordova fishers also bled (cleaned) and iced salmon on their boats, further increasing their value. They then sent their fish south by air. Each day during the fishing season, a Boeing 737, which became known colloquially as the "Salmon-Thirty-Salmon," carried salmon south. On the door of the Cordova airport, from which the salmon were shipped, are brass plaques engraved with the year and poundage airlifted to the outside world: 1984—1,226,658 pounds, 1985—1,646,091 pounds, 1986—1,307,388 pounds, and so forth.[87] In 2008–2009, Seattle restaurateur Jon Rawley, who had been instrumental in creating a market for Copper River salmon, sought to do the same for Yukon River salmon, in part as a way to help Yup'ik Eskimos, who were badly hurt by a decline in their catches.[88]

Copper River fishers were also among the first to take advantage of a 2005 Alaskan law allowing fishers to form regional seafood development associations. The associations were funded through self-taxation on catches and could use those revenues for just about any agreed-upon purpose. With 450 members in 2008, the Copper River association raised $350,000 annually, which it employed to expand marketing for its salmon. A similar association of Bristol Bay salmon fishers used its revenues to build new refrigeration facilities.[89] In 2008, it boasted 1,800 members. Another association, the Yukon River Drainage Fisheries Association, sought to unite fifty communities dependent on salmon fishing along the 2,300-mile Yukon River in the interest, its charter explained, of "ensur[ing] the long-term sustainability of the river . . . by promoting healthy, wild salmon fisheries."[90] About fifty fishers from Aleutian Island communities created the "Aleutia" brand for their salmon in 2003. According to a report five years later, "They adhere to strict quality and handling standards and have developed niche markets for Aleutia sockeye and king salmon." In 2008, they were poised to form a regional seafood development association, as were 486 salmon fishers in southeastern Alaska.[91]

Sustainable Salmon Fishing—At What Cost?

Alaskan salmon fishing became environmentally sustainable in the mid-1970s and later years. By limiting catches, Alaskans placed their salmon fisheries on a renewable basis and were recognized as having done so by the Marine Stewardship Council, the world's leading marine environmental group, in 2000. Alaskan salmon were among only a handful of fisheries worldwide to earn that organization's seal of approval for sustainability. The success Alaskans had in achieving sustainable fishing for salmon contrasts to the failure of Russians to do so in Kamchatka, just west across the Pacific. In Kamchatka, both over-fishing and habitat destruction destroyed salmon runs into the early 2000s. The lack of any regulatory regime of limited-entry fishing was especially harmful there.[92]

The achievement of sustainable salmon fishing in Alaska did not come easily. Only after precipitous declines in catches endangered their futures did

Alaskan fishers, fish processors, and government officials agree to move to limited-entry fishing. Although exact numbers are elusive, there were social costs, as some women and Alaskan Natives were excluded from the fishery. Still, the costs might have been higher, as the collapse of salmon fisheries in California and the Pacific Northwest has shown. As a consequence of continued over-fishing, many of those regions' salmon fisheries were closed to commercial fishing in the early 2000s, casting numerous fishers out of work.

Something of the same story as that which took place in Alaska's salmon fishery occurred in king-crab and bottom-fish harvesting, the topics of the next two chapters. Again, fishers, fish processors, and government officials agreed to move from open-access to closed fishing regimes, with sustainable fishing as the goal. And again there were social costs resulting from the switch to sustainable fishing. There were also, however, differences from what occurred in Alaska's salmon fishery. Because many king crabs and most bottom fish were harvested in waters well beyond Alaska's shores, federal officials played larger roles than state officials in regulating harvests. From the 1970s on, decisions by the NPFMC were of great significance in determining how king crabbers and bottom-fishers operated.

4

King Crabbing: Catch Limits and Price Setting

Returning to her home port of Cordova, Alaska, on 28 April 1976, the king-crab boat *Master Carl* encountered mechanical problems in the face of a fierce storm featuring waves thirty feet high. Water entered the vessel's hull as she passed near Montague Island just outside Prince William Sound, and at midnight the ship's flooded engine died. Tossed by waves, the *Master Carl* rolled onto her side and her captain and crew members had to abandon her. After donning insulated survival suits, they clambered into a life raft and, with great difficulty, cast off. Caught in the waves, the raft overturned on several occasions, spilling the men out into the rampaging sea. Against the odds, they climbed back in, and eventually two of the crewmen made it to shore. The captain and another crew member died. Once ashore, the two surviving men, exhausted and suffering from hypothermia, huddled together through a cold night. They were harassed by a grizzly bear, which they fended off by throwing rocks. After a horrific night they were rescued the next day by a coast guard helicopter.[1]

The loss of the *Master Carl* was all too typical of accidents afflicting king-crab vessels in Alaskan waters. In early 1983, the *Americus* and her sister ship, the *Altair*, sank in 85-mile-per-hour winds, costing the lives of thirteen men.[2] Even earlier, in the winter of 1962–63, thirteen king-crab boats were lost, most with all hands, in storms whose winds exceeded 140 miles per hour—a disaster that led Lowell Wakefield, one of the pioneers in Alaska's king-crab fishery, to lament that, while risks were always "the lot of those who follow the sea," the "final reckoning is never easy."[3]

In this chapter, I examine the development of commercial king crabbing, and later the pursuit of tanner crabs (smaller cousins of king crabs, often called snow crabs), in Alaskan waters.[4] A desire for high profits and adventure drove men, and occasionally women, to go king crabbing and to take risks that sometimes cost them their vessels and their lives, even more than was the case for salmon fishers. Among the fishers I profile are Lowell Wakefield, who developed America's king-crab fishery in the 1940s and 1950s, Spike Walker, who labored as a fisher during the 1970s and 1980s, and Andy and Johnathan Hillstrand, boat owners and fishers in the 1990s and early 2000s. The work and lives of these fishers, we shall see, illustrate changes occurring in their fishery. For crab fishers, pursuing profits came to partially trump other considerations, especially from the 1960s and 1970s onward. That pursuit of profit led to over-fishing and, in the early 2000s, the imposition of a quota system designed to make crabbing sustainable.

Unlike salmon and bottom-fish harvesting, king crabbing evolved very quickly. In little more than one generation following World War II, American fishers developed it into a mature fishery. American successes in the 1950s and 1960s attracted foreign competitors to Alaskan waters; some foreign fishers had taken crabs from them even earlier. Over-fishing occurred, as did a closely related growth of dangerous fishing methods. Regulation by state and federal government agencies followed, along with international agreements. Members of the North Pacific Fishery Management Council, pushed by crabbers and the heads of seafood processing firms, worried about the future of Alaska's crab fisheries, tried to place crab harvesting on a sustainable basis. First, the federal government excluded foreign crab fishers from American waters, a task largely completed in the 1960s and 1970s. Then, after ineffectively regulating catches by Americans in the 1970s and 1980s, the Council established tight controls over total crab catches in the early 2000s. Like salmon fishing, king crabbing underwent a fundamental alteration in its regulatory regime, as open-access fishing gave way to closed fishing. NPFMC allocated crab harvests to well-established fishers and processors—an action, I argue, that had the consequence of harming those fishers and, indeed, entire fishing communities excluded from the right to catch and process crabs. As in the other fisheries I analyze in this book, the nature of its regulatory regime greatly shaped how crab fishing was carried out.

Pioneering Developments, 1940s–1960s

Into the 1940s, king crabs were almost unknown to Americans. King crabs were so little understood that when secretary of commerce Elmo Roper suggested the possibility of establishing a king-crab fishery in Alaska to president Franklin D. Roosevelt in the early 1940s, the president practically laughed him out of the cabinet room. Only when he was presented with several whole crabs from Alaska did Roosevelt relent and support federal surveys to determine whether such a fishery could be created. During World War II, federal officials hoped that king crabs might become a source of inexpensive protein for men and women in the nation's armed forces, just as canned salmon had been in World War I. That plan did not work out, for it took into the 1950s for entrepreneurs to develop a king-crab fishery by trial and error.[5] It required time, as well, to win acceptance for this new type of seafood from the American public. Coastguardsman and fisher William McCloskey wrote of his discovery of king crabs in Alaska during the early 1950s: "This [king crab] was crab unbelievable . . . when I first visited Kodiak in 1952, in the Coast Guard, and then returned home to Chesapeake Bay country with a photo of myself holding a four-foot king crab across my middle, people thought I was playing a joke with paper mache."[6]

Leading the way in creating Alaska's king-crab fishery was Lowell Wakefield, who formed Wakefield Seafoods in late 1945, the first American company to pursue seriously king crabs. The son of a well-known Alaskan herring processor, Wakefield received a college education at the University of Washington and pursued graduate studies at Columbia University, working with the famed Franz Boas in anthropology. His studies with Boas may explain why Wakefield employed Aleut Natives in his company on equal terms with other workers, at a time when they often faced job discrimination in Alaska. Leaving Columbia, Wakefield was employed by the International Labor Defense, becoming involved in the bloody Harlan County, Kentucky, coal labor wars, which featured considerable violence by both strikers and thugs in the hire of the coal companies. In 1938, Wakefield returned to Alaska, where he joined his father and a brother in the family's herring business. Wakefield feared, however, that the herring fishery was "practically fished out" and thought that the salmon and halibut fisheries were "overcrowded." "Almost by elimination," Wakefield recalled, king crabs captured his attention. A young man, he wanted to strike out on his own and later stated that he was pursuing the "American dream in the pioneer tradition." He was well aware of the wartime crabbing surveys sponsored by the federal government—some took place practically on the doorstep of his family's herring plant—and thought of king crabbing as both a way to get ahead economically and a source of independence from his family.[7]

Figure 10. Coastguardsman William McCloskey holds a king crab in Kodiak in 1952.
Courtesy of William B. McCloskey, Jr.

Many of those joining Wakefield in forming his firm had been in the navy during World War II, often in Alaskan waters, and had become, as more than one put it, "water-oriented." Wakefield and the other founders were motivated by desires for profits and adventure. All believed that their company would be in the black within a few years. As one founding member explained, they all "expected to get rich overnight." In addition, they were seeking "a lot of glamour and excitement" and looked forward to "trying something that had never been done."[8] Romanticism tinged money making. Thus, even as he prospected new crab fishing grounds near Adak Island in the western Aleutians, Wakefield paused to contemplate the grandeur of the scene, the "predawn lighting of the sky" and the "snow clad cliffs."[9]

In their motives, the founders of Wakefield Seafoods closely resembled budding businessmen on earlier American frontiers, and Alaska was certainly a frontier economically and socially during the 1940s and 1950s. They were young men on the make. Like beaver trappers, cattlemen, farmers, and miners in the nineteenth-century trans-Mississippi West, they hoped to wrench a living—and, in fact, high profits—from the natural resources of a frontier region. They were all "expectant capitalists," desiring to put the resources of frontiers to productive use, with initially few thoughts about the future. Even farmers were real-estate speculators. Like earlier adventurers, the founders of Wakefield Seafoods also wanted to "see the elephant," as many gold-seekers expressed their reason for making the arduous trek to California in the 1840s and 1850s. That is, they wanted to participate in what was new and big in North America.[10]

While certainly risk-taking entrepreneurs, Wakefield and the others setting up Wakefield Seafoods depended on the federal government for help. The federal government's fishing surveys helped spur Wakefield to action. The passage of high tariffs protecting American king crab from foreign competition won their approval. Then too, Wakefield Seafoods depended on a loan from the Reconstruction Finance Corporation—a federal government agency formed in 1931 to help businesses, and the forerunner of the Small Business Administration—for over half of the initial financing of their company. (The remainder came from equity financing by Lowell Wakefield, his family, and his friends.) This partial reliance on the federal government was not surprising, or even unique. Far from it. At every step, federal-government employees helped develop America's frontiers: as explorers, military men, and surveyors, for example.[11]

Breaking with past experience, Wakefield had a single ship, the *Deep Sea,*

a 140-foot vessel specifically designed for fishing in Alaskan waters, which integrated catching, processing, and freezing king crabs. The vessel used high-
technology advances developed during or shortly after World War II by the
American military: radar, sonar (in the form of a fathometer to tell the depth
of the ocean), and loran (long range aid to navigation), a new navigational
system. Those few previous king-crab operations had employed small ships
to catch crabs, which were then transferred to shore plants or large mother
ships for processing and canning. Processing on board the *Deep Sea* was expected to greatly reduce costs by decreasing spoilage and by integrating previously separated stages of processing into one continuous-flow operation.
Freezing, which came into use for food processing in America in the 1930s
and 1940s, appealed to Wakefield as ultra-modern and a way to differentiate
his crab from the canned crab of competitors. After processing, the crab was
stored on board the ship in refrigerated holds until it could be packaged and
sent to market.[12]

Crab fishing was demanding work. Hours were long, with monotony setting in on voyages that might last for months with only rare shore leaves.

Figure 11. The trawler-processor *Deep Sea* pioneered industrial fishing in Alaskan
waters in the 1940s and 1950s. Author's collection.

Physical dangers were common. The *Deep Sea* generally fished through winds of 40 miles per hour and ten-to-twenty-foot seas. Under these conditions lifting the net onboard could become hazardous. The ship's captain later recalled, "The men became adept at not being killed," but bruises and cuts were the norm in heavy weather. Sometimes problems endangered the entire vessel. On one of her first voyages north, the *Deep Sea* encountered high winds and waves and began rolling. The captain later remembered that the vessel "hung over there on her side with a heavy sea bursting over her deck and through the companionway between the galley and processing room." Capsizing was imminent. It was, he thought, "a startling moment." Only one man was lost at sea from the *Deep Sea* during these years, but the circumstances of his death suggest the brutal conditions in which king-crab fishing took place. "We have been through one of the worst storms I have ever experienced at sea," the captain wrote home in April 1950. "The night Andy Peterson was lost was a nightmare," he continued; "The sea was 30–40 feet, wind NW 60–70 [knots, about 80 miles per hour], and it was snowing hard."[13]

The *Deep Sea* helped introduce industrial fishing to Alaskan waters. Crew members caught crabs in over-the-side (not stern) otter-trawling operations, making the ship a sidewinder in the parlance of the day. The *Deep Sea* dragged a large net along the ocean bottom, scooping up everything in its path. Only after her officers overcame many difficulties in catching, processing, and marketing king crabs did Wakefield Seafoods emerge as a profitable company during the 1950s. In 1948 the company faced liabilities of $432,000 with assets of just $141,000, mainly an unsold inventory of crab meat. Cash on hand had dwindled to a paltry $14. At this point, company officers and shareholders voted to disband and liquidate their firm, staying in business only when no buyer could be found for their ship. An emergency loan from the father of Lowell Wakefield and extraordinary luck finding crabs during the next few years saved the firm. It helped, too, that the company received a surveying charter from the federal government, which brought in sorely needed funds at this critical time.[14]

Developing markets also proved essential to the success of Wakefield Seafoods. Lacking sales outlets of its own, the company initially relied on those of the Red Salmon Packing Company and Pacific American Fisheries, well-known Pacific Northwest and Alaskan seafood processors. Deming and Gould, the sales agent for Pacific American Fisheries, quickly became the more significant of the two outlets, introducing king crabs to the important New York market in the summer of 1948. Deming and Gould in general

stressed the East Coast restaurant trade for king crabs. The goal was to position crab as an upscale Tiffany product. Gone were any thoughts of crab
meat as a low-cost source of protein for the masses. The major competition
came from lobsters and soft-shelled crabs. With its bright red skin and firm
white flesh, king crab meat closely resembled lobster in appearance, texture,
and taste (in fact, the Army-Navy Club in Washington, D.C., served king
crab as lobster for several years). Sales personnel thought king crab could
compete more successfully in eastern markets than in West Coast ones where
Dungeness crab, its major competitor there, had a very different and well-
established texture and taste.[15]

These early marketing arrangements did not work as well as those in
Wakefield Seafoods had hoped. The basic problem was that king crab was
a new and unknown product. A market had to be made for it, a much more
difficult task than anyone had anticipated. In the late 1940s, Wakefield executives severed their connections with Red Salmon Packing and Pacific American Fisheries. Those two processors had received a 6 percent commission for
their sales efforts, but they in turn had depended on many other independent
seafood brokers to move the crab meat. The problem from the point of view
of the managers of Wakefield Seafoods was that Red Salmon Packing and Pacific American Fisheries kept half the commission, passing on only the other
half, about 3 percent of the value of the sales, to the seafood brokers. Having
relatively little incentive to push the crab, most brokers did not. Now that they
knew more about markets, the officers of Wakefield Seafoods began working
directly with the brokers, paying them the full 6 percent. In line with their
conception of king crab as premium seafood, Wakefield also advertised in
stylish journals such as *Vogue* and *Ladies Home Journal*. Sales immediately
perked up.[16]

Wakefield Seafoods also resorted to publicity to stimulate consumer interest in the new product. In the fall of 1951, for example, the captain of the
Deep Sea conducted a three-month road trip through eastern seaboard and
southern states to try to open markets. Having fitted out the trunk of his
Mercury convertible with freezer containers to hold two or three cases of
crab meat, he traveled from city to city showing restaurant and hotel chefs
how to prepare king crabs and trying to sign up local food brokers to carry
the product. He was supplied by prearranged weekly refrigerated railroad
and truck shipments of crab meat. He sometimes resorted to gimmickry. In
Miami Beach, for instance, he billed himself as a sea captain from the Frozen
North and held a crab feed for brokers and the press in his hotel suite with

the air conditioning turned to its highest setting, an eccentricity duly noted in newspapers the next day.[17]

With its production and sales problems largely solved, Wakefield Seafoods emerged as a very successful firm in the 1950s and 1960s and attracted domestic competitors. Alaska's king-crab catch soared from 23,000 pounds in 1946, to 1.5 million pounds in 1950, 29 million pounds in 1960, and 160 million pounds in 1966, a high point. As competitors entered the crab fishery, the share of the catch accounted for by Wakefield Seafoods dropped from 70 percent in 1950 to just 18 percent in 1966. Thinking back to the early 1960s, Bud Ryan, then a young king-crabber, described the rapid expansion of the fishery, "It was like a fever sweeping the docks."[18]

From a peak in 1966, the total Alaskan catch collapsed to 60 million pounds in 1969 and 50 million pounds in 1974, probably as a result of over-fishing.[19] To deal with this and other problems, fishers took the initiative. Various groups of fishers turned to governments, and conservation measures often became tools for economic competition, just as had occurred earlier in the salmon industry. Throughout its history, interactions among fishers, law-makers, and scientists were important in the development of the king-crab industry. Public policies mattered a great deal, for they set the parameters within which the fishery functioned.

Of most immediate concern in the 1950s were regulations governing catching crabs within Alaska's three-mile limit. Most of the initial fishing regulations sought to mediate gear conflicts. Wakefield Seafood's ships were mainly trawlers. Until 1956, the *Deep Sea* dragged its nets fairly indiscriminately across the ocean floor. On the other hand, smaller boats manned by independent Alaskan fishers employed crab pots. Like very large lobster pots, they were lowered to the ocean floor. King crab pots were and are six to nine feet to the side (most are seven feet) and several feet deep. Initially most were round, but by the 1970s and 1980s they were square, a shape better able to resist the movement of ocean currents. Once crabs crawled into the baited pots through a funnel arrangement, they could not get out. Initially, pots were lifted to the ocean surface by winches and boom-and-deck-mounted haulers, a time-consuming procedure. This cumbersome method was soon replaced by the use of hydraulic pot lifters, which self-adjust to take up sudden slacks in lines to the pots in heavy seas. Power blocks greatly accelerated lifting pots, to the extent that a fully loaded crab pot weighing 3,000 pounds could be drawn up from a depth of 360 feet in just three minutes. Raised to the surface, the pots were emptied on board the boats, which then delivered crabs alive to processing plants. The catcher vessels had live tanks amidships containing seawater circulated by pumps to keep the crabs healthy.[20] As early as the mid-1950s, gear clashes occurred in parts of Cook Inlet not far from Anchorage. Local fishers claimed that the trawls were destroying prime fishing grounds and their crab pots. Federal and territorial authorities were able to work out compromises regulating when and where different types of gear could be employed.[21]

When Alaska gained statehood in 1959, control over near-shore fishing was transferred from the federal government to state agencies. Pushed by local Kodiak fishers, state officials banned trawling operations completely in 1961 and limited the movement of ships from one fishing area to another. As crab shortages appeared in some fishing areas, state agencies also sought to restrict the number of crab pots a boat could carry. This effort proved ineffective as a conservation measure, for it placed no restrictions on the number of boats entering the fisheries. Officials in Alaska's department of fish and game then began moving in the direction of limited-entry fishing, as desired by Lowell Wakefield and executives of other large companies.[22] However, little was achieved until after the crash in the crab catch in the late 1960s, for officers of smaller, local companies viewed limited-entry fishing as an infringement on their rights and opposed it. In the 1970s, state fish and game officials established a quota system by dividing Alaska's near-shore king-crab grounds into six areas, setting a maximum allowable catch for each and closing the grounds to fishing each season once the catch limit was reached. By 1976, the crab catch was back up to 106 million pounds, and in the late 1970s it averaged 180 million pounds per year.[23] This period was, as fisher and boat captain Sig Hansen called it, "the new Alaska gold rush," as many new people went north to harvest crabs.[24]

Foreign crabbers also reentered waters above Alaska's continental shelf in the 1950s. In 1958, American companies accounted for two-thirds of the king crabs caught from waters above Alaska's continental shelf, but by 1962 the American share of the catch had fallen to just half the total. In the mid-1960s, 190 American, Norwegian, Japanese, and Soviet vessels vied for crabs around Kodiak, and the value of the crab catch rivaled that of salmon. Bilateral agreements in 1964–65 greatly reduced the harvesting of king crabs from American waters by foreign fishers. Arguing that crabs were sedentary creatures on the continental shelf—American underwater filming seemed to show the crabs crawling, not swimming—U.S. negotiators succeeded in restricting foreign fishing under the terms of the 1958 United Nations Law of the Sea Convention. This convention, it will be recalled, gave coastal nations ownership of sedentary creatures on continental shelves to a depth of 200 meters. The negotiators also argued that American fishers were fully prepared to harvest the entire sustainable king-crab catch.

Until his death in 1977, Lowell Wakefield was an important adviser to American treaty negotiators and also served as an American delegate to Law of the Sea Conventions, taking with him his growing conviction that only through regulation could fishers avoid a tragedy of the commons in king crabs. In thoughts derived from observations during his fishing career of about thirty years, Wakefield encapsulated the fundamental shift occurring in much of the thinking globally about fisheries. From a person who had once viewed fisheries as limitless in extent and in need of only minimal supervision, by the 1970s Wakefield came to advocate tight national and even international controls over catches. In 1965, he observed in a thoughtful essay, "Commercial fishing has not progressed very far beyond buffalo hunting on the Western Plains." However, "just as homestead rights and grazing leases have stabilized and greatly increased production from the plains, some such

Figure 12. Picking king crabs from a pot. Courtesy of William B. McCloskey, Jr.

approach will one day come for the oceans. . . . The sort of thing that I can picture will be fishermen's cooperatives."[25]

The Fishery Conservation and Management Act and Alaska's Crab Fisheries

As in most American fisheries, government regulation introduced significant changes to Alaska's crab fisheries during the 1970s. Under FCMA, NPFMC regulated fishing 200 miles out from the coasts of Oregon, Washington, and Alaska. For crabs and bottom fish, the Council ruled the day, except for fish and crabs found in state waters, those close to the shore.[26] The Council quickly excluded most foreign fishing vessels from king-crab fisheries within 200 miles of Alaskan shores, concluding a process begun in the 1960s. However, in another crab fishery, which in the late 1970s and early 1980s was not fully utilized by American fishers, foreign fishers remained, at least for a while.

That fishery was the one for tanner crabs, sometimes called snow crabs. As the king-crab harvest declined in the mid-1960s, some American fishers turned to tanner crabs, smaller cousins of king crabs. However, tanner crabs were not as commercially desirable as king crabs, and American fishing for them was at first half-hearted. It was more difficult to remove flesh from the shells of tanner crabs than from those of king crabs, and at first no market existed for them. Only when king crabs grew scarce, and only after seafood processors and wholesalers renamed tanner crabs snow crabs, did sizeable markets develop. The allocation of snow crabs for foreign fishers (mainly Japanese) was initially large: 15,000 mt of the total 1978 catch of 17,268 mt. As Americans entered tanner-crab fishing, the foreign catch was limited in 1979 to 15,000 mt of a 68,556 mt catch.[27]

History and politics influenced the determination of which nations received crab-fishing allocations within American waters. Most important was a nation's history of fishing in a given region. Japanese and Soviet fishers had harvested crabs in the Bering Sea for decades by the 1960s and 1970s and so were given allocations for tanner crabs by the NPFMC. However, when American fishers showed that they could take large numbers of crabs, foreigners were excluded: in the 1970s for king crabs, in the 1980s for tanner crabs. Of significance, too, were geopolitical factors. Global politics, as played out in the Cold War, affected crab allocations. South Korea was a staunch ally of the United States during the Cold War and so received allocations for bottom fish, although not crabs. Trade issues played significant roles. In the late 1970s, for example, several members of the NPFMC sought to link giving Japanese fishers tanner-crab allocations to a lifting of import restrictions on surimi (fish paste) from the United States. However, international trade negotiators for the State Department opposed this method of coercing Japan to open its market, and Council proposals went nowhere.[28]

Members of the NPFMC—government officials, fishers, and fish processors—sought initially to regulate offshore American and foreign fishing for king crabs and snow crabs by setting minimum sizes for crabs, establishing requirements for fishing gear, and fixing closed seasons at some times of the year. The Alaska Department of Fish and Game established some catch limits for waters it controlled. However, officials did not at first establish individual fishing quotas, for many fishers opposed any suggestions that their freedoms be so curtailed. Only a handful yet embraced ideas put forward by Lowell Wakefield and a few others to limit American catches. As a result, king-crab and tanner-crab fisheries largely remained open-access fisheries for Americans through the 1980s and 1990s.

Excluded from catching king crabs and limited in their take of tanner crabs, Japanese seafood firms entered into joint ventures with Americans who caught the crabs, in moves similar to their formation in Alaska's salmon fisheries. Fishers used brand-new, expensive, high-tech ships designed specifically to pursue crabs during Alaska's stormy fall and winter crab-fishing seasons. From the late 1960s into the 1980s, many of these vessels were constructed by the Marine Design and Construction Company in Seattle. They were multimillion-dollar ships designed for just one purpose: to catch king and tanner crabs. Much of the financing for the new American king-crab vessels came from the Production Credit Association (PCA), a federal agency established as part of the federal government's effort to spur the development of American fisheries. Modeled after farm-subsidy programs, the programs of the PCA offered $80 million in low-interest loans to fishers to modernize their vessels or build new ones. Then too, federal legislation allowed fishers to invest profits they earned in fishing in boats without having to pay taxes on them.

As before, those in the king-crab industry viewed themselves as rugged individualists and entrepreneurs. However, they were eager to benefit from the actions of federal officials. They gleefully accepted federal loans and tax breaks and they benefited from the sonar and loran systems first developed by the military. Funds came as well from joint-venture partners. Japanese firms made heavy investments in most segments of Alaska's fisheries—salmon and bottom fish, as well as crab—in the 1970s and 1980s. These were expansive decades for the Japanese economy, in which consumerism ruled the day, including the eating of upscale seafood.[29]

The vessels entering the king-crab industry were of various sorts. There were extensive conversions of surplus military ships and shrimp boats from the Gulf of Mexico, especially as the spread of the dead zone there limited fishing—yet another example of the military's contribution to Alaskan fishing. More significant, however, were new vessels ninety feet or more in length designed specifically for king crabbing. Produced mainly in Seattle shipyards, they were "big, full, heavy boats—tailored to be stable all-weather work platforms—characterized by a large square deck for carrying a maximum number of pots, by equally large hold capacities to permit extended fishing without the need to return often to unload, and by a full bow structure that keeps the boat from plunging deeply in heavy seas." The vessels were powered by heavy-duty marine diesel engines, typically 575 and 1,200 horsepower for boats 90 and 120 feet long.[30]

The ships boasted the most advanced electronics of any fishing vessels of their time. Designed to take as many crabs as possible during short openings, these highly specialized vessels were prime examples of "technology stuffing." Writing about his experiences crabbing in the 1970s, Spike Walker described the $2–3-million-dollar vessels: "Inside, they added VHS sound systems. . . . They installed soda machines. . . . In the wheelhouse, they surrounded their plush leather chairs with an assortment of electronic gear that would rival the control panels of a NASA spacecraft. There were multiple assortments of radars, sonars, fathometers, CB and VHF radios, spinnaker windows, engine-temperature gauges, hydraulic valves, and the latest in automatic pilot and loran guidance systems. . . . Out on deck, they installed automatic coiling machines and herculean cranes with forty-foot arms that could lift and set a 750-pound crab pot into space just so thirty feet away and twenty feet overhead, even in the worst of seas."[31]

Walker disliked this type of vessel. "Some of us tried to argue with the times," he later recalled, for they felt that "there was no dignity in being a computer-age fisherman." However, such opposition accomplished little, for, as Walker also remembered, "We were forced to admit that no matter how good or experienced a crab fisherman and his crew were, they couldn't work a fifty-eight-foot wooden limit seiner in the Bering Sea in all weather. It couldn't be done."[32] The ship as a machine became an extension of competitive pressures.

Derby Fishing and Safety Issues

With demand for king crabs soaring in the 1970s, derby fishing resulted even more than in the salmon industry. Economic, safety, and regulatory issues were closely intertwined. Enjoying high profits, crabbers fished round-the-clock in dangerous conditions whenever there were openings for crabs. Walker described one such opening in 1979: "We cranked up the main engines, pulled anchor, and soon joined the long, foaming line of massive crab boats. . . . The battle had begun. The spectacle before me was a modern-day version of the Oklahoma Land Grab. The starting gun had sounded, and not until the entire quota was caught and the final whistle blown would anyone dare pause."[33]

A desire for high profits and earnings drove those in the industry. Captains and shipowners might earn $150,000 or more for a month or two of work, money sorely needed to service their multimillion-dollar shipbuilding loans. Crew members usually worked on a "share basis," paid a percentage of their boat's profits. It was not unheard-of for crew members on "highlining" boats (vessels catching the most crabs) to earn $60,000 or more for five or six weeks of work.[34] Sometimes their takes were much greater. Phil Harris, who later became a highlining skipper of a crab boat, fondly remembered his share of the profits from his first crabbing trip as a seventeen-year-old crew member: "It was the first trip of the crab season and in the next month I made $120,000."[35] Crew members on the *Americus* on her *very first day* of king crabbing in the Bering Sea in 1978 earned $14,000 apiece.[36] Greed occasionally even resulted in crab "rustling," as fishers stole crabs from each others' pots.[37]

In this boom-time situation, the nature of crab fishers changed somewhat. Patrick Dillon, a journalist who grew up among commercial fishermen in Puget Sound, has written about Alaskan king crabbers in the 1970s: "Vessels now took on crew members who had never met until they stepped on deck. Skippers were itinerant, owing their allegiances to no small towns or family bonds but only to the chance to make big money. Owners who had traditionally captained their vessels became absentee operators." Above all, according to Dillon, "The independent subsistence fishermen, the captains who fished to uphold family tradition, found no place in the king-crab fleet."[38] The inexperience of some crew members contributed to the dangers of fishing.

Even so, many of the factors motivating crab fishers remained unchanged. Walker asked in his reminiscences, "Why would anyone choose to venture into such a world, and take such risks?" He answered in words with which those on the *Deep Sea* would have agreed a generation earlier, "pride, freedom, and adventure." He also stressed that crewing on "highline crab boats" meant "taking home a $100,000 paycheck in a two-month season of crabbing."[39] However, more than money spurred Walker and other crab fishers, just as many elements motivated salmon fishers. Walker took tremendous pride in his work, writing, "We labored like proud beasts, ignored private aches, and tried not to draw attention to injuries that did not matter." Despite his individualism, Walker also liked laboring as part of a well-oiled team: "After several months of working together, we anticipated one another's moves like people with powers of telepathy." Then too, there was the thrill of crabbing, an adrenaline rush. Describing a storm, Walker observed, "Frightening as the waves were, there was something in their form and power that held me transfixed. I felt at once fearful and exhilarated." The beauty of Alaska attracted Walker. "Regardless of the urgency of our passing," he wrote of one trip, "the shore of the Alaskan mainland was not something to be ignored." In fact, Walker viewed Alaska as "an immense and rugged country . . . with hundreds of miles in wild and scenic accents of rock, glacier, volcano, valley, and plateau."[40] Romantic and utilitarian thoughts intermingled in Walker's mind, as they did in those of most fishers.

Walker's work as a crabber was physically and mentally demanding. At various points in his reminiscences, Walker complains about the lack of privacy and sense of claustrophobia on board crab boats, the monotony and drudgery of the work, sleep deprivation, and isolation from people other than his immediate crew members. Like many other fishers, he describes fishing for crab as being like battle. Injuries were common.[41]

The brothers Andy and Johnathan Hillstrand, crab-boat captains featured on the television reality show *Deadliest Catch* in the early 2000s, echoed many of the statements made by Walker in their 2008 reminiscences. Johnathan begins his account proudly with the statement, "I am a fisherman, an Alaskan fisherman, and a Bering Sea fisherman with thirty-seven years on commercial boats." Continuing, he observes: "I have fought forty-foot seas and seen rogue waves one hundred feet high. I work in water cold enough to kill a man in five minutes, and I have bent under the power of 120-knot Williwaw winds," winds blowing down from nearby mountains onto the sea. However, he counts himself lucky, writing, "I live like a king." The brothers grew up in Alaska, learning fishing from their father. Always optimistic individualists, they welcomed what they saw as the freedom and independence of fishing. Johnathan explained, "The cold wind and spray hissing against the wheelhouse windows gave me an almost overwhelming joy of freedom." Or, as Andy put it, "When I am out fishing, I am like the cowboy who rides off into the sunset at the end of movie, leaving the woman and kids, the ranch, the whole life behind." Still, like Walker, they eagerly awaited the high profits coming from their efforts and valued teamwork in their shipboard operations, noting that effective "crab fishing is like the military." They also describe the downsides of crabbing: a lack of sleep (it was a lack of free time that led them to christen their vessel *Time Bandit*), excessive drinking, divorces, and occasionally a feeling of insignificance. On the last point, Johnathan writes, "I feel small in the universe when I am at sea in an 80-knot blow. I am staring into the abyss."[42]

In his *Deadliest Catch*, published in 2008, Dan Weeks, director of the television series bearing the same title, printed interviews with crabbers active in the 1980s, 1990s, and early 2000s. Those captains and crew members emphasized many of the same points as did Walker and the Hillstrands. Almost uniformly they spoke of their desire for high profits, their yearning for adventure, the enjoyment they found in the physical act of fishing and the teamwork that accompanied it, and the sense of freedom they derived from fishing. Many of them also complained about injuries, boat sinkings, mental problems, and other types of stresses incurred in king crabbing.[43]

Sig Hansen—a crab fisher and then the highlining captain of his family's crab vessel *North by Northwestern*, yet another boat featured on the "Deadliest Catch"—agreed that risks were always present in king crabbing. Born the son of an Alaskan fisher in Seattle in 1966, Hansen first fished for salmon in Alaskan waters at the age of twelve, graduating to king crabs after he finished high school in 1984. While acknowledging the difficulties in crabbing, Hansen emphasized the rewards, psychic as well as monetary, writing in 2010: "My brothers and I learned to fish from our father when we were boys. He learned from his father, who learned from his father. I am proud of the life I have chosen is to work hard, to face the dangers of the seas, and to pull a living from the ocean, just as my father did, and those before him. The Hansens are a family of fishermen, of sailors, of captains."[44]

In the 1970s and early 1980s, safety received scant attention. As fishers noted, accidents, injuries, and deaths were even more common in the king-crab than in the salmon fishery. Abominable weather made a bad situation worse, especially since king-crabbing took place mainly in the fall and the season for catching snow crabs was primarily in the winter. Retired coastguardsman McCloskey aptly described the maritime Alaskan geography and climate: "This thin Aleutian barrier [the Aleutian Islands] is one of the world's most famous swirling points for foul weather. It is a clash line between the equatorial warmth pumped by the Japanese current along the Pacific side of the islands and the arctic cold that blows down across the Bering Sea. Sixty-knot winds are commonplace, hundred-knot storms to be expected, with fog and slanting rain or snow a virtually perpetual condition."[45]

Icing was a major problem. In stormy winter seas at freezing temperatures, spray almost instantly turned into ice on the superstructures of crab boats, especially since crab pots were often stacked five or six high on the vessels' sterns as the ships went to and from fishing grounds. Crew members routinely used baseball bats, mallets, and other implements to break ice off exposed parts of their vessels.[46] However, their efforts often fell short of what was needed, as ice accumulated faster than it could be removed. Ice raised boats' centers of gravity, making them top-heavy and sometimes causing them to capsize. Fishers did not last long in the frigid water, soon succumbing to hyperthermia. Even large vessels were far from stable fishing platforms at all times. The *Gemini*—a modern, 110-foot-long crab boat—was just one of a number which went down, covered in ice. Caught in high winds which splattered spray across her decks and crab pots, the *Gemini* made ice faster than her crew could knock it off. She sank about 120 miles southeast of Cold Bay on the Aleutian Islands on a blustery January day. Some crew members were rescued by the coast guard four days later, saved by their survival suits and raft they had been able to launch from their sinking vessel.[47] They were luckier than many fishers, for most boats did not carry survival suits and rafts at that time.

Typical of the new king-crab vessels, and the problems they faced, were ships owned by Jeff Hendricks. First off the shipway was the *Antares*, constructed in 1977 at a cost of $3 million. This steel-hulled vessel was 124 feet long and 32 feet wide, with a depth amidships of 14 feet. She burned to her waterline in an accident at sea five years later, a total loss. Next was the *Americus*, a near duplicate of the *Antares*, launched in 1978. Finally, came the *Altair*, a copy of the *Americus,* which first pursued crabs in 1980. Both the *Americus* and the *Altair* boasted 1,120-horsepower, turbocharged engines, and both had state-of-the-art electronics gear. Both carried about 200 crab pots. Both were lost at sea in February, 1983, just north of Dutch Harbor. Neither sent out a distress signal, and there were no survivors, as all fourteen crewmen perished. Both ships were later found overturned, drifting on the waves. After twenty-five months of hearings and investigations, the coast guard found that the two ships had been unstable because of the heavy weight of crabbing gear on deck, mistakes made in flooding live tanks for crabs, and errors in distributing fuel in tanks throughout the vessels. The coast guard's investigatory board concluded with understatement, "There is convincing evidence that commercial fishermen in general lack an appreciation of the principles of stability."[48] The technologies of shipbuilding had outrun practical knowledge of how to deal with them.

Commercial fishing was the most dangerous American occupation, with a mortality rate in the mid-1970s seventy-five times greater than the national average of on-the-job deaths. King-crabbing was the deadliest of all. In 1982, king-crab fishing had a mortality rate twenty-five times greater than the rest of fishing, and nine times higher than that for mining and farming, the next-most-dangerous occupations.[49] One captain later recalled, "When I quit fishing in Alaska was when I realized I could no longer watch out for others. That's when you no longer belong in the wheelhouse. I didn't want to be the one to make the mistake to cost people their lives."[50] Many fishers, however, accepted death and injury as parts of their jobs. Don Lane, a fifty-five-year-old king-crab fisher from Homer, Alaska, observed, "It will kill a certain number of people. It always has. You have to be really careful you are not one of them. You can't make money in bad weather." Jim Herbert, a sixty-year-old fisher from Seward, made much the same point, noting, "It was part of the game, and fate will have its way." In 1987, he had skippered a boat that capsized when hit by large waves, killing one crew member.[51]

Only after several well-publicized sinkings increased insurance rates for ship owners and outraged the mothers of young men lost at sea did Congress pass the Commercial Fishing Industry Vessel Safety Act in 1988. The loss of Peter Barry, a twenty-year-old anthropology student from Yale University, while out summer fishing on the Alaskan purse seiner *Western Star* in 1985 was particularly notorious. Crewing aboard the leaking wooden vessel skippered by a cocaine-snorting captain, Barry went down on a boat that had little survival gear. His death mobilized his parents, especially his mother, to mount a crusade for increased safety on commercial fishing vessels. Peggy Barry testified in a public hearing on the bill: "On August fifteenth of last year, the *Western Star* left the harbor of Kodiak, Alaska, to fish for salmon. Something happened; we will never know what. . . . But we do know that the wooden-hulled vessel was seventy years old, that some of the structure was rotten, that it probably had a loose hatch cover, that it had only a hand-operated pump . . . and that it had a heavy, diesel-powered skiff lashed to the deck, making it top heavy. We know that there were no life rafts, no EPIRBs [automatic beacons] and no survival suits." Then too, annual insurance premiums soared from $34,000 in 1976 to $169,000 a decade later for a typical fishing vessel with seven crew members.[52]

The safety legislation passed in 1988 required that American fishing vessels carry survival suits and rafts for all crew members and that they have automatic radio beacons called Emergency Position Indicating Radio Beacons (EPIRBs) to signal for help should they sink. The legislation was a compromise. Because of the opposition of defense lawyers and some fishers, it did not contain any licensing requirements for ship captains, as desired by coast guard officials. Nor were there any requirements that ships be inspected and undergo stability tests, as had also been desired by the coast guard. In the early 1990s, the coast guard began requiring vessels to offer safety training, including monthly drills, and began offering a dockside program to reduce stability problems on some vessels.[53]

With the passage of the safety act and the end of most derby fishing (discussed below), the work of fishers became safer. Between 2003 and 2008, an average of eleven fishers died on the job in Alaskan waters each year, down from an average of thirty-seven in the 1980s. Overall, the number of annual fatalities in Alaska's commercial fishing industry halved between 1990 and 2006. Even so, fishing continued to take place in dangerous, stormy seasons in the Bering Sea, and some captains still drove their boats and crews hard to be the first on the crab when seasons opened, although the economic incentive to do so lessened with the enactment of new types of fishing regulations. The mortality rate for king crabbers was thirty times higher than that for workers in all American jobs in 2006–2008. In 2008, Alaska remained the most dangerous state in the Union in which to work.[54] A leading crab-boat captain summed up his philosophy about safety in mid-2009 with the words, "Rule number one is stay on the boat, and rule number two is to keep the water on the outside of the boat, always."[55] Sig Hansen agreed, saying that, "Safety is a fulltime job."[56]

In the wake of continuing fishing deaths and boat sinkings, many still resulting from capsizing, the coast guard sought to tighten safety requirements for commercial fishers in 2008–2009. In the summer of 2008, coast guard officers proposed extending rules that required larger fishing vessels to carry rafts and EPIRBs to all fishing boats, even very small ones. Many fishers objected. "It would require survival craft on any commercial fishing vessel, even seine skiffs. That doesn't make sense," said Mark Vinsel, executive director of United Fishermen of Alaska, representing thirty-seven fishing groups. Another person who identified herself as "fisherlady" was blunt: "Every day you find out another stupid thing they have forced on us unawares."[57] In a curiously American fashion, ideas about autonomy mixed uneasily with thoughts about government regulation to produce statements such as these.

A Fisherman's Fisherman: William B. McCloskey, Jr.

The hard work and danger of crab fishing comes through in the fictional works of William B. "Bill" McCloskey, Jr., a "fisherman's fisherman." From the 1970s through the 1990s, he hauled nets and pulled pots from the North Atlantic to the Indian Ocean to the North Pacific. Much of his fishing occurred in Alaskan waters, where he pursued bottom fish, shrimp, salmon, and crabs. In a trilogy of novels featuring the fictitious fisher Hank Crawford as protagonist, McCloskey presents a compelling look at the lives of fishers in the North, especially king crabbers.[58]

Born in Baltimore, Maryland in 1928, McCloskey attended public schools there. After high school, he attended the Carnegie Institute of Technology (later renamed Carnegie Mellon University) in Pittsburgh, majoring in drama. However, McCloskey left Carnegie Mellon to join the merchant marine. He "yearned to see the world," the "wide open spaces." He worked as an ordinary seaman for one year on ships operating out of Baltimore, visiting Rumania, Russia, the Persian Gulf, and South America.[59] McCloskey next attended Columbia University, which fit in with his growing interest in art, music, and acting. For McCloskey, "New York was the hub of the universe; I majored in New York"—the "waterfront, theaters, museums, opera, ballet, and art." In 1951, McCloskey graduated with a B.S. in creative writing.

With the Korean War underway, McCloskey joined the coast guard, graduating from that service's accelerated officer candidate school as an ensign. When the Coast Guard Academy considered assignment requests, McCloskey expressed an interest in Alaska: "Alaska was there . . . I wanted a ship, and I wanted Alaska." McCloskey was assigned to the *Sweetbrier*, a coast guard cutter based in Ketchikan (and later Cordova). The ship serviced navigation aids, conducted fishery inspections, and performed rescue work throughout Alaskan waters. A high point for McCloskey was the role his ship played in opening Alaskan waters to Japanese fishers, a move undertaken in June, 1952, at Adak. McCloskey was the ship's communications officer. The *Sweetbrier* picked up a Japanese-American in Adak to go out and meet the incoming Japanese fleet "in utmost secrecy," with no photographs allowed. McCloskey served his enlistment and left the coast guard in 1953.

Back in Baltimore, McCloskey became a reporter for the *Baltimore Sun*, writing about police and court activities for two years. However, McCloskey experienced wanderlust. After saving $700, he travelled in Europe, cycling around parts of France and Spain. Returning again to Baltimore, McCloskey secured a position with Black & Decker, the tool maker, to start that company's public relations department, a job he held for two and one-half years. Then he journeyed to Europe again, coming down with hepatitis, which forced him to convalesce in Florence. Other positions followed his recovery: one as an officer with the United States Information Agency in India, another in public relations at the Martin Marietta Company. Even before his second trip to Europe, McCloskey had met Ann, his future wife. He married her after returning from Europe in 1956. McCloskey next worked at the Johns Hopkins University's Applied Physics Laboratory (APL) in public relations. The APL was largely government-funded, developing military devices for the Cold War. McCloskey served as the APL's congressional liaison and in other positions, often working on classified projects. It was at the APL that McCloskey made his career, staying there for several decades.

With the full support of his wife and on leave at various times from the APL, McCloskey turned to fishing in the 1970s, casting nets around the world over the next three decades and writing accounts about his experiences. He ascribed his love of fishing to "atavism," "self-indulgence," and perhaps age (mid-forties).[60] His earlier duty in the coast guard left him especially attracted to Alaska. So he traveled there on a coast guard vessel and then "walked the docks," looking for work. "Fish-boating," he later said, "seemed the ultimate kind [of seafaring], because you're in a small boat with your nose right in the water."

Some of McCloskey's Alaskan fishing was for salmon and halibut. His first position was in the summer of 1975 as a crew member on a fifteen-foot-long "Siwash" salmon gillnetter, operating out of Kodiak. "Siwash," McCloskey has noted, was an Indian-derived term for fishing without machinery. The boat used no hydraulics, no power block, to pull in the net. Everything was done by hand: "When we pulled in salmon, they were literally beating around our legs." In the summer of 1976, McCloskey worked on a larger salmon seiner, again operating out of Kodiak, and during several summers in the 1980s he labored on Bristol Bay gillnetters. The nets were hauled in over a power drum on the stern where the salmon were picked out by hand, "an acquired skill." McCloskey also long lined for halibut. He later observed that this type of fishing was "Olympic" or "trophy" fishing, featuring short openings of twenty-four to forty-eight hours: "All of the boats went out and competed at the same time." During the openings, there was little time for sleep: "You didn't sleep, you fished." Consequently, fatigue could make the work "very dangerous."

McCloskey was most enamored with king crabbing. He crewed on the *American Beauty* in the winter of 1976–77, operating out of Dutch Harbor, a real "adventure." The ship was a 108-foot-long, all-steel vessel. Work was intense, for crabs had to be taken during limited openings and be delivered to processing plants alive. McCloskey later remembered working twenty hours or more at a stretch, lifting strings of fifty to sixty pots. He was sometimes so exhausted that he slept in his oilskins and boots. The work was "very strenuous," causing "tremendous tendonitis" in his arms. Crew members relieved social tensions by "a lot of practical jokes," such as tossing sea creatures that came up in the crab pots at each other. They also unwound ashore. In Dutch Harbor at a bar called the Elbow Room, McCloskey was "six-packed" by the other crew members after his first trip. That meant being served six "tall glasses of neat of Scotch." "I just laughed," McCloskey later observed, "and passed it around." Asked in 2009 if he would engage in fishing again, with all of its hardships and dangers, he replied: "Of course, I love seafaring and consider fishing the ultimate communication with the sea."

An accomplished, published author, McCloskey has written about three major topics: the sea, the culture of Southeast Asia, and opera. About fishing he has published *Highliners* (1979), *Fish Decks* (1990), *Their Fathers' Work* (1998), *Breakers* (2004), and *Raiders* (2004). In describing fishing, McCloskey said that, "I was following what I love, that's all."

In his first fictional account about fishing, *Highliners*, McCloskey introduces Hank Crawford as a handsome but naïve nineteen-year-old sophomore from Johns Hopkins University. Working first in a salmon cannery on Kodiak Island in the summer of 1963, Crawford soon lands a job on a salmon seiner, beginning his fishing education and adventures. On board the purse seiner *Rondelay* he experiences derby fishing and runs into competition with Russian fishers near Kodiak. Crawford listens, as another crew member explains, "Russian trawler cocksuckers are dragging nets practically across the harbor, and the best we can do is route all the time to keep watch."[61] With salmon fishing finished for the season, Crawford returns to college, where he spends a "restless" winter. He eagerly returns to Kodiak for winter king crabbing on the converted *Rondelay*.[62]

After finishing college and serving in the navy during the Vietnam conflict, the fictional Crawford returns to Alaska in 1970 determined to become a career fisherman. He is sobered by the words of a former crewmate, "When you go out in the winter, there ain't much fun left in fishing. You do it to make payments."[63] Nonetheless, he crews on shrimp and halibut boats. He suffers in the dangerous work. By 1972, "There were scars on his face from maverick crab pots and hooks, and the hand that held his glass had a finger missing."[64] But, he learns the ropes and becomes the skipper of the seventy-eight-foot *Nestor* operating out of Dutch Harbor. Additional positions on other boats culminate in Crawford's captaining the *Adele III*, a state-of-the-art vessel designed for king crabbing in the Bering Sea. In that capacity, he participates in an unsuccessful rescue attempt of another fishing boat lost when she ices up. Crawford marries during one of his breaks ashore, and his thoughts turn to owning his own vessel, even though he is dismayed by the high prices of new crabbing boats.

McCloskey's second novel, *Breakers*, picks up Crawford's life in 1978, depicting him at first as running a tender delivering salmon from fishing boats to canneries. Crawford takes on this task to help pay for a 108-foot-long king-crab boat named the *Jody Dawn* he has ordered from a Seattle shipyard. Bank officials, recognizing his abilities as a highliner, are willing to loan Crawford the $1.6 million needed to pay for the ship. The vessel has "the usual radar, loran, and depth sounder, as well as king crabbing gear considered basic—pot handler, pot launcher, and line coiler."[65] In addition, she has an engine with the horsepower needed to trawl for pollock, 1,150 versus the normal 850, and the "latest in electronic color-display trackers." Although he disdains bottom fish, Crawford wants to have a ship prepared to pursue them if need be.[66]

Fishing out of Dutch Harbor in the fall of 1978, Crawford works his crew hard, allowing them only five or six hours of sleep per day and launching and retrieving crab pots every six or seven minutes when fishing. His boat is swamped with crabs, and Crawford emerges as the number-one highliner for the season. These flush times do not last. In the early 1980s, Crawford faces typical challenges Alaskan king-crabbers experienced: a crash in the crab population and resultant money problems in paying down large debts, along with heavy seas and injured crew members. Despite heroic efforts on his part, Crawford also loses a close friend and mentor, when his salmon boat sinks in Bristol Bay, pounded to pieces on a sand bar. Faced with myriad difficulties,

Crawford reluctantly enters a joint-venture with a Japanese seafood firm. In return for the Japanese company paying all of his debts, Crawford agrees to sell crab and fish only to that firm's processing ships and plants.

In the final novel of the trilogy, *Raiders*, McCloskey has Crawford spend most of his time captaining fishing vessels taking bottom fish—halibut, sablefish, and pollock—for the Japanese processor in the early 1980s. As American vessels increased their take of bottom fish, Japanese firms found their quotas progressively reduced by the North Pacific Fishery Management Council. They had, increasingly, to rely on American catchers for their fish. The relationship between Crawford and the Japanese is tense, full of misunderstandings and under-the-table dealings. Meanwhile, Crawford's wife becomes captain of a fifty-eight-foot salmon seiner. After growing friction with the Japanese, Crawford breaks with them and begins anew as an independent fisher, considerably chastened by his experiences.[67] In this outcome, the fictional Hank Crawford is more fortunate than many real-life American crab fishers, who failed and left the fishery.

In his three novels, McCloskey captures basic changes occurring in Alaskan king crabbing over about two decades. From a boom-time enterprise, he shows, the crab fishery became increasingly rationalized, with a growing role for the federal government as both promoter and regulator. However, even in the early 1980s, when McCloskey ends his third account, federal officials had not yet instituted overall catch limits for crabs or allocated crab harvests among individual fishers. It required experiences with still more booms and busts for many fishers and fish processors to accept those actions.

The Movement Toward Sustainable Crab Fishing

Fluctuations in Alaska's king-crab catch followed intensified American fishing pressure. After expanding in the late 1970s, the catch collapsed, falling by about 80 percent in 1981. In that year, the catch came to only 28 million pounds, far down from 130 million pounds in 1980. "No one could find a crab," remembered Sig Hansen.[68] Controversy continued into the early 2000s about the cause of the crash in the crab catch.

Marine biologists could not agree on the reasons for the slump. Natural events may have contributed to the rapid decline. One possibility is that the same rise in sea temperature that salmon could tolerate caused some plankton to disappear. Tiny copepod and krill, which feed on plankton, lessened in numbers. Crabs, deprived of copepod and krill as food, faced lean times and also decreased in number.[69] Even so, it is likely that at least part of the problem was over-fishing and the inadvertent destruction of crab grounds by fishers. C. Braxton Dew, a leading marine biologist specializing in king crabs, has argued that over-fishing was the culprit. For decades, crab fishers had observed a no-trawling zone in a section of Bristol Bay containing much of the Bering Sea brood stock of mature female king crabs. In the late 1970s and early 1980s, however, trawlers in American-Soviet joint ventures—indirectly encouraged by the exclusion of Soviet fishers from the region by the 1976 Fishery Conservation and Management Act—heavily worked over the region in search of bottom fish. Between 1980 and 1984, Dew has shown, some 5,000 commercial bottom-fish trawls invaded what had been the no-trawling zone. The inadvertent catch of king crabs greatly increased, and most of the crabs caught were female, creating problems for the future harvesting of king crabs in Bristol Bay and more generally the Bering Sea.[70] However, not all scientists have accepted Dew's findings, and in 2009 Dew noted that they remained "controversial."[71]

Some recovery occurred in the mid-1980s, but it was only temporary. King crabs, one Alaskan fishery specialist observed, once more became a "bonanza fishery," in the mid-1980s, with catches reaching 185 million pounds annually. But by 1988 the harvest had dropped to just 18 million pounds, at which level it remained in the late 1990s. As before, the reason for the drop was unclear. "It doesn't really matter why the crab aren't here," wrote fisher-turned-journalist Brad Matsen, "They just aren't." He noted, "It could be the water temperature. It could be overfishing. It could be that the cod and pollock ate them five years ago when they were small. Who knows?" In 1998, McCloskey observed, "King crabs are only now returning to the Bering Sea, but in modest numbers that can support only a few boats for a short season." Whatever the reason, the crab catch fell dramatically. Alaska's crab catch (for king and snow crabs combined) plummeted from 400 million pounds in 1991 to just 45 million pounds in 2000.[72]

As a result of their continuing problems, many in the crab industry came in the early 2000s to favor setting total allowable catches (TACs) and individual transferable quotas (ITQs) for crab fishers and processors. In 2001, the North Pacific Management Council—many of whose voting members, it will be remembered, were themselves fishers or fish processors—considered new ways to regulate the crab catch and a year later decided that restructuring the fishery around seasonal TACs and ITQs was more desirable than other alternatives. Council members observed that their proposed plan would protect established fishers and the crab stock. "In recent years," they noted, "substantial investments of participants in the Bering Sea/Aleutian Islands (BSAI) crab fisheries, together with stock declines, have resulted in a race for fish, complicating stock management and causing economic hardship." To remedy the situation, they recommended adopting limits on harvests for the various types of crabs, along with allocations of the catches among established fishers and processors.[73]

Still, achieving those recommendations took time, for there was considerable opposition. "This program is certainly not without controversy," Council members noted, with masterly understatement, in the summer of 2002.[74] A seemingly neutral and, for many, "natural" goal, the "rationalization" of the king-crab fishery, as the proposed changes were called by proponents, implied the achievement of efficiency and stabilization. But, it was much more. By limiting crab harvests as a whole and catches allowed by individual fishers, rationalization promised (threatened) to basically reshape the king-crab industry by limiting catches and entry into it. Rationalization was a highly politicized process. In fact, the proposed quota system came under attack. Fishers and processors who had not been in the crab industry for the required length of time—three to five years—would receive no allocations. Many fishers protested, and twenty-four Alaskan communities passed resolutions against the plan.[75] Council members were still seeking in 2003 ways to make Alaska's king-crab fishery sustainable. "The goal of rationalization," one of the council's reports on the king-crab fishery reiterated, "is to end the race for fish and solve the problems of overcapacity while providing for a balanced distribution of benefits and improving fisheries management and resource conservation."[76]

After holding numerous public hearings and modifying its original scheme, the Council achieved rationalization with a plan implemented in 2005. More fishers and more fishing communities received allocations in this rendition of the plan than in earlier proposals. Partly satisfied, fishers lessened their opposition, and many established fishers supported the new regulations. They came to see controls as useful, even necessary, for the future of their fishery. Moreover, representatives of fish-processing companies accepted the prospect of tighter government regulations, if their industry were to continue into the future. Together, a growing number of fishers, fish processors, and scientists favored the plan.

Under the plan's terms, the North Pacific Fishery Management Council set harvest limits for the crab species each year. Owners of fishing boats were issued Individual Fishing Quotas (IFQs), which were guaranteed shares of the harvests, with the assumption being that the boats could actually catch the crabs. Under this scheme, derby fishing became unnecessary, for fishing generally continued until the harvests were finished. Processors in turn were guaranteed specific shares of the catch to freeze or can. These shares were called Individual Processing Quotas (IPQs). The Council divided the Bering Sea and Aleutian Island fisheries into eight districts and required that fishers deliver 90 percent of their crabs on a set schedule to designated processors in their districts. Council members hoped that allowing fishers to deliver the remaining 10 percent wherever they desired would keep an element of competition in what, they realized, was fast becoming a noncompetitive fishery regime.[77]

In reality, regulators and rules largely supplanted the market. In the new regulatory regime representatives of arbitration organizations for fishers and processors determined crab prices at the start of each fishing season, with mandatory, binding arbitration available to break deadlocks. A major goal was to avoid fishers' "strikes" that might shut down processing, as they had at various times in the past. (So, it is not surprising to find fish processors as supporters of regulation.) Only boat owners and processors who could show that they had been commercially active in Alaska's crab industry for a number of consecutive years received quotas to catch and process crabs. The exact number of years varied by district, but was four or five years for fishers and three or four for processors.[78]

Defined by the Council as "Eligible Crab Communities," nine villages and towns dependent on king-crab fishing received some guarantees that fishers and processors in their communities would receive quotas. This last proviso was a response to the protests against the earlier plans, which contained few such provisions. It also illustrated the difference in Council decision making between maximum sustainable yields and optimum yields. In the latter, which was the course the Council ultimately adopted, economic and social, as well as biological, factors could be considered. Even so, some fishers and communities were excluded from crabbing, and protests, especially by fishers, continued.[79]

In 2010, the jury was still out on the outcomes of the new crab-regulation scheme. It led, as expected, to consolidation. The number of boats fishing for crabs fell from 252 in 2002 to 75 just five years later, and the number of crew members dropped from roughly 1,500 to only 418. Conservation was another matter. Whether or how soon the crab catch would recover was in doubt. Several crab-fishery areas were closed. The allowable harvest of king crabs was lowered 15 percent in 2007 to encourage recovery, and the American catch that year came to only 15.5 million pounds.[80] In late 2009, the NPFMC considered lowering the next year's catch of snow crabs by 73 percent.[81]

Fishers' Laments

There was a chorus of opposition to parts of the scheme. A review of the program conducted by the NPFMC in 2007 concluded, "Many participants from both sectors [fishers and processors] (but not all) believe that the program is a substantial improvement on the pre-rationalization fishery."[82] Not surprisingly, holders of individual fishing and processing quotas liked the favored places they acquired in the fishery. The Council suggested that only minor changes should be made. In fact, there was more dissatisfaction than the review suggested. Open access to the crab industry disappeared with rationalization, upsetting many Alaskans. It became expensive for newcomers to enter fishing or processing, for they had to buy or lease quotas from established fishers or processors at high prices. In mid-2007, the trade journal *Seafood Business* noted, "In the Alaskan crab fishery, the fleet has been reduced by two-thirds, much to the dismay of Alaskan fishermen and crewmembers who didn't make the cut. The few who did, though, now have plenty of money to hire lobbyists."[83] Established boat owners received almost all of the fishing quotas; only 3 percent of them were set aside for boat captains, and none for crew members.

Residents from some coastal communities joined the outrage. Rationalization resulted in entire villages and towns, except those nine designated as eligible crab communities, being excluded from crab fishing. An anthropologist who studied the impacts of the crab-rationalization program on False Pass, Akutan, and King Cove in the Aleutian Islands concluded, "The findings on direct impacts of crab rationalization on the study communities include loss of crab fishing crew jobs, fewer boats delivering crab, and lower sales for support businesses."[84] Fishers in these communities were outspoken. One complained, "All those boat owners ended up with this quota and it was built by guys like myself; guys that were on deck all those years—they didn't get anything out of it." Another observed, "It was put together by a group of too many special interests which captured the fishery for themselves;

it had nothing to do with the people that participated."[85] In 2008, Terry Haines—a Kodiak city councilman, former deckhand, and member of Fish Heads, an advocacy group concerned about the impact of rationalization on communities—wrote: "In the years since implementation of crab rationalization the council [the NPFMC] has done very little to look back at what happens to towns like Kodiak when you tie up two-thirds of the boats, suck 75 percent of the money out of the paychecks and make the free market illegal."[86] The *Anchorage Daily News* observed in 2009 that throughout the previous year "disenfranchised crab crew continued efforts to obtain a share of the crab quotas."[87]

Even some boat owners who possessed quotas lamented that their earlier free-and-easy way of life was vanishing, a victim of rationalization. Bart Eaton, a longtime king-crab fisherman, later a vice president in Trident Seafoods, asked, "Do we really want a failsafe society? With regulations that tell you where to fish and when, guys feel more and more like they're spare gear in a big bureaucratic machine."[88] Highlining captains and boat owners Andy and Johnathan Hillstrand complained in 2008, "We are afraid of becoming hourly salaried workers with the adventure, traditions and romance of crabbing buried under pages of quotas and regulations. We do not want to be part of bureaucracy." They concluded, "The Bering [Sea] then is our last frontier. It is our Wild West, our Lonesome Dove, played out on waves."[89] Most fishers, however, probably agreed with Sig Hansen, who stated in 2010, "These days, fishermen work together with the agencies to ensure a healthy fishery. We realize that, if over fished, there is no future for us, either."[90]

Questioning led members of the NPFMC to review their plans. They considered various ways by which "some community concerns could be alleviated." They recognized, too, that "the benefits received by shareholders . . . have been at the expense of crew more than others" and that "the current program lacks mechanism for natural progression of crew in fishery from deck to wheelhouse to vessel ownership." The state of Alaska and some private banks implemented programs to try to help individuals and communities acquire fishing quotas, through the formation of fishing cooperatives, for example. How successful they will be remains to be seen.[91]

Resource Usage in the Twenty-First Century

The choices Alaskans faced about harvesting crabs will, most likely, be repeated by Americans and by people around the globe. How to best exploit renewable natural resources in the interests of sustainability is one of humankind's most pressing issues. The example of crab fishing in Alaskan waters suggests that there are no easy answers. Any choices involve winners and losers, as an industry moves from open access to closure. The resource may be conserved, but often only by incurring human and community costs. This shift occurred in king crabbing, just as it did in salmon fishing. Some crab fishers and some communities lost out. Even so, all fishers and processors would have probably suffered much more, if no caps had been placed on crab harvests. The shift from crabbing as a boom time to a mature industry, already apparent by the mid-1960s when crab catches first plummeted, signaled the need for a new type of regulatory regime. Lowell Wakefield was a leader among those who recognized that new regulations were necessary. However, most king crabbers were staunch individualists, and many resisted catch limits and allocations until the early 2000s, when collapsing harvests threatened to put them out of business.

Some of these same issues surfaced as well in taking bottom fish in Alaskan seas, which I explore in the next chapter. Here too, I argue, issues of environmental sustainability sometimes clashed with those of environmental justice. In taking bottom fish, as with salmon and crabs, governmental regulatory bodies played supreme roles in deciding how fishing would be done. Still, there were differences stemming from the various types of fish stocks, gear, and locations.

5

Bottom Fishing: Quotas and Sustainability

When Americans first began fishing in a serious way for sablefish (black cod) and pollock in Alaskan waters in the 1980s, they encountered an unusual problem. In their trawling operations, they caught so many bottom fish that they had great difficulty hauling their nets back to the surface, even with power winches. In fact, several crews found their boats "anchored" to the sea bottom by over-full, "slugged" nets. Unwilling or unable to quickly release their nets, several boats, incapable of moving, foundered in heavy seas. Most captains soon learned, however, to avoid the extensive red blotches that showed up on their electronic fathometer screens as indications of large quantities of the fish. They trawled around the edges of the concentrations and still brought up thousands of tons of fish from the sea bottom.[1]

The bottom-fish story in Pacific Northwest and Alaskan waters is one of increasing American efforts and capabilities, starting in the late 1970s—boosted by governmental actions—and decreasing foreign participation. The declaration of an exclusive economic zone 200 miles out to sea by the 1976 Fishery Conservation and Management Act made a tremendous difference for U.S. fishers. Five fishery experts observed in 1983 that "In the Northeast Pacific the most dramatic change has affected Groundfish resources, where *all* species have for the first time come under the management authority of two coastal states [the United States and Canada]."[2] The tale is also one of a movement toward sustainable fishing. American bottom-fish operators responded to growing scarcity of their resource in the 1990s and early 2000s by devising quota systems similar to those in Alaska's salmon and crab fisheries.

Two salient points stand out about the development of the American bottom-fish industry: the tremendous importance of government policy in shaping the fishery and the fishery's global scope. In this chapter, I examine first the boom-time, open-access fisheries for Pacific cod, halibut, pollock, and other bottom fish and then the achievement of sustainable fishing and its meaning for coastal residents. The very nature of fishing was altered as new laws, technologies, and economic conditions intertwined—as can be seen in the careers of Cathy McCarthy and Margaret Kohler, a mother-daughter fishing team, and Derek Lawson, who pursued halibut. I close this chapter by moving beyond bottom fish to a more general assessment of the factors involved in the attainment of sustainable fishing for salmon, crab, and bottom fish in Alaskan waters and a comparison of those successes to failures elsewhere.

Early Bottom-Fish Harvesting: Halibut and Cod

Commercial halibut fishing began in Alaska in 1888, when sailing ships started traveling north seasonally from Seattle and Vancouver. Just as they did in the North Atlantic, fishers worked from two-person, oared dories lowered each day from their mother ships, sail-powered schooners. Fishers in the dories dropped long, baited lines to the sea bottom and "soaked" them there for several hours to attract halibut. They pulled up the lines hand-over-hand or through hand-cranked rollers, took the fish off the hooks, and rowed or sailed back to their schooners, where they cleaned and iced the halibut before returning to port. Hours were long, and work was physically demanding. Fog and stormy weather sometimes caused dories to be separated from their schooners, with fishers lost at sea. One observer wrote, "The work was excruciatingly hard, and so dangerous in the capricious northern seas that many men and dories were lost each year." Around the time of World War I, diesel engines replaced sails on many schooners, making it possible for the vessels to drag many long lines right over their sides. Dories were no longer needed. Dory ships gave way to diesel-powered wooden schooners typically fifty to eighty feet long. However, most schooners kept sails as a source of auxiliary power.[3] Ballard, a section of Seattle, was home port for as many as 200 of the Northwest's 300 halibut schooners in the 1920s and 1930s.[4]

With some modifications, schooners remained the backbone of the American and Canadian halibut fleets into the 1970s. Coastguardsman and fisher William McCloskey lovingly described them as "sturdy white-hulled vessels, their bows straight with simple grace," and explained how halibut fishing was conducted: "In the halibut fishing process, called long lining, hooks are baited and set in three-hundred-fathom units called 'skates.' . . . The roller mechanism that brings in the fish-weighted line is still called the gurdy after the hand-cranked version aboard the dories, which worked like the hurdy-gurdies of the time." He concluded, "Now that the gurdy is mechanically driven, ten or more skates are usually tied into a multimile string." As before, halibut were cleaned and iced soon after they were caught. Beginning crew members were called "inbreakers," for they broke the ice in ships' holds and stowed the halibut in it, onerous chores. More experienced crew members handled the fishing lines.[5]

Fisher Joe Upton described the daily routine of halibut fishing in his 1977 account, *Alaska Blues*: "Longline gear for halibut consists of long lengths of line, usually quarter-inch nylon, set on the bottom and buoyed and anchored at either end. . . . At intervals in the line are leaders and hooks, baited with pieces of herring, octopus or even salmon. . . . One unit—or skate—of gear consists typically of 1,800 feet of line with a hundred hooks." Skates might be "set singly, but it is more common for several skates to be tied together to make up a mile or more of line." He concluded, "Traditionally, much of the halibut has been caught by distinctive white schooners, 50 to 80 feet long. These boats once ranged as far as the Bering Sea on trips of up to 30 days, fishing 50 to 60 skates of gear a day."[6]

In the early and mid-twentieth century, most Pacific halibut were taken from Alaskan waters around Kodiak Island and from fishing grounds off British Columbia. Canadian and American boats shared the fishery, landing their catches mainly at Prince Rupert, British Columbia, and the Alaskan ports of Kodiak, Seward, and Petersburg. However, when fast-fresh and bulk-frozen seafood shipments became possible in the 1960s and 1970s, Seattle replaced the Alaskan ports as the principal American halibut-landing port.

Halibut fishing has had a lengthy politics. Beginning in 1925, Halibut stocks were managed jointly by Americans and Canadians through the International Pacific Halibut Commission (IPHC) in the interests of achieving the maximum sustainable yield. The Commission set total catch limits by area and allocated catches between American and Canadian fishers. This joint effort successfully nursed halibut stocks, which had been declining, back to health, with American and Canadian fishers taking about 50–60 million pounds of dressed (gutted) halibut each year.[7] The entrance of Japanese and Soviet fishers onto the Northeast Pacific halibut grounds in the 1950s and 1960s upset this equilibrium. Over-fishing occurred and the overall halibut catch in Alaskan and Canadian waters plummeted to 20 million pounds in

1974.[8] Al Pruter, deputy director of the National Marine Fisheries Service Northwest Fisheries Center observed the change in an interview conducted in 1976: "The halibut situation has also had a great adverse effect on United States fishermen. As long as it was just United States and Canada, the resource was under good control." Problems began, he thought, when Japanese and other foreign fishers started harvesting halibut, either as their target catches or as accidental bycatches when trawling for other types of fish. Halibut, he noted, "are on the grounds at the same time as many of those target species [such as cod and pollock] for foreign fleets." As a result, "a lot of halibut were taken incidentally."[9]

The halibut fishery recovered, when the North Pacific Fishery Management Council largely excluded Japanese and Soviet vessels from Alaskan waters in the late 1970s and 1980s. Natural factors, as well as government regulation, were also probably involved, although scientists do not agree on this point. The declines in king crabs in the early 1980s may have boosted halibut numbers, for crabs eat small halibut and other bottom fish. With crabs largely gone, halibut and cod flourished. Consequently, more boats entered the halibut fishery, which in turn led to some over-fishing and cuts in the length of halibut-fishing openings. Some old-time vessels still long lined for halibut in the early 1980s. However, these ships were joined by many newer ones converted from king crabbing and salmon fishing. With crabs, and at times salmon, scarce, fishers sought other options to earn money. Bottom fish, desired especially by Japanese processors for their nation's market, beckoned. Long liners required a work deck up forward, not astern as on the crab boats, a situation that often required moving cabin structures from boats. As in other fisheries, many of the alterations were financed by funding from federal agencies or joint-venture partners, especially Japanese ones.[10]

There was something of a boom in demand for halibut during and after the 1970s. With new technologies, especially refrigerated cargo ships and airplanes that could deliver fish to markets in good shape fresh or frozen, and increased marketing by fish processors and wholesalers, halibut became more a prestige seafood than it had earlier been. Served fresh, halibut was particularly fashionable in upscale restaurants, and frozen halibut became a supermarket staple as a prepared dinner entree. One American processor to pursue halibut and other bottom fish in Alaskan waters was the New England Fish Company, which relocated from Gloucester to Seattle in 1931. In response to the FCMA promise of limitations on fishing of foreigners, the company geared up to pursue bottom fish, in 1980 sending a 110-foot-long trawler fitted out for year-round work into Alaskan waters. Chairman C. Reid Waters explained his firm's increasing presence in bottom-fish harvesting as a way to regularize company operations. "I decided," he said in 1979, that "it was the best way to get this company on a stable basis, away from seasonal products [such as crabs and salmon] and into products with a 365-days-a-year supply."[11]

To meet this demand, derby fishing developed, just as it had in salmon fishing and king crabbing. Serving aboard the *Sue Ann*, a halibut long liner, in June 1992, fisher-journalist Brad Matsen prepared an account of derby fishing. Those on the vessel, he noted, "have been fishing without a break for fifteen hours. They are shivering in their own sweat under gore-splattered raingear, hungry to the point of nausea, and alternately giddy and silent with fatigue." They were fishing a twenty-four-hour opening, one of only two such openings for halibut that year, the other being in September. On those two days alone, fishers landed 65 million pounds of Alaskan halibut. "Some fishermen," Matsen thought, "like the gamble, the quick money, the thick, primitive rhythms of this kind of competition, [but] not many like the danger, the waste, or the dark hours of that long night." And, there was danger: "The Derby may kill you with an assist from a vagrant gale, an overloaded boat, or the grim consequences of a careless moment around flying hooks, lines, and anchors that are tools of your trade."[12]

Cod was less important than halibut in early bottom fishing in the North Pacific. The cod fishery also extended across national boundaries, raising issues of global competition and cooperation. Writing in 1974, fisheries expert Robert Browning observed that Pacific cod, "something of a Johnny-come-lately to the world's attention" had not achieved the high place held by its Atlantic cousin. Still, he noted, "it has contributed a substantial fishery through the years."[13]

The nineteenth-century Pacific cod fishery was headquartered in San Francisco. Beginning in 1863, large schooners from that city sailed thousands of miles across the Pacific to the Sea of Okhotsk to catch cod. A few years later, cod were discovered in waters along the Aleutian Islands, where they could be exploited by smaller vessels. As in the halibut fishery, fishers dangling hand lines from dories lowered from schooners took the fish, which were cleaned and salted onboard the schooners. Catches were "salted in the hold, 'bundled,' boxed boneless." Between 1865 and 1880, about 970 tons of dressed (cleaned) cod were landed in San Francisco each year.[14] From San Francisco the cod were transshipped to markets throughout the United States—the completion of America's first transcontinental railroad in 1869 helped open markets—and the Pacific. For decades, cod reached markets dried and salted. I can remember my mother soaking dried cod from Alaska to rehydrate it preparatory to cooking the fish for my father for breakfast in Seattle in the 1950s. The entire downstairs of our house smelled of cod for days at a time.

Partial mechanization led to some expansion of the cod-fishing industry in the early twentieth century, similar to that in harvesting halibut, but large-scale development occurred only after World War II, and especially in the 1970s and 1980s. Like halibut, Pacific cod became a more upscale fishery when artificial refrigeration allowed shipment of fresh and frozen cod to supermarkets and restaurants from the 1970s on. Even so, this development took decades to complete. In 1979, for example, Oral Burch, a Montana miner turned Alaskan fisher, found it difficult to find a market for his cod and other bottom fish. Returning to Kodiak in the spring of that year with ten tons of cod, flounder, perch, and pollock—the results of trawling operations at depths to 500 feet—he found that buyers for Kodiak processing plants would purchase only part of his catch. Crabs and salmon still ruled the day.[15]

Americans developed few other Pacific Coast bottom-fish fisheries until after World War II, and not really until the 1970s and 1980s. Nor did pollock, soon to become a leading global fishery, elicit much attention. As Browning wrote in 1974, "pollack promises a substantial fishery for Americans and Canadians although to date, it has not been exploited by either of them." He observed that "Asians, especially the Japanese take tremendous tonnages of pollack every year from the waters both north and south of the Aleutians."[16] Only from the 1980s on did Americans pursue pollock in major way.

From Open-Access to Closed Fishing Regimes

From the mid-1970s, fishers long lining and trawling in Alaskan waters generally operated under management regimes set by the North Pacific Fishery Management Council. The Council set policies only after considering reports from scientific advisory committees and holding extensive public hearings at which fishers and representatives of fishing groups testified. They were, of course, in part speaking to other fishers and fish processors, who, we have seen, often composed many of the voting members of the Council. In the 1970s, and even into the 1980s, many Alaskan fishers disdained bottom fish, as other types of seafood were much more profitable to catch and more glamorous as well. To be a salmon or king-crab fisher had more "jazz" and appeal than to be a harvester of bottom fish. To go after crabs and salmon was to be like the (imagined) cowboy of the nineteenth-century Wild West: fearless, individualistic, and daring.

Hank Crawford, the protagonist of McCloskey's novels, captures this common attitude. Told by a cannery superintendent in 1978 that "Groundfish may be your future," Crawford replied, "What? Cent-a-pound trash the Japs make into fish paste? With good crab and fish out there? I catch critters big enough to wrestle with. Real food, not mush." The reference to "mush" was a derogatory comment about the tendency of pollock to spoil quickly. Another captain made similar disparaging remarks about "shitty little pollack that gets you two cents a pound, versus king crab that bring, what, sometime two *bucks* a pound?"[17] These attitudes initially left most of the bottom fish to foreign fishers, mainly Japanese, Soviets, and South Koreans, who together accounted for 95 percent of the bottom-fish catch in Alaskan waters in the early 1970s.[18]

The disdain with which many American fishers viewed bottom fish— other than, perhaps, cod and halibut—did not eliminate conflicts with foreign fishers. In the 1970s and 1980s, the NPFMC granted allocations to foreign fishers to harvest certain species, such as pollock and sablefish, which most Americans ignored, in designated Alaskan and Pacific Northwest waters. Those foreigners often fished with trawlers that supplied nearby factory ships. Dragging their nets across the ocean bottom, the trawlers sometimes destroyed pots laid out by American vessels seeking crabs, resulting in acrimonious gear conflicts.[19]

In time, American attitudes changed. Reflecting new realities, especially a dearth of king crabs, the fictional Crawford equipped his vessel the *Jody Dawn* to go after pollock as well as king crabs. Crawford, who had just a few years earlier disparaged bottom fish, observed of them in 1980, "High volume, all those little fish, there could be money in it."[20] In 1982, Crawford, beset with debts, entered a joint venture with a Japanese seafood company. In return for payment of his debts, Crawford agreed to sell his takes of halibut, cod, pollock, and sablefish only to the Japanese firm. With their fishing quotas for bottom fish reduced and then eliminated altogether as Americans expanded their bottom-fish harvests, Japanese companies needed American catches to supply their factory ships for the Japanese market. A fictional Japanese executive explained matters, "Without more quotas from Americans for my company in the Bering Sea, it is *banzai!*" Americans, he contended, "have no use for this fish that Japanese need." Bottom fish "belong to the world, not only to Americans."[21]

Typically, catcher vessels supplying bottom fish for Japanese processing ships caught the pollock and other species in trawling or long-lining operations. Trawling became most common, especially for pollock. The trawler's crew hauled the nets to the surface as "bulging bags." Never actually landed on the trawlers, the nets with the fish in them were picked up in the water by tenders and towed to the mother ships. There the nets were hauled up stern ramps and unloaded. Next, the fish was cleaned and processed, usually being turned into surimi (fish paste) and fish cakes. Meanwhile, the trawler was already fishing with a second net. The tender returned the first net, once it was emptied.[22]

Americans differed in their early assessments of arrangements with foreign firms, including joint ventures with Japanese companies. Testimony at public hearings in 1983 was revealing. At issue was whether the NPFMC should set a specific date to phase out all foreign fishing, a step taken six years later. There were divisions of opinion. Many Americans and Japanese thought their joint ventures were valuable. The American owner of the 125-foot trawler *Great Pacific* observed, "My trawling operation was managed for seven years by a salmon company, and it brought us to our knees. Now we're fishing for Taiyo, and we're getting high tonnage and a fair price. We see joint ventures as an important way of Americanizing the grounds." Another Alaskan joint-venture boat owner explained, "You talk about needing to provide an attractive investment environment, but that seems to be true about a date-certain phase-out only if you're a processor." A representative of Japanese fishing companies in the United States claimed, "The people behind me [executives of Japanese seafood firms] are the best friends the U.S. fishing industry has. The processors' push to run them off the grounds is not based on analysis of the market or economics. They think phase-out will force the Japanese to buy from them."[23] On the other hand, a member of the NPFMC who was an American seafood processor stated, "With regard to the Japanese who may be put out of work, better them than us." Similarly, an Alaskan labor leader, a member of an advisory panel to the NPFMC, asked rhetorically, "How do I explain to that work force [Alaskan workers] that out of 5 billion pounds of seafood taken in the U.S. zone off Alaska, 4 billion pounds went to foreign processing fleets in direct foreign fishing and joint ventures?"[24]

The federal government's management of bottom-fish resources proved more successful in Alaskan waters than in waters off Washington, Oregon, and California. The center for West Coast bottom fishing lay offshore of Oregon. There fishing had developed in much the same ways as it had off Alaska,

Figure 13. Japanese pollock fishing in the Bering Sea in 1976. Courtesy of William B. McCloskey, Jr.

with foreign vessels taking much of the catches by the early 1970s. With the U.S. declaration of a 200-mile exclusive economic zone in 1976, Soviet and Japanese bottom fishers could be forced out of West Coast waters if American fishers boosted their harvests, and federal and state officials soon tried to convince fishers to do just that. It did not happen overnight. In 1979, for example, the optimum annual yield for West Coast hake, a bottom fish, was 198,000 mt. The harvest of American fishers was only 50,000 mt, with 67,000 mt going to Soviet fishers, 19,000 mt to Polish fishers, and 6,000 mt to Mexican fishers. It was much the same for other bottom-fish species.[25] This situation changed, however, as American fishers received government aid, especially in the form of boat loans to expand their efforts and push foreign fishers out.

State governments helped with marketing, as fishers and processors tried to create consumer demand for fish species earlier considered "trash." The Oregon state legislature made it legal to rename "snapper" as "butterfish" and "sablefish" as "black cod." As always, political actions proved important. A major goal of Americans pursuing bottom fish was to move their catches upscale by changing public perceptions about bottom fish. Here the Oregon state government certainly helped.[26] Branding was important, of course, in changing the images of many types of seafood—Copper River salmon, Chatham cod, and snow (rather than tanner) crabs—as, in general, American seafood operators sought to move their products upscale from the 1970s onward.

Boats to meet the burgeoning demand for bottom fish were expensive. Vessels harvesting common West-Coast bottom fish cost about $1–3 million, factory trawlers (vessels that caught and processed fish) $18–22 million. Federal agencies stepped in to provide much of the financing. Production credit associations set up by the federal government under the terms of the FCMA made direct low-interest loans to fishers and processors. Tax-deferral programs allowed favorable tax treatment for capital improvements in the construction of fishing vessels.[27]

Thus, federal and state governments financed, regulated, and promoted harvesting bottom fish in Pacific Northwestern waters. Regulation and development went hand in hand. Even as a federal commission set total harvests and individual fishing quotas, another federal agency provided low-cost financing for Americans to build or renovate fishing vessels. Both federal bodies derived their powers from the 1976 Fishery Conservation and Management Act, whose goals were to help Americans achieve sustainable fishing, while excluding foreigners.

Unfortunately, the federal agency managing West-Coast bottom-fish harvesting set catches that were too high to be sustainable, similar to what had
occurred for cod in the Northwest Atlantic. In 2000, the U.S. Department
of Commerce declared that because of over-fishing West-Coast bottom fish
were in a "state of disaster." Five of the major species "were at less than fifteen percent of their pre-exploitation abundance." This dismal situation led,
perhaps ironically, to increased federal presence in the fisheries, for the declaration cleared the way for some fishing communities to qualify for federal
disaster relief funds.[28]

Federal regulators experienced more success in achieving sustainability
farther north. The NPFMC began to regulate the taking of bottom fish in the
Gulf of Alaska in 1978 and in waters of the Bering Sea and Aleutian Islands
four years later. Council members started to allocate harvests for most bottom fish solely to American fishers in 1990, excluding foreign fishers from
within the 200-mile zone, a step debated at public hearings since the early
1980s. They added harvest limits and fishing quotas for halibut and sablefish
in 1995–96, although not for Pacific cod or pollock, which were still relatively
plentiful.[29]

Limits on catches perhaps most immediately affected halibut fishing. In
1990, American owners of 7,000 boats held halibut-catching permits, 5,000
of which were actively fished that year. As late as 1995, 3,500 American fishers chased halibut in a season only seventy-two hours long. Fisher-and-
writer Brad Matsen observed, "The fishery resembles a street fight instead
of a respectable effort on the part of the community to gather food." Many
established fishers agreed. "It all adds up to a bad situation," said one, "most
fishermen now support some form of limiting access to the fleet." A sixteen-
year veteran of halibut fishing approvingly observed, "An IFQ [individual
fishing quota] system means I could own access to a certain amount of halibut catch forever." Limits on halibut harvests and the allocation of those harvests as individual fishing quotas to American fishers began in 1996. This
new quota fishing altered the situation dramatically. "Once Alaska halibut
fishermen changed to the IFQ system," observed a writer for the trade journal
Seafood Business, "the fishery was transformed." Only those commercial fishers who had taken halibut in 1988, 1989, or 1990 were allocated quotas. She
noted that "the harvest stabilized and value increased."[30]

The new regulatory regime affected marketing as well as fishing. Under
the older derby fishing situation, millions of pounds of halibut might be
landed from fishing vessels in a single day. Product quality suffered, for there

was not enough time to properly dress (clean and trim) and ice the fish. In fact, only a small proportion of the catch could be marketed as upscale, fresh halibut. Fishers, as a consequence, received only about $1.25 per pound at the dock for their catches in 2006. However, under the quota system, derby fishing in short openings disappeared, replaced by a longer fishing season, until each holder of an individual fishing quota caught his or her share of the catch. Fishers were now able to space out their deliveries, and halibut reached markets in much better shape than before. The writer for *Seafood Business* concluded, "the markets for fresh halibut increased." Laura Fleming, spokesperson for the Alaska Seafood Marketing Institute, concurred: "That was a big breakthrough in getting [halibut] on menus throughout the country and in getting seafood cases throughout the country." By 2008, fishers received $5.25 per pound for halibut at the dock, much more than in earlier years. Despite the onset of a nationwide recession, dockside halibut prices still stood at $4.25 per pound in 2009.[31]

In 2010, the owners of schooners pursuing halibut and black cod held quota permits worth $2–6 million apiece. Vessel captains and crew members might earn $100,000 per fishing season. The fish had become a highly desired dish on many American tables. Seattle's leading newspaper explained the change: "The value of the halibut catch is more than triple that of a few decades ago and reflects halibut's transformation from a blue-collar staple to a pricey seafood that retails for more—often much more—than $10 a pound."[32]

U.S. government actions went even farther in the boosting pollock fishing. Two steps were most important. In 1980, Congress passed the American Fisheries Promotion Act, with the intent to spur the growth of U.S. fisheries by persuading foreign nations and companies to help in its development. While important for many types of bottom fish, this legislation was especially significant for pollock. Officials of the Commerce and State departments, working in tandem for once, adopted what became known as "fish and chips" criteria for foreign fishers harvesting seafood in American waters. Under the terms of the act, if foreigners wanted to fish in American waters, their governments had to lower trade barriers to allow more American seafood into their markets. Then too, their fishery firms had to invest in and transfer technologies to American fisheries. Both of these requirements were usually met through the formation of joint ventures. "Growth of the domestic pollock fishery" geographer Becky Mansfield has written, "was the first and most dramatic success of the fish and chips policy."[33] The catch of pollock by Americans soared from almost nothing in 1980 to 1 mmt just six years later. From 1990 to 1997, United States fishers annually harvested an average of 1.4 mmt of pollock, and in 1997 pollock products composed the largest individual category of seafood exports from the United States. Most pollock was processed into surimi, fish sticks, or other battered fish products.[34] Then too, the American Fisheries Act, passed by Congress in 1998, reduced the number of American pollock-fishing vessels to about a dozen and eliminated derby fishing. The legislation also increased the minimum domestic owner- ship requirement of vessels in the interest of creating a fully owned American catcher fleet.[35]

More generally, NPFMC members worked hard to protect established bottom-fish boat owners. In 2008, for example, they eliminated unused trawl- ing licenses for Alaskan waters. Council members argued, "Trawl vessel owners who have made significant investments, have long catch histories and are de- pendent on BSAI [Bering Sea and Aleutian Island] and GOA [Gulf of Alaska] groundfish resources need protection from others who have little or no recent history with the ability to increase their participation in the fisheries."[36]

The American pollock fishery was oriented to the world from its out- set, with major markets located overseas. "In one of the first joint-venture operations for pollock," Mansfield has noted, "US fishermen caught fish for Soviet processing vessels. The fish was taken to the Soviet Union, then trans- shipped aboard a Japanese freighter to South Korea, where it went through the initial processing stages. From there, the pollock was shipped back to the USA for final processing."[37] The resulting products might well find markets in Japan. Between 1992 and 1998, American firms exported an annual average of nearly 100,000 mt of surimi valued at $260 million to Japan, 12 percent of all American seafood exports. Later joint ventures also resulted from the fish and chips policy, with Japanese companies maintaining both processing ships and onshore processing plants in Alaska. Two of Japan's largest seafood processors, Nippon Suisan and Taiyo (later Maruha), agreed to build major surimi plants in Alaskan as early as 1985. By 1998, four of the eight pollock- processing plants in Alaska were wholly owned by Japanese seafood firms.[38]

Much changed, but much also remained the same in catching cod, halibut, and pollock in the early 2000s. New technologies—automatic hook baiters, GPS systems, and the like—continued to make fishing increasingly efficient. So did the imposition of harvest limits and individual fishing quotas. Fewer boats went after more fish, as various species recovered from over-fishing. Even so, fishing to catch quotas remained hard work. New regulations did not end the strenuous and sometimes dangerous labor involved in fishing, especially since those regulations sometimes seemed distant on the vessels far out at sea.

One fisher has left his impressions of pursuing halibut in 2004–2005. Arriving at fishing grounds off Sitka in southeastern Alaska in late March 2004, he observed: "We set two strings of twenty skates on the halibut grounds. Without wasting any time we ran out to the deeper blackcod grounds and set two blackcod strings. After that we ran back into the halibut zone and began hauling for the flat ones." The following four days saw intense work. "Our strings are 25 skates long, with 180 to 200 hooks per skate, for an approximate 4,500 hooks per string," he explained. On the final day, he and his crew lifted their strings, took the fish off the hooks, and began running their vessel south to Bellingham, Washington, where they thought they might receive higher prices than in Alaskan towns.[39]

About a year later, he fished for black cod on the Portland Bank in the Gulf of Alaska. Here he ran into the potential problem of icing. Fishing in winds of thirty-five knots, which lifted freezing spray from eighteen-foot waves, he and his crew members prudently retired to a sheltered cove to wait out the storm. He described their reasoning, "The *Discovery* is an excellent sea boat, and we have been out in 35-knot blows many times. But if a boat accumulates freezing spray, it builds up a layer of ice on everything above the waterline." Ice accumulation could lead to disaster. "Even a skinny, weightless rigging cable or antenna mast can accumulate a couple of inches of ice all the way around, adding a lot of weight way up above the waterline. This can cause the boat to roll over, and then it is too bad for everyone on aboard." It was, he concluded, "best to use extreme caution when conditions call for freezing spray."[40] King crabbers were not the only fishers to fear icing.

Not all the fisher's time was spent in work. After delivering his catch in Seward, Alaska in late March 2005, he walked quickly to the nearest bar, "filled with fishermen," who he thought were "so predictable." "Here are four or five different boats in town at the same time, and we all show up at the same bar and do the same thing—drink." As he explained, "There was a lot of booze there—I don't know who was buying drinks, or why, but we all had them lined up in front of us. Then a couple of drunks rang the bell for two more drinks." He was probably more cautious than most fishers: "I gave my drinks away and switched to drinking water around midnight, because I knew we had two more strings to bait the next morning."[41]

As in all Alaskan fisheries, temporary workers—people who crewed on boats and labored in processing plants for short periods of time, not for

Figure 14. Sorting pollock and cod on an American boat in Alaska in 1987. Courtesy of William B. McCloskey, Jr.

careers—were important. Derek Lawson was one of those many.[42] Born in Oklahoma, he moved with his family to a suburb of Columbus, Ohio, at an early age, graduating from high school in 2002. From high school, Lawson went on to Hocking Technical College in southern Ohio, graduating from its program in ecotourism and adventure travel. His studies there involved a stay in the Bahaman Islands, which sparked his interest in traveling and the sea, as did subsequent work with sixth-graders in Los Angeles in an outdoors education program.

Lawson decided to go commercial fishing in Alaska, influenced by the television program "Deadliest Catch" and by stories a friend had told him about fishing up north. Lawson later recalled that he was interested in "money and travel." He bought an airplane ticket and flew to Kodiak, where he lived in a campground for several days. He put his name up on a bulletin board in a coffee shop, and he "walked the docks" four or five times a day looking for a berth on a boat. On the third day—7 June 2008—he was hired as a green crew member on the *Zenith*. He was told "to grab his bags and hop in the truck" to get to the boat. He picked up some supplies at a store and went. Lawson earned a $100 per day on his first trip, but more on his later ones.

Figure 15. Derek Lawson with a mid-sized halibut. Courtesy of Derek Lawson.

The *Zenith* was a fifty-eight-foot limit boat formerly used in salmon fishing. She was all-steel in construction, with a deep bow, well designed for Alaskan waters. The cabin was aft, having the bridge on top, with full windows giving a wide view. The vessel boasted advanced electronics, including a state-of-the-art GPS, a fathometer (depth finder), and radar. She also had a full galley, with food held in nets to avoid spillage in heavy seas, a television, and a table; "tiny-little" staterooms for the crew (Lawson shared his with one other person); a head (bathroom) with a shower and pump toilet; and a washer-drier.

The *Zenith* long lined for bottom fish. Lawson fished mainly for halibut, but also for black cod and Pacific cod. He later recalled ten-day trips with harvests of 40,000 pounds of halibut and 20,000 pounds of black cod. Some Pacific cod was taken, along with some ling cod, skates, and rock fish. In addition, "now and again we pulled up a crab for dinner." The *Zenith* was typically at sea for a week and a half at a time, but made one trip of three weeks in duration. The fish were delivered mainly to facilities in Sand Point, Dutch Harbor, and Unalaska. It was at these ports that the ship picked up supplies, for the canneries "had everything."

There were numerous tasks for the *Zenith*'s captain, five deckhands, and engineer. The captain had the fifth-highest individual fishing quota for Alaskan halibut, and his major job was to "find the fish." Crew members' jobs included sorting hooks and coils of line using a rack system; baiting hooks, made easier by an automatic baiter; laying out the long lines for fishing, done in long strings with multiple shackles, with hooks about three feet apart; mechanically playing the line over the stern, with "ten hooks a second going over" as sets were laid down; pulling in the lines after they had been in the sea, typically for three hours, but sometimes for up to twelve hours; cleaning the fish; and icing the fish in bins in the holds.

Lawson worked hard, but not usually around the clock, although he did fish for thirty hours straight on one occasion. "There was never a lack of jobs," he remembered. He was usually able to get four hours of sleep each day, and there were regular breaks for snacks and meals. The meals were, he recalled, "great," including peach-mango salmon. The *Zenith* had deep freezers, which allowed "snacks galore," and there was always coffee available. No drugs or alcohol were allowed on board. Lawson fished during the summer and early fall, during which time his ship encountered no problems with icing. His vessel carried survival suits for all crew members, who practiced once in putting them on, and had an emergency beacon. Lawson later recalled that there were a "couple of storms" when he was fishing and that on one occasion a large wave hit the *Zenith*, causing concern: "One wave, I thought we were going over."

Asked if he would go fishing in Alaska again, Lawson replied that he would probably not engage in commercial fishing. He clearly enjoyed the hard physical work and liked the closeness to nature—even though this included an erupting volcano in the Aleutians, which covered the boat with ash and forced crew members to wear respirators. He particularly liked seeing wildlife, such as porpoises and humpback whales. However, he disliked what he viewed as environmental damage done by commercial fishing. He observed with dismay that the *Zenith* used six gallons of bleach each trip, along with metal brightener and other "nasty chemicals" that ended up in the ocean. Lawson said that he would like to go to Alaska for enjoyment, perhaps sport fishing—"definitely to Alaska . . . I loved it."

Even with new regulations, harvesting bottom-fish remained dangerous. Lawson was more fortunate than some. Much of the fishing was conducted in the winter and spring in the Bering Sea, subjecting vessels to the same problems crab ships faced, such as icing. Not all fishers were prudent. Particularly startling to Alaskans was the well-publicized sinking of the 203-foot *Alaska*

Ranger, a large catcher-processor, 120 miles west of Dutch Harbor in late March 2008, with the death of the captain and four crew members. A coast guard helicopter and nearby ship plucked forty-two other crew members out of the sea. "It was a textbook worst-case scenario," recalled Lt. Steve Bonn, who piloted the helicopter: "There were people just floating everywhere," and "driving snow and rain and 30 mph winds sharply reduced visibility." Moreover, "pounding waves crested to 20 feet, sometimes 30 feet." All the survivors wore survival suits, which fishing vessels had been required to carry since 1988.[43]

Just seven months later, the *Katmai*, a 93-foot cod-fishing vessel, sank in Amchitka Pass in the Aleutian Islands, fully loaded with 120,000 pounds of fish. Again, a coast guard rescue helicopter was able to lift four crewmen, all of whom had been able to don survival suits and scramble into a ship's life raft. Weather conditions during the search included "50–knot winds from the north, seas rising 17 feet, with a mix of rain and snow." Coast guard helicopters carried rescue swimmers who jumped into the water to get to fishers and place them in baskets, which were then hoisted up into the helicopters. One such swimmer described his ordeal trying to reach the life raft in which crew members from the *Katmai* huddled: "I wasn't making much headway. I don't know how long I was in the water trying to swim to it. I finally got up to the guys on the life raft. I would swim up to it, get a little bit closer and they would try to grab me, and a swell would come out and take them about five feet away from me again." He finally reached the raft and succeeded in putting the men into the basket. One at a time, they were lifted into the helicopter. Seven other crew members were lost at sea, with the floating bodies of five of them found later by several ships.[44] The *Anchorage Daily News* averred, "The Katmai is the fourth head-and-gut vessel to suffer catastrophe this decade, beginning with the 2001 sinking of the Arctic Rose in the Bering Sea, killing all 15 crewmen."[45]

Addressing Community Concerns

Worries that had surfaced about closing access in salmon and crab fishing also punctuated discussions about bottom-fish rationalization. Fishers and residents in fishing communities, especially Alaskan Natives, excluded from bottom fishing by the various rules put in place in the 1980s and 1990s, were vocal in their concerns. In 1992, representatives for the state of Alaska, the

U.S. Marine Fisheries Service, and the NPFMC responded by jointly establishing community quotas for villages, primarily inhabited by Alaskan Natives, in western Alaska.[46] Then, as revised in 1996, the Fishery Conservation and Management Act required in its "Standard 8" that community concerns be given greater consideration in establishing total allowable catches and individual fishing quotas than before.

Optimum yields, which considered social and economic community issues, especially job creation and destruction, were to take precedence over maximum sustainable yields, which looked only at biological matters. One result of the growing sensitively was the Western Alaska Community Development Quota Program, which used funds derived from payments for individual fishing quotas to aid in community development. The plan fell short of what some community-development activists wanted.[47] Responding to continuing community concerns, Congress placed a temporary moratorium on creation of rationalization plans in 1998–99, only to lift it a few years later.[48]

Worries on the part of some village residents remained, leading members of the NPFMC to boost the Quota Program, which allocated "a percentage of all Bering Sea and Aleutian Islands quotas for groundfish, prohibited species, halibut, and crab to eligible communities."[49] The program vested sixty-five coastal villages from Nome to Naknek, inhabited mainly by Alaskan Natives, with 10 percent of the revenues from Bering Sea fish and crab harvests. The Natives did not catch the fish and crabs themselves. Rather, they leased their fishing rights to six companies that did the actual fishing. Villagers typically used their fishing lease revenues to build processing plants, improve village health facilities, and provide scholarships for young people.[50]

Writing in 2003, Terry Johnson, an Alaskan fisheries expert, concluded that while little income from the bottom fish industry reached local residents in the 1970s and 1980s, "That changed significantly in the 1990s, when Community Development Quotas (CDQs) went into effect, channeling a percentage of the Groundfish harvest to people living in tiny communities in the Bering Sea coastal region." In 2007, the fishing companies generated $170 million in income and possessed assets of $534 million. Some $17 million went to the villagers. In that year, the coordinator of the Bristol Bay Economic Development Corporation, representing seventeen villages of Alaskan Natives, concluded that the Community Development Program had given people "hope and pride."[51]

Two years later, twenty southwestern Alaska communities composing one of the CDQ groups, with a total population of 8,700, announced that the group was opening a $35 million salmon-processing facility in the village of Platinum, financed by profits from pollock fisheries. The plant would employ 125 people. By this time, "Pollock Provides" had become the slogan of that community development quota group.[52]

Nonetheless, the NPFMC actions in restricting overall catches and limiting individual quotas still left some Alaskans, especially non-Natives, out of such programs. Another program, proposed for residents of Gulf of Alaska villages in 2000 and enacted five years later, was designed to make it easier for members of some communities to purchase individual fishing quotas for sablefish and halibut. However, for most, prices were still too high. One person testifying about the program observed, "As it sits now, it is set to fail. The price of the IFQ is so great that it is virtually impossible to make money." Another complained, "People who grew up in the coast communities had salmon, crab, halibut, whatever, available to them and should still have it available." He asserted, "It is not right that we have to buy into this. It is God given for the people who live here." Likewise, the head of the Gulf of Alaska Coastal Communities Coalition lamented "the steady and serious erosion of local fishery opportunities—often brought about by the inadvertent effects of the regulatory system." An anthropologist studying the situation found in 2007 that residents of small communities on Kodiak Island associated the fishing quotas for bottom fish with village depopulation and a lack of involvement in fishing by young people.[53]

In early 2009, the Alaska state legislature passed a resolution urging NPFMC to keep Pacific cod fisheries open to all state residents. Rep. Alan Austerman of Kodiak, a sponsor of the resolution, explained: "The NPFMC should know that the Alaska State Legislature supports a policy of broad participation in the fisheries harvest. . . . We want to encourage them wholeheartedly to oppose any amendment package that would reduce meaningful access opportunities for young fishermen and Alaskans."[54]

One town that definitely benefited from bottom-fish harvesting and king crabbing was Dutch Harbor/Unalaska on Adak Island in the western Aleutians. In 2007, Dutch Harbor was the leading fishing port, as measured by tonnage of fish landed, in the United States for the nineteenth year in a row. About 777 million pounds of seafood worth $174 million, led by landings of pollock, were unloaded at the town's docks. Kodiak was the nation's number-four port, with landings of 320 million pounds of seafood worth $126 million.[55] Long the heart and soul of commercial fishing in Alaska, Kodiak was home to the annual meeting of fisher poets, described by the town's newspaper in 2009 as "Kodiak Out Loud, Fishing and the Sea." The line-up that year included a woman salmon fisher, a male salmon fisher inspired by the annual meeting of cowboy poets in Elko, Nevada, a fisher from Chinook, Washington, a salmon fisher who was also an adjunct professor of English at Kodiak College, and several others.[56]

Mixed Fishing: Cathy McCarthy and Peggy Kohler

Many fishers who pursued bottom fish also went after crabs and salmon. Mixed fishing was common in Alaskan waters, as exemplified by the experiences of Catherine McCarthy and her daughter, Margaret Kohler.[57] Operating out of Kodiak most of the time, they were among those who engaged in many types of fishing, and, inevitably, they found their fishing careers affected by government regulations.

Kohler moved to Alaska when she was two. McCarthy moved to Alaska in 1957 and taught special education in Dillingham, Koliganek, Kenai, and Anchorage, becoming principal of an elementary school in Kodiak. With her second husband, she left education to enter fishing. Their boat, the *Anna D*, was steel hulled, forty-six by sixteen feet, and diesel powered (and could make about 6–7 knots), with a live tank for crabs amidships. The electronics included Loran C, radar, an autopilot, and a color fish finder (NavCom). There were a head (bathroom) and a galley, a launcher for tanner-crab pots, and a hydraulic lift for pulling the pots up. McCarthy owned the boat for three years after her husband died of cancer, during which time she tendered the boat in barebones leases to other captains. She "dry leased it for halibut." Lessees paid their own insurance and other expenses.

McCarthy began fishing on the *Anna D* as part of the family business, harvesting Dungeness crab, tanner crab, and halibut, the latter taken by long lining. McCarthy and Kohler (and her sisters) worked on the deck. They fished around Kodiak Island and opposite the island across Shelikof Strait in inlets on the Kenai Peninsula (Katmai National Park), hiring extra crew members as needed. McCarthy remembered that her husband kept "voluminous notebooks" identifying good fishing places and returned to them year after year. Doing so was, she thought, a common practice: "You didn't tell other people about it."

They also tendered for salmon, taking the salmon off fish boats and transporting it to canneries. In tendering, they worked for canneries—such as All Alaskan Seafoods, Cook Inlet Processing, Bumble Bee, and Whitney Fidalgo—with contracts covering each season. The canneries paid them on a per pound basis for salmon. As was typical, they negotiated contracts with the canneries and were responsible for paying their crews. Always venturesome, McCarthy also flew with her husband, a pilot, in a DC3 they owned to pick up salmon caught by other fishers. Landing on beaches, they loaded salmon into the plane and ferried it to canneries or to airports for shipment south. McCarthy observed that some independent fishers used their services as part of an effort to ship fresh salmon directly to Seattle restaurants. Kohler also worked on a salmon slime line for a processor on the Alaskan Peninsula. It was hard work with long shifts, sometimes twenty-four hours straight, often resulting in swollen hands and an aching back

The *Anna D* carried about 300 Dungeness crab pots at a time, but the family had 1,000 pots, stashing many at beaches along the Kenai Peninsula. Each weighed about 150 pounds empty. They fished "about 200 or 300 pots a day," "a lot of work." Their vessel could carry about fifteen tanner-crab pots, each six feet by six feet. Each weighed about 1,000 pounds empty. They fished for tanner crabs, not king crabs, and hired extra crew members for tanner-crab fishing. They typically soaked tanner-crab pots for about twelve hours. They might soak Dungeness-crab pots for several days. Dungeness-crab pots used biodegradable twine for their traps that would eventually disintegrate; so the pots would not fish forever if lost. Both women later remembered having sore hands from dealing with 300 Dungeness-crab pots per day. Dungeness crabs also hurt when they pinched, even through gloves.

Fishing could get "real rough," especially crossing Shelikof Strait, McCarthy recalled. There were other downsides. McCarthy and Kohler were often tired and lacked sleep; they were sometimes "pretty wrung out," as Kohler put it. They took tanner crabs in January, when "it was freezing cold." At that time of the year, they had to use baseball bats to break ice off their vessel. Kohler later remembered the openings for halibut as "nightmares." The openings were short, sometimes only a day or two, in which they fished round the clock, with perhaps four of every twenty-four hours to sleep. "You worked like a maniac." The *Anna D* used large tubs to hold the long lines. "We had them all set up, exactly right," Kohler recalled. Bait was octopus or fish. Two people snapped the bait on the line, which "went over a huge reel at the back of the boat." Kohler explained that you had to be "really careful" baiting the hooks so as not to take a hook in your hand. "You also did not want to get anything caught on the longline going out, because that's really dangerous."

Only skilled people baited, which was very hard work at a time when the "weather was usually bad."

In these conditions, safety always was a concern. "There was nothing [in the way of safety measures] when we started," McCarthy remembered. Bad accidents in 1987–88 changed this, she recalled. McCarthy strongly supported all the safety measures—rafts, survival suits, mini-beacons on suits, and ship beacons—and her vessel had them before required by law. She also remembered, "You had to train your crew." She and her crew members practiced putting on survival suits and jumping in the water with suits on. No alcohol was allowed on board, "a big change" from earlier times. Even with precautions, fishing could be dangerous. McCarthy later described the sinking of a friend's halibut boat. People on that vessel had survival suits, but not mini-beacons. Some were never found: "The others drifted away and they couldn't find them and they died of hyperthermia." McCarthy and Kohler observed that their main safety problem actually came from bears on the Alaskan Peninsula. McCarthy explained, "Our biggest experience was on the beach with the bears." More than once, when cleaning crab pots on shore or digging for cockles, they had frightening run-ins with bears on the beaches. Kohler remembered meeting a "monster bear" at close quarters.

As a boat owner, McCarthy qualified for individual fishing quotas and had them. However, she harbored reservations about government-mandated quotas and the federal loan programs: "I was very much opposed to them." In fact, she recalled, "A lot of fishermen fought against them very hard." Individual quotas, she thought, "benefited people who had a lot of money." This situation, she concluded, was unfair to newcomers wanting to go into fishing, and to captains and crew members, who "really got nothing." Quotas hurt women, she believed. "There weren't many women fishermen." Still, when McCarthy retired from fishing, she sold her halibut quota for as much as her boat, which she also sold.

Despite the danger, hard work, and economic ups and downs, the two women loved fishing as a way of life. They liked being out in the elements, the hard physical labor. "I loved being out in the middle of nowhere, with the fresh air," Kohler later stated. They liked making at times "lots of money." Kohler put herself through Oberlin College and Eastman School of Music with funds earned fishing. Both stressed that despite the problems they had had "a lot of good times" on Alaskan waters.

Sustainable Bottom-Fish Fishing in Alaska

In 2008, the NPFMC adopted rules to make bottom fishing more environmentally sustainable than it had been. Some 180,000 square miles of the Bering Sea were closed to all trawling operations, bringing the total size of such closed areas in the Pacific Ocean to 830,000 square miles. (Other newly restricted areas were off the coasts of Washington, Oregon, and California.) Environmental groups such as Oceana and Greenpeace had long sought bans on trawling. "It basically is taking a net and raking it on the bottom and anything that sticks up from the bottom gets bulldozed over," testified Chris Krenz, Oceana's Arctic project manager. "It is similar to forest clear-cutting," he claimed. About 150,000 square miles remained open to trawling in Alaskan waters, mainly around the Aleutian and Pribilof Islands. Representatives for the Groundfish Forum, a trade association of six companies engaged in trawling in Alaskan waters, said that the body's members could live with the closure, but that it might hurt them in the future.[58]

Fishing controversies continued in 2008–2009. In one instance,the NPFMC began resolving a fifteen-year feud between commercial fishers and charter-boat (sports) fishers over access to Alaska's halibut catch. A drop in the halibut catch made resolution of the issue timely. In public hearings before the Council, fishers presented self-serving arguments. Commercial fishers observed that they had made costly investments in their vessels and that their catches supported major onshore processing plants, creating numerous jobs. Charter-boat operators countered that their businesses were an important segment of the growing tourist industry in Alaska and should be supported as part of the wave of the state's future. Conflict became ugly at times, with bumper stickers in Homer and Sitka declaring, "Die Charter Scum." In the end, members of the Council sided mainly with commercial fishers, voting 10–1 to limit sports fishers to one halibut per day, not the two desired by charter-boat owners, whenever the halibut population was deemed as being low. The ruling covered southeast and south-central Alaska. Responses were predictable. The lone Council member voting against the ruling was Ed Dersham, who operated a salmon and halibut charter business out of Anchor Point. He complained that the plan "does not meet the test of [being] fair and equitable." Council member Gerry Merrigan, a commercial halibut fisher from Petersburg, who approved of the ruling,stated that it "establishes a line in the sand that I think is long overdue."[59]

A second major controversy swirled around pollock. In late 2008, the environmental group Greenpeace began running advertisements on Alaskan television stations featuring a "sad-looking, bearded fisherman in a yellow rain slicker—the spitting image of the guy on Gorton's fish stick frozen meals—wander[ing] the streets with a big sign that claims the crash of a Bering Sea fishery made him homeless." The fishery in question was the Bering Sea pollock fishery. In 2008, stocks of Alaskan pollock indeed shrank by about one-half. Whether this decline resulted from natural fluctuation or over-fishing was unclear.[60] In December 2008, the NPFMC responded to the drop by setting the pollock harvest for the coming year at 815,000 mt, an 18.5 percent reduction from 2008, and a 45 percent reduction from its peak in 2004.[61]

National and local environmental activists desired a smaller pollock catch of 458,000 mt, saying that their review of federal marine science "found weaknesses in the pollock stock that could lead to collapse, depending on climate change." "This is a time when you need to be extra cautious because there's not a lot of insurance," observed Chris Krenz of Oceana. Phil Kline, a commercial fisher for twenty-nine years and a senior oceans campaigner for Greenpeace, agreed. "Now is the time to back off the fishery," he argued. "It's about protecting not just the pollock but the function of the ecosystem and the people who rely on it." Doug Mecum, a member of the NPFMC, countered, "The harvest strategy that's in place has resulted in a sustainable harvest for quite a long time."[62] A leading executive of Trident Seafoods also argued that the downturn in pollock catches was simply cyclical. Pollock, he argued, was a well managed resource needing no further cutbacks in harvests. The past few years happened to be a down period for pollock, with recovery expected soon.[63]

In 2009, commercial fishing in the Arctic was banned. Influenced by the decline in the number of bottom fish in nearby seas and by the testimony of environmentalists, the NPFMC voted unanimously in early 2009 to forbid all commercial fishing in American waters in the Arctic Ocean. The Council adopted an "Arctic Fishery Management Plan," on which it had been working for two years, which outlawed commercial fishing across the entire Arctic region from the Canadian border to the Bering Strait separating Alaska from Russia. Little commercial fishing had yet occurred in those waters. However, Council members believed that as a result of global warming some cold-water species such as king crabs and pollock might migrate northward into Arctic waters. Their beliefs reflected findings by scientists of the UN Food and Agriculture Organization, who concluded in 2008 that "climate change is modifying the distribution of marine and freshwater species." More specifically, they discovered that some "species are being displaced toward the poles and experiencing changes in habitat size and productivity."[64] The Council's plan called for more study before commercial fishing might be permitted in the Arctic regions. The area could be opened to commercial fishing if research showed that it could be conducted without hurting "an ecosystem populated with seabirds, seals, whales, and other species important to Native residents as subsistence food."[65]

Both fishery groups and environmental bodies praised the decision. "Climate change is having a significant effect on the Arctic, opening ice-covered waters and drawing cold-water species farther north," observed Dave Benton of the Juneau-based Marine Conservation Alliance, which represented fishing companies, processors, and environmental groups. Oceana leader Krenz called the ruling "a great example for other nations." In fact, in 2008 Congress passed a joint resolution calling on the United States, Canada, Russia, Norway, and other nations to negotiate how to manage migratory and transboundary fish stocks in the Arctic Ocean. Not everyone was pleased with the ruling, however. In a blog, one Alaskan wrote sarcastically, "Yeah, let the Russians and Japanese fish . . . by all means, we don't need the industry." Another blogger, disgusted with what he/she thought was over-fishing in the Bering Sea, commented, "The Bering Sea is going bald so we'll close the Arctic. Does this sound like a fake end run around or what. Those guys [members of the Council] are scary."[66]

Sustainable and Unsustainable Fishing in American Waters

The entrance of environmentalists into debates about commercial fishing issues in Alaska added a new, public dimension to decision making in the early 2000s, paralleling—with some delay—the growing importance of environmentalists in many other such debates in the United States. For instance, environmentalists and scientists came to play greater roles in deciding how the Bureau of Land Management administered the hundreds of millions of acres composing the nation's public domain. Ranchers, miners, and timber operators, the original "constituency" of the Bureau, no longer determined by themselves how lands should be utilized. To the contrary, broader input resulted in the adoption of multiple-use and watershed-management schemes.[67]

It took longer for this shift to occur in fisheries management, and in the early 2000s it was not nearly as complete as in many other fields. Commercial fishing simply did not attract as much public and environmental attention as most other similar issues. Fish were not as glamorous as, for example, whales. Public outrage in the United States and many other nations led to fairly successful efforts to restrict commercial whaling, with environmental groups such as Greenpeace taking leading roles. There were relatively few such actions with regard to fish. Instead, commercial fishing agreements long tended to be compromises among fishers, fish processors, and government officials, with only limited public input. Of course, scientists staffing advisory panels offered their findings to bodies like the NPFMC, and the Council held public hearings; but decision making was usually dominated by participants in the seafood industry.

Those decisions directly affected how fishing was carried out, species by species. Comparisons of developments in the various American fisheries discussed here reveal complexities in fishing and over-fishing. Over-fishing was commonest in the long-established fisheries of the Northwest Atlantic, such as those for cod and blue-fin tuna. The application of industrial fishing methods after the Second World War intensified large-scale fishing that had begun earlier. The failure of the New England Fishery Management Council and International Commission for the Conservation of Atlantic Tuna to provide adequate regulation made a bad situation worse, leading to the near demise of Atlantic cod and blue-fin tuna as commercial fish stocks. In the Pacific Northwest and California, the erosion of major salmon runs, such as those for the Sacramento and Columbia Rivers, resulted from habitat destruction, over-fishing, and natural events. Poorly informed government regulation hurt bottom-fish fishing off the West Coast.

Farther north in Alaskan waters, salmon benefited from less habitat destruction and more sustainable regulation of fishing, especially from the mid-1970s. Alaskan salmon also proved able to cope with natural changes such as the increase in ocean water temperatures. On the other hand, king crabs suffered from over-fishing, an initial lack of adequate regulation by the NPFMC, and possibly environmental changes. Even with the implementation of a rationalization plan in 2005, the future of crab fishing was uncertain. Plans did seem to have placed harvesting major commercial species of bottom fish on a sustainable basis. Pacific cod did not seem to be going the way of its Atlantic cousin. Nor, despite some decline, possibly only temporary, did pollock or other bottom fish. A leading officer in Trident Seafoods noted in 2009 that Alaska's bottom-fish fisheries had become much more efficient and rational than ever before. The move to quota fishing in them was, he concluded, the most successful fisheries management change that had taken place.[68]

As we have seen, the Marine Stewardship Council (MSC), the independent British environmental group, began certifying fish stocks as being managed in sustainable ways in the mid-1990s. By mid-2005, eleven fisheries around the globe produced fish bearing the MSC label, including halibut and most Pacific cod caught in Alaskan waters.[69] Bering Sea pollock achieved certification in 2007. By mid-2008, some twenty-six fisheries had secured certification worldwide, impressively including all Alaskan pollock, salmon, halibut, and sablefish, and most Alaskan cod.[70] In mid-2008, EcoNews, a branch of Environmental Communications, Inc., featured Kodiak, Alaska, especially its pollock fishery, in one of its documentaries to be shown over seventy government-access stations in the United States. On the other hand, in early 2009 representatives of Greenpeace and Oceana called on the MSC to reconsider its approval of Alaskan pollock.[71]

Most of Alaska's fisheries had developed as bonanza enterprises, and they remained open-access fisheries as late as the 1960s. However, beginning in the 1970s and continuing in the early 2000s, Alaska's fisheries became among the most highly regulated industries in the United States, altering the nature of fishing in fundamental ways. Government bodies set overall catches, allocated individual fishing quotas (and for crabs processing quotas as well), and sometimes even supervised the setting of prices. Fishers, processors, the residents of fishing communities (along with community activists), environmentalists, and scientists all played roles in bringing about this change.

However, it was well-established fishers and processors who were most influential. Rightly worried about the long-term future of their industry, they drove sustainable fishing forward. One knowledgeable observer noted in 2007, "Alaska fisheries, once faced with depleted salmon runs and domination by foreign boats, are renowned today for many healthy fisheries in a world hungry for nutritionally rich foods."[72] A felt need for stability and permanence—especially on the parts of well-established fishers and large processors—trumped earlier desires for quick gains, making most of the fisheries sustainable. The availability of better science, younger fisheries, and the very negative example of Northwest Atlantic cod fisheries spurred the NPFMC to positive actions not taken by the NEFMC.

Sustainability meant limiting catches and the number of fishers. For people in a nation ostensibly committed to the preeminent individual who worked through markets, this shift was dramatic. It meant accurately determining and stringently enforcing total allowable catches and individual fishing quotas. These actions broke the downward spiral so often caused by overcapacity in fisheries. Processors benefited from the steady flow of raw fish to their plants. Some Alaskan fishers lost their jobs and some communities suffered. However, the situation could have been much worse. Certainly, there was pain in Alaska as some were excluded from fishing, but none as severe as in Newfoundland and parts of New England, homes to fishers of the collapsed cod fisheries there, as discussed in Chapter 2.

In 2008, fishing remained, as it had long been, one of Alaska's leading industries. Between 2002 and 2007, the average annual dockside value (the amount paid fishers) for Pacific cod and pollock landed in Alaska came to $520 million. The comparable sum for salmon was $320 million; for halibut and black cod $264 million; and for other bottom fish $175 million. The dockside value of shellfish was $132 million.[73] In 2008, the number of fishers peaked at 20,137 per month during the summer salmon runs, with another 54,000 workers employed in processing, transporting, and otherwise directly supporting fishing.[74]

New issues about sustainability arose in 2007–2010. These concerns had less to do with environmental than with economic sustainability. A leading economist dealing with Alaskan fisheries asked in September, 2008, "Now what do we do with the notion of sustainable economic development?" He observed, "With fuel prices near all-time highs, many of Alaska's seafood harvesters and processors are hurting." As a consequence, "Unless fuel prices drop dramatically, the state might soon find itself under even more pressure to 'sustain' Alaska's archetypical sustainable industry, seafood, with money from its archetypical unsustainable industry, oil and gas." In fact, high fuel prices idled about one-fifth of Kodiak's trawlers, and fishers were by then seeking state aid in the forms of tax credits and tax waivers.[75] There were also fears that economic difficulties in Japan, Alaska's most important seafood customer, might hurt sales, but that situation remained impossible to predict. "It is important not to jump to conclusions when it comes to predicting how that will affect fish sales," observed one well-respected commentator.[76]

Even as fishers faced new challenges from the 1970s on, so did processors of seafood for the American market—firms like the Red Chamber Company, Trident Seafoods, and the Pacific Seafood Group, the three largest in 2006. The growing scarcity of some fish species affected the full lengths of seafood chains, including processing and selling, as well as catching, fish. Concerns about the availability of some types of seafood, for example, led the officers of processing firms to rework corporate strategies and structures. The executives continued, and in some cases, accelerated the vertical integration of their companies backward to control their sources of raw seafood, a topic I deal with in the next section of this book.

PART III

Changing the Food Chain

6

The Companies: Controlling Food Chains

In 2003, Frank Dulcich, Jr., who headed the Pacific Seafood Group, then the fifth-largest supplier of seafood to the American market, expressed concerns to an interviewer about over-fishing. Talking about West Coast processors, he observed, "We're losing retail and food service business because they [retail outlets for seafood, such as restaurants and grocery stores] want consistent supply." Still, when asked whether he thought there was "light at the end of the tunnel," Dulcich replied, "there's lots of fish out there, we're seeing lots of salmon." In fact, "most all species except for a few rockfish species" were "stable or increasing." The seafood business, he concluded, was not "going to go away."[1] Dulcich's somewhat contradictory statements about the supply of seafood captured well the challenges facing processors, wholesalers, and retailers: some marketable species of seafood were over-fished and in short supply, and others thrived. Companies supplying American markets with seafood faced especially volatile economic, environmental, and political circumstances, as they grappled with issues of resource scarcity and the new regulatory regimes established to deal with the shortages. In an effort to master these changes, seafood processors adopted new approaches to their firms and their industry.

In this chapter I examine the changing nature of the major suppliers of seafood to the American market. These companies, such as Dulcich's Pacific Seafood Group, were processors and distributors that exerted considerable clout over seafood chains. I show that by the late 1990s and early 2000s the leading processors were family owned and operated, privately held businesses—a real change from the more diversified, publicly held corporations that had dominated the seafood industry in earlier decades. (As noted earlier, common stock in privately held firms is not available for sale to the general public; in publicly held firms it is.) I argue that the officers of these family firms focused on seafood, like Frank Dulcich, had intimate knowledge of the sources for raw fish and crabs, giving their companies a competitive advantage over more diversified, broadly focused, publicly held corporations that dealt in a range of products, causing many of the latter to exit seafood processing. The actions of company officers—spurred by scarcity and by regulations designed to alleviate scarcity—partly reshaped, I contend, the organization of America's seafood industry in the late twentieth and early twenty-first centuries.[2]

In this chapter and the following one, which examines how these companies changed the ways they actually processed and marketed seafood in light of scarcities, I argue that seafood food chains have become increasingly global in scope and are likely to remain so.[3] That globalization has taken numerous forms. Fish caught in Pacific Northwestern and Alaskan waters have long reached some markets around the world. Since the 1970s, however, seafood companies have increasingly operated across national boundaries by entering into joint ventures, as Japanese processors did with American fishers, moves unintentionally encouraged by the U.S. declaration of a 200-mile economic exclusive zone. We have viewed those connections in previous chapters. Then too, as I show in this chapter, both American and Japanese processors acquired foreign subsidiaries to be close to their major overseas markets. Finally, both Japanese and American processors established foreign plants of their own around the world.

The executives of companies controlling food chains, including those for seafood, have been very potent agents of economic globalization. At the level of the business firm, they have encouraged a movement toward global vertical integration. In vertical integration, company officers join the various stages in their businesses, from raw materials to production through sales. In the late nineteenth century, for example, steelmaker Andrew Carnegie made sure that his firm had its own supplies of iron ore and coal, iron smelters, steel works, and sales outlets. His goal was twofold: to control raw materials needed for steel production at times of peak demand and to keep all the profits in his company. Recently, linkages among fishers, processors, and retailers have been tightening, especially as some processors have vertically integrated their firms backward to try to ensure sources of raw seafood. In 2010, Trident Seafoods, one of the largest American processors, had as its company slogan: "From the source to the plate." Moving beyond American borders, I discuss in this chapter as well how Japanese companies, the largest seafood firms in the world, have also adopted strategies of cross-border vertical integration and ownership as means of controlling their seafood sources. Altogether, significant shifts occurred in processing and distributing seafood across the world, in large part due to scarcities of fish and crabs and the politics involved in trying to end those scarcities.

Shifts in Seafood Processing

A relatively small number of suppliers and processors came to control gateways in the American seafood industry—firms like the Red Chamber Company, Trident Seafoods, and the Pacific Seafood Group. They purchased fish from thousands of fishers, processed it, and then distributed it to additional thousands of retail outlets, mainly grocery stores and restaurants. In 2009, about 600 fresh and frozen seafood processors served American markets. The fifty largest processors were responsible for about half the total market. Frozen fish accounted for about 30 percent of seafood processing revenues, frozen shellfish another 20 percent, fresh fish and shellfish an additional 15 percent, and canned seafood another 15 percent.[4] The seafood industry was part of the larger United States food chain, involving something like 20 percent of American workers and having products worth $5 trillion at retail— half sold by stores, the other half by restaurants, including fast-food outlets.[5]

The concentration seen in seafood processing was typical of the processors of other food products in the United States. A handful of processors, often using capital-intensive machinery and plants, typically gathered raw food products from many farmers or ranchers, processed them, and distributed them to many retail outlets. Only a few firms, such as Swift and Armour, historically had the resources and knowledge to undertake these tasks. In these firms, machinery (which required capital funds) replaced workers in turning out food products. The goals of company owners were to lower production costs, avoid labor disruption (machines do not strike), and increase profits. Among meat, fruit, vegetable, and milk producers, concentration became increasingly common in the twentieth century. The degree of concentration varied from field to field, but because machinery required capital, some concentration occurred in all of them. Unable to afford machinery, small producers often merged or sold out to larger ones. Sometimes, the processors engaged in vertical integration. American meat packers and egg distributors established "cold chains" of chilled warehouses and transportation facilities across national and international boundaries.[6]

Over-fishing and attempts to deal with it through regulation affected decisions of seafood processors about corporate strategies and structures.[7] The quest for raw seafood, along with the growing use of machinery on fish and crab processing lines, sped up a movement toward vertical integration dating back to the nineteenth century. That trend might well have been expected. Yet, there were also unexpected consequences of the recent seafood shortages. My examination of the largest suppliers for the U.S. seafood market (as measured by sales) between 1999 and 2006 reveals both continuity and change in their operations (see Appendix). Some of these processing firms were American companies; some were not, as explained below. The sales figures are their total sales. Most of the sales made by these firms went into the United States market, but some sales were made in overseas markets, especially the Japanese market.

The elements of continuity in suppliers have been several. The top twenty-five suppliers accounted for roughly the same proportion of wholesale seafood sales made by suppliers for the American market between 1999 and 2006: $11 billion of a total $24 billion in 1999 and $13 billion of $33 billion in 2006. Numerous smaller suppliers provided the remainder. The largest five or six suppliers remained about the same in size, ranging between about $500 million to $1 billion apiece in annual sales. Then too, throughout the early 2000s suppliers participated, as in earlier years, in the global economy. They both imported and exported seafood, with imports running ahead of exports by about 3:1. In 2007, imports accounted for 80 percent of the fish consumed in the United States. Seafood exports in 2007 picked up a bit, especially sales of Alaskan pollock to Europe, as a result of the decline in the value of the American dollar compared to the Euro.[8]

By 2006, about 21 percent of the seafood imported into the United States came from China, as that nation crowded more traditional exporters such as Japan. China had great success, for example, in boosting its exports of farm-raised tilapia to the United States, with its share of tilapia exported to America rising from 24 to 70 percent of the total between 2001 and 2007. To achieve those gains, Chinese tilapia raisers placed, an investigator for *Seafood Business* explained, a "surprisingly strong and improving focus on quality." Reacting to the concerns of American buyers, Chinese raisers reworked their production systems to minimize viruses, contaminants, and other aquaculture problems. By the early 2000s, Chinese tilapia production works were in full compliance with United States Food and Drug Administration regulations, which had been greatly tightened in 1997.[9] How the American market affected raising tilapia in China is a good example of how rules created in one nation could extend to the details of production in another.

Annual global seafood sales by United States companies in 2006 were much less than the $8.4 billion in combined seafood sales by the Japanese giants the Maruha Group and the Nichiro Corporation. Then the world's largest and third-largest suppliers of seafood, the two companies began merging late that year, with the merger finalized in 2007, creating Maruha Nichiro Holdings Inc. That combination controlled eight Pacific Northwest companies: Aleyeska Seafoods, Golden Alaska Seafoods, Orca Bay Seafoods, Peter Pan Seafoods, Premier Pacific Seafoods, Supreme Alaska Seafoods, Trans-Ocean Products, and Westward Seafoods. Even before the merger, Maruha consisted of "more than 200 companies active in almost every aspect of fisheries production, processing, distribution, and marketing." In 1996, the Maruha Group was composed of "9 fishing companies, 20 wholesale auction houses, 29 food processors and distribution companies, 16 cold storage companies, 12 aquaculture firms, 9 marine transport companies," and other miscellaneous enterprises. Global in its reach, Maruha was fully vertically integrated. In 2009, the Maruha Group had four major divisions—fishery operations, food operations, meat and other products, and storage and logistics—but derived three-quarters of its revenue from its fishery division. One American analyst aptly labeled Maruha, "the big tuna on Japan's sushi tray."[10]

The second-largest global seller was Nippon Suisan Kaisha, Ltd., another Japanese company. Fishing operations accounted for 43 percent of the firm's sales in 2008, with the remainder from pharmaceuticals, chemicals, shipbuilding, and restaurants. An American subsidiary, Nippon Suisan USA, owned American suppliers Fishking, Gorton's Seafoods, Unisea, and several others. About 80 percent of Nippon Suisan's sales occurred in Japan, but the firm made about 12 percent of its global sales in North America in 2008.[11]

These and other Japanese companies, such as Kyokuyo Company, Ltd., pursued the strategy of backward vertical integration; they sought to control their sources of raw seafood, especially in times of short supply.[12] To that end, they entered into joint-venture agreements with American fishers whenever possible. American salmon, crab, and bottom-fish fishers supplied Japanese firms with much of the Alaskan seafood catch from the late 1970s well into the 1980s. As we have seen, the Japanese firms sought joint ventures when their fishing was limited by the 1976 Fishery Conservation and Management Act, which ended most foreign fishing within 200 miles of American shores. As American processors increasingly challenged their Japanese counterparts, joint ventures became less tenable. The 2005 Alaskan crab rationalization plan, for example, shut out Japanese processors in favor of American ones. However, in other fields, such as some types of bottom fish, Japanese processors remained active in Alaskan waters. They owned, for example, some of the major onshore pollock-processing plants in Alaska in the 1990s, a topic examined in more detail in the next chapter. Like the changed realm of fishers, policy decisions penetrated deeply into food-processing operations.

Those same regulations helped determine who actually processed fish. Few of the processors that had been at the top of the list of firms supplying the American market with seafood in 1999 remained there in 2006. Of course, companies have often changed positions as processors and distributors of seafood for the American market. Still, the shifts between 1999 and 2006 were especially notable.[13]

Most of the large diversified American companies dropped out of seafood-processing over these seven years. By 2007, StarKist Seafoods, the world's leading packer of canned tuna, was the *only* top-ten seafood producer owned by a big, diversified American firm, Del Monte Foods, and then not for long. In mid-2008, Del Monte sold StarKist, as Del Monte sought to attain "sharpened strategic focus." A South Korean food company snapped up StarKist. What happened to Bumble Bee Seafoods, another major producer of canned tuna, was similar. Owned by International Home Foods of Parsippany, New Jersey, Bumble Bee became part of ConAgra Foods, a diversified food company based in Omaha, when ConAgra purchased International Home Foods in 2000—but again, not for long. ConAgra divested Bumble Bee as part of its general exit from seafood processing and distribution in 2004–2006. Run by the same people who had been managing it as part of ConAgra, Bumble Bee became the core of the seafood-focused Connors Brothers Income Fund.[14] In 2008, Connors Brothers in turn sold Bumble Bee to Centre Partners Management LLC of New York.

Other diversified American firms also left the wholesale seafood business. Sysco, a food-products company with an inventory of 275,000 items and serving 300,000 retail outlets, left the top-ten list in 2000. Some foreign firms that owned American seafood subsidiaries followed suit. Unilever, a global multinational, sold Gorton's Seafood, the largest U.S. producer of frozen seafood products, in 2001. Gorton's did not become an independent firm, however, but was acquired by Nippon Suisan USA.[15]

Managers of many of the large, diversified food companies found that they lacked the specialized knowledge and access to raw seafood needed to

prosper in the tough times of increased product scarcity and regulatory regime change. Financial muscle was not by itself sufficient. Fishery-industry
commentators observed, for instance, that ConAgra's exit from seafood was
"part of ConAgra Foods' plan to drive consistent and sustainable growth by
concentrating in those areas where it has the strongest competitive positions."
In addition to selling Bumble Bee, ConAgra sold its surimi (fish paste) business to Trident Seafoods.[16] ConAgra tried to pull back to its core capabilities, which did not include seafood.[17] The trend toward divestiture of seafood
businesses by large diversified companies was widespread. A writer for the
trade journal *Seafood Business* noted in mid-2005 that "all but a few top 25
contenders [leading seafood processors] are privately held companies either
in the United States or owned by foreign parent companies." A year later another writer for the same journal observed that "the food conglomerates . . .
are bailing out."[18]

In the rapidly changing times, Frank Dulcich, head of the Pacific Seafood
Group, argued that the appropriate "business model" was "to be vertically
integrated from boat to throat."[19] Only by engaging in fishing could firms be
sure of having the seafood they wanted to sell. An outside industry commentator made much the same point, observing in 2009, "Large companies have
advantages in vertical operations and economies of scale."[20] Vertical integration was (and is) a hallmark of many of the largest suppliers of seafood for the
American market.

The Major Companies

The three top firms serving the American market in 2006—Red Chamber,
Trident Seafoods, and Pacific Seafood Group—shared historical and structural characteristics. From humble origins they expanded through internal
growth and acquisitions, with family funds and retained earnings the main
sources of capital, at least initially. They became vertically integrated, assuring
that they would have access to seafood supplies; Alaskan waters were major
sources. They were headquartered on the West Coast and dealt only in seafood, about which their owners had intimate knowledge.

These focused, privately held, family seafood companies replaced diversified, publicly owned food giants as the top processors and wholesalers of
seafood for the American market. As in some other industries in the United
States and abroad, then, the trend in business strategy in the seafood industry

was to return to what companies did best, "to get back to the knitting."[21] Moving away from diversification was part of that trend, a reversal of an earlier movement toward the development of large, diversified, multidivisional corporations such as General Motors and DuPont.[22]

Red Chamber, the industry leader, originated in a family restaurant in the Los Angeles area in 1973.[23] The firm was owned by a Chinese American family; its officers in 2008 were Shan Chun Kou and Shu Chin Kou as co-chairmen, Ming Bin Kou as president, and Ming Shin Kou as chief financial officer. Headquartered in Vernon, California (part of Los Angeles), Red Chamber took its name from the mid-eighteenth-century Chinese literary classic, *The Dream of the Red Chamber*. By 2006, the firm possessed seafood-processing and cold-storage plants capable of holding sixty million pounds of finished goods on the East Coast, the West Coast, the Gulf of Mexico, and abroad. Red Chamber's owners boasted that their company "could process seafood in every conceivable method"; and the list of their company's products was long indeed, embracing Pacific cod, haddock, halibut, pollock, mahi-mahi, orange roughy, catfish, shrimp, crab, salmon, surimi, scallops, lobsters, and specialty items such as octopus, squid, and mussels. In 2006, the company purchased some of the seafood operations ConAgra was divesting. A year later, Red Chamber had 1,600 employees and ranked 236th on the *Forbes* list of private companies. In 2008, the company had an estimated $1.76 billion in sales, up from $1.58 billion in 2005.[24]

Trident Seafoods, the second-largest supplier for the American market, was formed as a partnership by several Alaskan king crabbers in 1973, with Chuck Bundrant the sparkplug. Described by a colleague at Trident as hardworking, focused, and driven, Bundrant grew up in Tennessee, where he attended a community college. In his early twenties, he was looking for a break from his studies and went to Alaska, where he worked on a processing line on a floating processor in Adak. He crewed on several boats before finally buying his own vessel. He also had work experiences with Vita Foods, a food processor, in the 1970s. So, Bundrant understood several aspects of food production. He also probably knew about the *Deep Sea* and Wakefield Seafoods. Bundrant began Trident Seafoods with the *Billikan* ("Good Luck"), a combined 135-foot catcher-processor for crab, which was financially successful.[25]

In starting Trident, Bundrant was joined by several others. Kaare Ness and Mike Jacobson, also king crabbers, were partners from the outset. Ness had been fishing for scallops, but switched to crab. According to him there was only one speed in Alaskan waters, "full speed." Ed Perry of San Juan

Figure 16. Three of the founders of Wakefield Seafoods in the Aleutian Islands in the early 1950s, with Lowell Wakefield on the left. Author's collection.

Seafoods, a processor in Bellingham, just north of Seattle, joined Trident in 1974; and Bart Eaton, who arrived in Alaska's canneries with no prior fishing experience in the 1960s and went on to become a highliner, did so decade later. Headquartered in the Ballard area of Seattle, a longtime neighborhood for fishers, Trident developed rapidly over the next three decades. "It began with one boat," Bundrant recalled, "We asked why we couldn't catch crab and process crab on the same vessel." The *Bountiful*, a second catcher-processor for crabs, joined the *Billikan* in the late 1970s.[26]

From the first, Bundrant wanted his firm to be more than just a harvesting or crab company. He was interested in diversifying the types of seafood Trident handled, perhaps on the advice of Jacobson, who warned that one should never rely on just single species. Trident was soon involved in freezing salmon at Bristol Bay, one of the first processors to do so. The company acquired land in Akutan in 1982, on which it built one of the largest seafood-processing facilities in the world to the present day. Trident initially put up Pacific cod and crabs at Akutan, adding pollock in the mid-1980s. The plant was unusual in that it could process pollock into both surimi and fillets. The fillets were quick-frozen. Trident made a large capital investment to expand the plant's output of pollock in the late 1980s.[27]

Acquisitions, along with expansion of established plants, contributed to Trident's growth. Trident's Chief Legal Counsel Joseph Plesha remembered two purchases as watershed issues. First, Trident merged its seafood assets with those of ConAgra in 1987, with Trident shareholders buying out those assets in the mid-1990s. Second, Trident purchased Tyson's seafood businesses in 1999.[28] Smaller acquisitions included Far West Fisheries in 1992. Financing came from a combination of retained earnings and borrowing. It did not include government loans. In 2000, Trident employed 4,000 people.

Further expansion occurred in the early 2000s. Between 1999 and 2006, Trident increased its annual sales from $600 million to $925 million, with much of the growth coming from sales of pollock. Acquisitions also accounted for some continuing expansion. In 2001, Trident purchased some of the assets of the Depoe Bay Fish Company, giving it increased capacity to supply surimi for that product's expanding market. Three years later, Trident bought NorQuest Seafoods of Seattle, an Alaskan salmon producer, an action which by some reports made Trident the largest buyer of Alaskan salmon. In 2006, Trident acquired Louis Kemp Seafood, which owned the leading retail surimi brand in the United States, from ConAgra. Trident failed, however, to purchase Ocean Beauty Seafoods, the eleventh-largest supplier of seafood for the American market. As Bundrant explained at the time, "We simply were not able to reach an agreement on this transaction."[29]

Purchases continued throughout 2007 and 2008. Trident bought Bear & Wolf Salmon of Seattle, which increased its capabilities in sockeye and pink salmon production through the acquisition of a Cordova, Alaska, processing plant, and Japan's Kako Foods, which processed salmon for the Japanese market.[30] Just as Japanese processors owned American subsidiaries, American firms sometimes had Japanese subsidiaries, as they both sought to get close to their markets. In mid-2008, Trident bought Wrangell Seafoods in Wrangell, Alaska, for $4.4 million, boosting still further its capabilities in salmon.[31] That fall, Trident joined with Russian pollock harvester Gidrostroy Holding

Company to harvest, process, and distribute pollock from the Russian Far East under the trademark "Russian Certifish."[32] By this time, Trident had annual sales of about $1 billion, and had diversified production to include tilapia, swordfish, mahi-mahi, Wahoo, and lobster to supplement operations in staple Alaskan and Pacific Northwest species.[33]

Trident was able to become a partially vertically integrated firm, with the degree of integration varying by species. In 2008–2009, Trident's catcher-processor vessels for pollock were totally integrated, catching the same fish they processed. Its shore plants secured about 55 percent of the pollock they processed from Trident catcher boats. The firm's catcher vessels accounted for a somewhat higher percentage of the cod and about 10–20 percent of the crab its facilities processed. None of the halibut or salmon processed by Trident came from its own catcher boats, for fishing regulations and quota agreements forbade processors from catching halibut or salmon, but what its processing vessels and plants could not obtain from the company's own catcher boats they purchased from independent fishers. Trident sought to maintain tight relationships with its independent fishers by providing them with financing and various services. For example, Trident gave short-term loans to salmon fishers in the form of seasonal pack loans. These loans covered items such as ships' stores and supplies, which federal loan programs did not include.[34]

In fact, Trident quickly became known for taking good care of fishers delivering to its plants, for the high quality of its seafood packs, and for being totally owned by Americans. Bundrant remained the driving force behind Trident's operations as the firm expanded, described by William McCloskey in 1995 as "wired, but coolly in charge" and as an operator who "personifies the new Bristol Bay of international markets and opportunity." In 2009, Trident possessed a fleet of more than thirty catcher boats and processing ships working mainly in Alaskan waters, along with twenty onshore processing plants scattered throughout the West Coast and Alaska.[35]

Not surprisingly, company officers, such as Plesha and Bundrant, generally worked for catch limits and quota systems to try to ensure the future of their firm's raw seafood supplies. Committed to maintaining its sources of fish and crab, Trident's officers lobbied hard before the NPFMC and other bodies to protect their firm's interests. Far from all Alaskans favored such political activities by commercial fishers and processors. As we have seen, sports and commercial fishers often found themselves at loggerheads. Members of the North Pacific Fishery Management Coalition, a private organization of

Alaskan sport charter fishers, viewed Trident as "an evil empire" which, they claimed "will stop at nothing" to limit sports fishing in Alaskan waters.[36]

Like Red Chamber, Trident sold its products at home and abroad, winning an Export Achievement Certificate from the U.S. Department of Commerce for its export efforts in 2003.[37] Just how global Trident's operations had become became apparent in 2005. In that year, the company shipped thirty million pounds of salmon caught in Alaskan waters to China, where bones were removed by hand at one-fifth the cost of doing so in the United States. Trident froze the salmon within hours of harvest and shipped them to China, where they were thawed to 40 degrees F., deboned., and shipped back to the United States. The journey to China and back took two months.[38] This interaction between Trident and Chinese workers was, of course, yet another example of globalization of seafood chains.

As Trident grew, its officers both expanded and streamlined operations. NorQuest was fully integrated with Trident, and a new salmon division was created. Sales teams operated from offices throughout Europe and Japan. Nonetheless, Trident remained a privately held family company, with Chuck Bundrant, the founder, serving as the chairman of the board and his son, Joe Bundrant, acting as the executive vice president in early 2011.[39] According to its Internet website, Trident was "fast becoming a global company with an entrepreneurial heart and soul." It was a place, the website claimed, where "you won't find a lot of suits and ties, but [where] you might hear business being conducted in more than half a dozen different languages." Alaskan sourcing, however, remained at the company's core. Chuck Bundrant noted in 2009, "We are fortunate to have the rich waters of the North Pacific literally at our doorstep," allowing his firm to acquire its seafood "from sustainable fisheries."[40]

Trident's major Alaskan processing plants included the large Akutan facility, capable of freezing 3 million pounds of mixed species of bottom fish each day. Trident's Ketchikan plant put up 500,000 cases of canned salmon each year, and its processing operation at St. Paul in the Bering Sea was the largest crab production facility in the world, with a daily capacity of 450,000 pounds of crab. The firm's plant at Sand Point, Alaska, 580 miles southwest of Anchorage in the Aleutians, could put up 600,000 pounds of cod, 1.2 million pounds of pollock, or 350,000 pounds of salmon per day.[41]

The Pacific Seafood Group, the third-largest supplier of the American market in 2006, advertised itself as "a family-owned, vertically integrated seafood company . . . which performs all operations from dock to dinner table."[42]

Frank Dulcich, Jr., the grandson of the firm's founder and in 2003 the president and chief executive officer, explained that Pacific Seafood Group's goal was to be fully vertically integrated.[43] For about three decades, the company pursued that objective, always trying to match increases in its distribution capacities with similar increases in its ability to process seafood. Company officers hoped this balancing act would allow them to provide customers with high-quality fish at reasonable prices. Vertical integration, which included close relationships with fishers, was seen as a key to low costs and solid profits.

Frank Dulcich, Sr., started the Pacific Seafood Group with his son Dominic in 1941. A Croatian immigrant to the United States in the 1920s, Dulcich began by operating a small retail counter selling fish in Portland, Oregon.[44] Growth was initially slow, with the firm having only eighteen employees in 1978. At this point Frank Dulcich, Jr., a college graduate trained in child psychology at Portland State University and grandson of the firm's founder, joined the company. In the late 1970s and early 1980s, Pacific Seafood faced numerous challenges: a newly built plant at Clackamas, Oregon, experienced "product flow and systems difficulties"; high interest rates ruined many fishers and processors alike; key suppliers for Pacific Seafood (one was Ocean Beauty) went into business for themselves as competitors; and Dulcich, Sr., the founder, died. Most upsetting, the Pacific Seafood Group lost about 70 percent of its business when an El Niño event destroyed fish harvests in 1982–83.[45]

Rather than fold, the company expanded operations, buying its first processing plant for $5,000, twice the firm's monthly operating revenues of $2,500. An entrepreneur, Frank Dulcich, Jr., bet his company on a series of expansion moves beginning in the mid-1980s. He did so at the right time. Americans bought more seafood for health reasons, and interest rates declined dramatically, enabling Dulcich to finance the purchases. Expansion continued in the 1990s with thirteen acquisitions, and in the early 2000s with several more. In 2005, the Pacific Seafood Group operated twenty-eight plants up and down the West Coast and distributed its seafood, mainly Pacific fish and shellfish, throughout much of the United States. Having about 1,000 employees, the company also exported to Asia, Europe, and the Middle East. Growth continued over the next few years, including the acquisition of East Coast Seafood in late 2007.[46] In 2008, the Pacific Seafood Group owned forty companies, operated thirty-six processing and distribution facilities from Alaska to Mexico, and employed about 1,800 people. Its 12,000 customers were evenly split between major food retailers and restaurants.[47] An outside

observer noted that the Pacific Seafood Group was "always fishing for acquisitions" and had "built up a vertically integrated company by snapping up
competitors."[48]

Many of the largest American processors entered fish farming in the early
2000s, as they sought assured sources of raw seafood. In 2006, Trident Seafoods began buying farmed salmon from Marine Harvest of Pompano Beach,
Florida, distributing the fish under both companies' labels. In the same year,
Icicle Seafoods—another Alaskan processor, the eighteenth-largest supplier
of the American seafood market then—entered into a partnership with a
Chilean fish-farming company to sell farmed salmon in the United States.
"There isn't a wild seafood company out there that doesn't use farmed seafood
products in some way," commented one observer.[49] Indeed, in 2008 the Pacific Seafood Group bought a steelhead-raising facility on the Columbia River
below the Grand Coulee Dam. Located on land owned by the Confederated
Tribes of the Colville Reservation, the farm produced about 2 million pounds
of fish annually. Pacific Seafood Group executives hoped to increase production to 7 million pounds per year by 2010. Attuned to environmental issues
in fish farming, they said they would use feed made from sustainable sources
and employ no growth hormones, growth-promoting antibiotics, pesticides,
or herbicides.[50]

Red Chamber, Trident, and the Pacific Seafood Group dominated much
of the processing and distribution of seafood in the American market. Vertically integrated and family owned, these private companies succeeded in a
competitive global industry. One source of their strength was access to sus-
tainably caught seafood from Alaskan waters. Realizing the importance of
that seafood, their executives, especially those from Trident Seafoods and Pacific Seafood, supported (indeed often encouraged) the work of the NPFMC
and may have sometimes used their positions on the Council to place their
firms at competitive advantages over sport-fishing companies.

The Other Top-Ten Seafood Firms

However, not all United States leading seafood suppliers were privately held
American family firms, as a brief review of the next largest seven reveals.
Some were foreign-owned companies, and some were publicly held.

Headquartered in Markham, Ontario, the Connors Brothers Income
Fund was the fourth-largest supplier in 2006, a ranking it retained a year later.

Established in 2004, it owned Bumble Bee Foods and had a 10 percent stake in the Thai tuna processor the Sea Value Company. Connors Brothers also sold beef and poultry products produced by subsidiaries acquired from other firms. However, meat recalls in 2007 led the company to sell several of its operations in that area. At the same time, it mounted an aggressive marketing campaign for tuna. Yet, just a year later, as the global economic downturn took hold, the Fund sold its operating subsidiaries, including Bumble Bee, to Centre Partners of New York for $423 million.[51]

Tri-Marine International, with headquarters in Bellevue, Washington, just east of Seattle, was the fifth-largest supplier of the American seafood market in 2006, and the third-largest a year later. The firm was founded in 1972 by a group of companies owned by the Italian government, which sold out in 1986. Tri-Marine was another major supplier of canned tuna to the American market, owning a fleet of seven tuna-catching boats and chartering another ten reefer (refrigerated) vessels in 2006. It added four more catcher-boats in 2007, and another in 2008. It had seven processing plants in Colombia, Ecuador, China, Kenya, Mauritius, and the Solomon Islands, in addition to one in San Pedro, California. In 2007, Tri-Marine handled more than 550,000 mt of tuna, up 15 percent from the previous year.[52]

The remainder of the ten-largest suppliers of seafood for the U.S. market presented mixed pictures. Nippon Suisan USA—formed in 1974, and the sixth-largest supplier to the American seafood market in 2006—was a wholly owned subsidiary of the large Japanese seafood processor Nippon Suisan and owned many American subsidiaries. It "grew quietly" in 2007, "steadily expanding its U.S. presence," but its sales fell slightly in 2008. Thai Union International, established in 2000 in Thailand, was the seventh-largest supplier in 2006, with three major U.S. subsidiaries: Chicken of the Sea International, which had been purchased from Tri-Marine in 2000 and dealt in tuna; Empress International, a major shrimp importer acquired in 2003; and Chicken of the Sea Frozen Foods, set up in 2006 to market frozen shrimp and other products. Fishery Products International, eighth-largest seafood supplier in American markets, with headquarters in St. John's, Newfoundland, was Canadian. Established in 1984, the firm dealt in a broad range of seafood, including cod, halibut, crab, pollock, salmon, shrimp, and tilapia. However, shareholders split up the company in 2007, with some of its assets going to rival Canadian firms Ocean Choice and High Liner Foods. StarKist, the ninth-largest supplier, went through numerous ownership changes, ending up as a subsidiary of a South Korean seafood business. Founded in 1988, and reorganized in 2000, the American Seafoods Group, the tenth largest supplier, was jointly owned by the Coastal Villages Regional Fund of Anchorage, Alaska (one of thirteen Alaskan Native corporations set up in the 1980s to invest oil money) and an outside management group.[53]. Based in Seattle, it sold Pacific cod, hake, pollock, scallops, sole, and for a while catfish. It bought Southern Pride Catfish in 2002, but it sold the company to Heartland Catfish six years later. In 2007 and 2008, American Seafoods was the largest U.S. largest harvester and at-sea processor of pollock and hake.

Serving American Markets in Volatile Times

Industry observers wrote approvingly of the changed nature of the companies. "Generally speaking, seafood companies are as healthy as I've seen them," noted Tim Antilla, a vice president for Wells Fargo Bank in Seattle, in mid-2007. "They're more efficient, better capitalized, and more liquid than five to ten years ago."[54] In June 2007, Scott Etzel, a seafood industry consultant, observed that the "most successful players have strong access to the resource [fish], and it's been a long road for them to get to that point. Seafood doesn't lend itself well to a neat, tidy balance sheet. It isn't easy to predict."[55] Commentators saw the American seafood business as strong in mid-2008, continuing to expand despite American economic difficulties. "The seafood business," the industry's leading trade journal reported, "is growing organically by garnering new customers and launching new products."[56] The financial problems of 2008 and 2009 dimmed, but did not extinguish, hopes executives had for bright futures for their seafood firms.

The top ten suppliers of seafood for the American market were diverse in their operations and structures. Nonetheless, they shared some strategies. Most were at least partially vertically integrated, and becoming more so, as in Tri-Marine's expanding ownership of catcher boats to supply its processing plants worldwide with tuna. They wanted direct access to fish, crabs, and other types of seafood. In fact, the executives of seafood processing companies adjusted to and shaped changes in seafood supplies in a variety of ways, with concerns about scarcity running through many of their actions. Like those in charge of Red Chamber, Trident, and Pacific Seafood, the top three processors of seafood for the American market in 2006, the officers of the next largest seven dealt almost exclusively in seafood, were worldwide in their reach, and had multiple sources of their raw products. Concerned about the long-term futures of fish stocks, the executives of some processors worked for the creation of sustainable regimes for wild fish. Some also took their companies into fish farming.

Unlike the largest three suppliers of seafood for the American market, many of the other seven processors were not family-owned. Four were sub-sidiaries of foreign companies. The seafood industry and its food chains were truly global in scope. American firms owned foreign subsidiaries and had various types of joint ventures with foreign firms. Some Trident salmon was caught in Bristol Bay, processed in China, and marketed in the United States.

The seafood processors controlled the gateways through which fish passed on their way to consumers. Like major processors of meat, fruit, vegetables, and milk, seafood processing companies were, arguably, the most powerful elements in their food chains. Many processors tightened controls over raw seafood via vertical integration, tying contracts with suppliers of raw seafood, and other ways. As I explain in the next chapter, hygiene, product safety, and the environment were affected, as seafood moved from ships to consumers. Similarly, in the following chapter I also argue that significant changes came to retailing seafood in American markets, as restaurants and grocery stores found they had to alter their sourcing methods in the face of the growing scarcity of wild fish.

7

Reaching Consumers:
From Processing to Retailing

Faced with localized shortages of desirable species of seafood, the upscale Waterfront Restaurant on Maui reached tying agreements with local fishers. Its owners advertised in 2008 that, "Every day Maui fishermen call Chef Bob to tell him what they're bringing in, which gives him and his kitchen staff the freshest fish available. Since we are right on Ma'alea Harbor, Chef Bob can inspect fish even before it's off the boat."[1] Few restaurants went that far in securing fish supplies, but many changed their sourcing methods in the faces of over-fishing and new regulatory regimes set up to deal with that crisis. In this chapter, I argue that many of the links in seafood chains, not just harvesting, have been affected by over-fishing. In Chapter 6, I examined the impact of over-fishing on the structures of the leading seafood firms; here I look at how over-fishing and government regulations led those firms to alter some of the ways they processed and sold seafood.[2]

I explore especially how salmon, crab, and bottom fish caught in Alaskan waters have been processed and distributed to consumers in the United States and elsewhere, delving into matters of quality control and hygienic safety, both of which have influenced seafood chains. I examine as well the retailing of seafood in American markets by looking at the changing operations of restaurants, fast-food establishments, and grocery stores. In some respects, at least, seafood consumption became more sustainable than in times past. Large retailers, in particular, required that the seafood they sold come only from sustainable sources, a real shift from past practices.

Processing Seafood: Quests for Efficiencies and Profits

The processors examined in the last chapter—companies like Red Chamber, Trident Seafoods, and Pacific Seafood Group—generally controlled the food chains for American seafood. The shift to fishing quotas led them, in many instances, to alter processing methods. The scarcity of some seafood especially highlighted the need to achieve efficiencies in production, to waste as little as possible of the raw seafood. There were, we shall see, additional consequences for the processing and selling of seafood resulting from the movement to sustainable fishing, some expected, others not fully anticipated.

The food chains for seafood bound for the American market were (and are) complicated, varying by species of fish and by the places where the fish were (are) caught. However, the journey salmon harvested in Alaska took to market in the early 2000s suggests well the many interlinked steps involved in turning wild fish into consumer products. That journey needs to be relatively short, for fish deteriorate more quickly than do many other perishables. While some fruits and vegetables can remain fresh for weeks in refrigerators, fish cannot. Enzymes and bacteria in fish have evolved to function in cold aquatic environments, so refrigeration has only a limited effect on them. Exactly how quickly fish spoil depends on several factors: fatty species such as salmon spoil faster than leaner ones, species from temperate waters faster than those from tropical waters, and those from salt-water seas and oceans faster than those from fresh-water lakes and rivers. Fish must be taken fresh to markets or be preserved by canning, freezing, or some other method within a few hours or at most a few days of being caught.[3]

Taken by trollers, gillnetters, or purse seiners, Alaskan salmon were soon transferred to a much larger salmon-tender vessel. On the tender, the fish were placed in a large box, weighed, and stored in chilled seawater tanks. Within minutes, the core temperature of the salmon dropped to about 31° F. William McCloskey described a typical salmon tender as a "floating box, chilled seawater worth its weight. She holds four hundred thousand pounds if you distribute it right." Once her tanks were full, the tender weighed anchor and headed for a processing plant onshore. At the plant, the salmon were lifted out of the tender in net bags or were pumped through hoses into a large container, which was then hoisted onto the dock. Beyond taking salmon from fishers, tenders operated as floating stores, providing fishers with groceries, laundry and soap privileges, and spare parts for boat engines.[4]

Workers onshore sorted the fish by species and quality, placed them in "totes," and wheeled them in the totes to a "slime line" in the processing plant. On the slime line workers used machines and hand labor to behead, gut, and wash each fish at long tables served by conveyers and rows of cold-water spray nozzles. Especially important was a machine pejoratively nicknamed the "Iron Chink," which mechanically butchered salmon, cutting off their heads and tails. Developed in the early twentieth century, the Iron Chink was named after Chinese workers who had previously performed these tasks by hand. It was a labor-saving device: proponents claimed that two machine operators replaced ten to twenty hand workers. The machine was introduced to salmon canneries in the Pacific Northwest and Alaska in 1903, but came into use gradually. Hand cuts wasted less salmon flesh, for skilled salmon butchers adjusted more easily than machines to different-size fish. Still, by the 1920s and 1930s Iron Chinks were in fairly common use, especially in Alaskan regions where salmon runs of homogeneous fish were long.[5] Hand work complemented machine labor. Workers eviscerated and cleaned the fish carcasses coming from the Iron Chinks with brushes, knives, and hoses.[6] At this point, too, workers removed eggs from female salmon for sale in Japan, where raw salmon eggs were considered a delicacy.[7] Meanwhile, one observer explained, "Farther on, clattering machinery stamped cans into shape and pushed them along overhead racks to belts where chattering native women filled the cans with fish."[8]

The goal was high-volume, low-cost production. Salmon fisher Bert Bender left a first-hand account of work in a cannery on the shore of Alaska's Cook Inlet during the 1960s, 1970s, and 1980s. He wrote: "The cannery's social hierarchy, its division of labor, and such mechanisms as a quart [of whiskey] helped it run smoothly, almost as parts of the well-oiled, belt-driven machinery that clattered along the processing lines or the room above the warehouse where new cans were stamped into shape." He noted that "Everyone worked together in ways that seemed natural and just to achieve the single purpose of catching and processing as many fish as possible."[9]

In his novel *Highliners*, McCloskey presents a vivid picture of salmon-cannery work during the same decades: "Even with a layman's eye, he [Hank Crawford, a new cannery worker] could trace the progress of the salmon from deep bins, where men sorted them onto running belts and others lined them head-to-head, into big machines with water spraying them in all directions that transformed them from creatures into slabs of food, to lines where people with knives and brushes dressed them further." "The fish then disappeared into other machines and emerged as chunks in cans." Machines filled the cans with salmon at the rate of 125 cans per minute, a mass-production level. The filled cans then passed through exhaust boxes and vacuum sealers that "pulled vacuum and made the final seal." Next came cooking: "the cans—with lids now on top—went into steaming cookers" called retorts. In the retorts, the canned salmon was cooked by steam under pressure for about eighty minutes at 240° F. to kill all bacteria. (In earlier times before the use of retorts, the cans had to be boiled for six to seven hours.) Finally, the cooked cans of salmon, "one pound tall" or "half pound" cans, were packaged and sent to market.[10]

Not all canneries were as mechanized as the one written about by McCloskey. In his novel *The Fisherman's Son*, set in northern California after World War II, Michael Koepf describes less-mechanized salmon cannery operations: "The air reeked of fish. Pipe hissed. Metal scraped against metal. Men in black boots pushed the carts of uncooked salmon into long cylindrical pressure cookers." The salmon were cooked before being placed in cans, and much more hand labor was used: "Beyond the cookers, his mother stood with other women. They wore black rubber aprons and white hats. Cooked fish moved past them on conveyer belts. . . . The women plucked the flesh from the moving carcasses and placed it in shiny metal cans that moved like a metal river on tracks above the conveyer belt. Bone, tails, skin, and heads tumbled from the end of another belt, into a bin. . . . His mother worked in an awful place, standing for hours in a steamy stench, plucking clean the bones of fish."[11] Much smaller in its operations than most Alaskan plants, this California one used more hand labor and less machinery.

Even with the extensive use of machinery, cannery labor was tedious, messy, backbreaking work. Trident Seafoods explained on its Internet site in 2009 to prospective employees, "The work of processing seafood is physically demanding, cold, wet, and repetitive. . . . Generally you can expect the weather in Alaska to be miserable most of the time. Processing is hard work and definitely not for everyone." Moreover, "living conditions can be cramped," and "mail delivery varies depending on the weather and can be very erratic." More positively, the firm's posting said that workers would be flown to and from Alaska at company expense, that Trident would provide room and board for workers, that workers could expect many hours of overtime, and that workers would be able to save most of their earnings, since there were few places to spend money "in these remote areas of Alaska."[12]

Several destinations awaited the salmon processed in Alaska. Canned salmon was sold mainly in the American South and Midwest, and in Western

Figure 17. Processing salmon roe. With the permission of Richard Newman.

Europe (especially the United Kingdom) and Australia. Pink salmon were used particularly for canning. However, many of the fish, an increasing proportion from the 1970s on, went to market fresh or frozen. Some were flown fresh for sale in Tokyo's huge Tsukiji Market, and speed and efficiency were especially important in these instances. Chinook and larger Coho salmon often also went fresh or frozen to smokers in Japan, Europe, and the eastern United States, which processed them into lox. Still others were flown fresh directly to restaurants throughout the United States, served on plates only a few days after being caught.[13]

By the 1970s and 1980s, many of the gutted salmon were being frozen in large freezers in the processing plants. The shift to freezing resulted in large part from the growing demand by Japanese consumers for high-quality frozen salmon and a declining willingness to accept canned varieties. "The market for salmon shifted," explained one fisher, "from canned to fresh-frozen fish that were highly prized in Japan." He observed that, "Salmon suddenly became much more valuable." In fact, "the Japanese market for frozen salmon displaced the market for canned salmon."[14] Thus, a switch in tastes of consumers in one nation dramatically altered production techniques in another, a vivid example of the potency of globalization. Nor was freezing limited to salmon. Many obstacles had to be overcome in developing methods to freeze fish, but by the early 2000s freezing was common worldwide. In 2006, about half the wild fish harvested globally went to market fresh. The rest was processed before marketing, with freezing the commonest form of processing for fish destined for human consumption.[15]

Developing mechanical techniques to freeze fish proved difficult. A major problem was that early methods froze fish too slowly, allowing moisture in the flesh to form large crystals that eventually ruptured cell membranes. "Upon thawing," one scholar observed, "water leaks out, the cells collapse, and fish tastes like mush."[16] In 1862, the first U.S. patent was issued for a brine-freezing method. The technique involved freezing salmon on racks beneath pans of ice and salt, which chilled the fish faster than cold air could and prevented the absorption of salt. After they were frozen, the salmon were dipped into water to receive a protective glaze. This method spread from Maine, where it was developed, to Alaska, where the first salmon-freezing plant opened in 1902. Still, freezing was laborious and slow. As late as 1939, Alaskan packers put up only $303,000 worth of frozen salmon. Clarence Birdseye began solving these problems with his "quick-freezing" methods during the 1920s, and was paid $22 million for his process and plant by the Postum Company (later known as

General Foods) in 1929. Birdseye froze fish fillets, not whole fish, by pressing them between two hollow ammonia-chilled metal plates, with surface temperatures of −25° F.[17]

More was involved in reaching consumers with frozen fish, however, than developing freezing techniques. General Foods and other companies developed "cold chains" of refrigerated warehouses and transportation vehicles. They persuaded grocers to put freezer cabinets in their stores to carry frozen foods, including fish, for consumers. As early as 1937, Birds Eye frozen food reached consumers via 3,000 wholesale and retail outlets. Long-haul refrigerated trucking was very important, with mechanical refrigeration used in truck vans in a major way in the 1950s. Faster and more flexible than railroads, trucks opened new markets. Business historian Shane Hamilton has written: "By the mid-1950s, the integration of long-haul reefer trucking and modern warehousing significantly reduced the cost of frozen food distribution, paving the way for the mass consumption of the product for the first time in history."[18] Then too, Americans, mainly middle-class urbanites, bought mechanically driven refrigerators in which fish and other goods could be kept cold. For them, refrigerators replaced old-style ice boxes in the 1930s and 1940s. Cheaper electricity and the development of Freon as a nontoxic, nonflammable refrigerant were crucial in stimulating demand for refrigerators. So was mass production, which lowered the average price of an electric refrigerator to $154 in 1940, by which time over half of American households had one.[19]

Between 1949 and 1956, consumer purchases of frozen food in the United States soared to $2 billion, almost 4 percent of total food sales in the later year.[20] Frozen foods continued to increase in popularity in later decades. Known for improved tastes and desired for convenience, especially as more women joined the American workforce, frozen foods became staples in the United States.

Salmon were, as one Alaskan fishery expert has explained, "frozen solid as cordwood and glazed with maple sugar to prevent dehydration and oxidation." Depending on market demands, some salmon were filleted before freezing. By the 1970s, processors froze salmon in several ways. Fish placed in "sharp" freezers were put on shelves composed of coils through which the freezing medium was pumped. Fish frozen in "multiple" freezers were placed between two freezing plates, a process used especially for fillets and steaks. In "blast" freezers cold air was forced around fish and packaged fish at high velocity. "Immersion" freezers used brine chilled by ammonia or Freon to freeze fish in the round. Some salmon were prepared this way, but immersion freezing was used especially for tuna frozen on boats.[21]

Frozen salmon were packed in cardboard boxes and stored in freezer vans, and shipped by barge to Seattle and other Pacific Coast ports, where they were held temporarily in huge cold-storage facilities. According to the U.S. Department of Agriculture "Capacity of Refrigerated Warehouses Report," which surveyed public and private facilities, there were 1,464 major cold-storage facilities in the United States in 1998 and 1,578 in 2010. The director of marketing and communications for the Global Cold Chain Alliance observed in the latter year that, "There's been an increase in cold-storage capacity of over 1 billion cubic feet in the last decade." The American cold-storage business generated annual revenues of $4 billion in 2009.[22]

Next, the salmon were transported by containerships or jumbo jets to market destinations in Japan, the United States, and elsewhere. From the 1970s on, frozen and fresh seafood—salmon surely, but also many other types of fish, crabs, and clams—traveled long distances as air freight to their markets. In the early 2000s, some airlines, such as Alaskan Airlines, provided special training to their employees in how to manage cold chains. According to the vice-president in charge of cargo at Alaskan Airlines in 2009, "We try to keep the cold chain an efficient, fluid motion, so that cargo doesn't get backed up. It's a carefully choreographed dance between us, the processors, and their customers or couriers at the destination." Similarly, Federal Express paired with Periship to ensure that seafood reached its markets in mint condition. Periship's director of operations stressed the comprehensive nature of transportation planning for perishable seafood: "We'll help the customer find a proper packaging system, and when he's ready to ship, we'll monitor variables like weather and transportation equipment, exchanging internal information with FedEx around the clock. If there are any problems, we resolve them by working with FedEx and giving the customer frequent updates." In the various markets additional middlemen broke down the shipments and placed the salmon and other seafood into grocery stores and restaurants.[23] The goals were to handle salmon as efficiently and quickly as possible—to get the salmon, especially fresh salmon, to markets in good condition capable of commanding high prices.

Facing different markets from salmon, other Alaskan seafood passed through a variety of steps from boats to dining tables. Sablefish (black cod) went mainly to Japan, where it was smoked, and followed paths similar to those of salmon going to that island nation. Halibut was sold primarily in

American markets as fresh fish, beheaded and filleted. Some halibut, however, was frozen and later cut into steaks with band saws. McCloskey offers
an account of processing and freezing halibut in the 1960s and 1970s. The fish
were gutted by hand. "At the end of the slime line the fish emerged from their
washing to be weighed and placed in various carts by size. The weigher jabbed
a color-coded tag into each tail." The fish were next transferred to freezing
lockers. "The freezer gang wore extra hoods and sweaters. . . . They hefted the
fish from the carts to tiers of frosty shelves, forty-to-sixty-pounders overhead,
two-hundred-plus-pounders at ground level. It was a strange, fettered place,
akin to working undersea. Each job had its tricks."[24]

Other bottom fish—sole, Pacific cod, and pollock—were caught by trawlers and quickly delivered to onshore plants or floating processors, where
the fish were cleaned and filleted before possible freezing. Most fillets were
packed fresh between sheets of waxed paper in boxes called "shatter packs."
However, some fillets were quickly "flash" frozen and packed as "individu-
ally quick-frozen" portions, which were growing in popularity. Some Pacific
cod and other flatfish fillets were airlifted to markets in the United States and
abroad as fresh fish. However, many pollock and Pacific cod were also processed into fillets or blocks, which went to fast-food restaurants throughout
the United States and to reprocessors, which turned them into fish sticks and
other products.[25]

King and snow crabs were usually cooked in the shell in shore plants or
aboard floating processing vessels. The crab meat was sometimes later extracted by processors outside Alaska.[26] Processing as accomplished aboard
the *Deep Sea*, the Wakefield Seafoods catcher-processor vessel, in the 1940s
and 1950s set precedents followed for decades. The *Deep Sea* functioned as a
floating factory. Operations began with landing the trawl net amidships and
emptying the crabs on the deck. The deck crew, which worked the net, butchered the crabs by hand. Next, the deck gang cooked the crabs in the shell
and passed them on to the processing crew, which separated the meat from
the shell. Problems initially occurred in both cooking and processing. The
ship's continuous cooker proved inadequate, and it became necessary to cook
the crabs in large batches rather than continuously, as had been planned. In
processing the crabs the major bottleneck lay in removing the meat from the
shell, done initially by time-consuming, costly hand labor. In 1949, however,
the ship's chief engineer perfected a mechanical device that proved to be a
major breakthrough. One person using this "crab shaker" could remove three
to five times as much crab meat as a person working by hand. Once cooked,

the crabs were frozen as meat in the shell or underwent additional processing, after which the meat, separated from the shell, was placed in molds and frozen. In either case, the crab meat was fast frozen in trays designed to exclude air to avoid freezer burn and deterioration. Refrigerated holds received the frozen crab meat for storage until the *Deep Sea* could transship it or return to port.[27]

By the 1960s and 1970s, processing usually involved several steps performed in Alaskan shore plants, many of them similar to those pioneered earlier on the *Deep Sea*. First, workers butchered the king crabs. Wearing hard chest protectors, a butcher held up the live crab—all crabs had to be delivered alive to the plants; dead ones decomposed quickly and were not accepted—to his chest, two legs in each hand. As one observer described the action, the butcher "pressed the shells against his chest and the undersides against a metal wedge, then with a snap of his arms tore them in two. Crab entrails dripped everywhere." Butchering was a demanding job: "There was pressure to maintain speed, because the entire processing line depended on the crab halves." From time to time, workers paused to hose off the offal, called "gurry," that splattered onto their faces and arms, lest skin rashes develop from contact with it.[28]

Workers next removed meat from the legs, which contained the edible meat. As on the *Deep Sea*, machines replaced hand picking. Rollers squeezed meat out of the lower legs. Blowers shot a mixture of compressed air and water through the main leg shells to remove meat there. Finally, workers on the "shake line" used flips of their wrists to remove meat from the shells closest to the crab bodies. Any shell fragments still in the meat were taken out by hand. The crab meat was then frozen or canned. Preservation had its own problems. McCloskey has noted, "Canning and later freezing problems included discoloration in the can and much thawed legs, needing adjustments—e.g., in cooking time, volume of washes, degree of brine quick freeze."[29] Butchering, processing, and cooking snow crabs involved similar steps, with Americans learning how to extract meat from the thin snow-crab legs from the Japanese.

Wakefield Seafoods tried to minimize processing problems. At shore plants, established in the 1950s and 1960s, cooking was performed as a single-stage, continuous operation, as glitches encountered earlier on the *Deep Sea* were ironed out. The crabs were cooked for twenty to twenty-six minutes at 212° F., the boiling point of water. (Companies canning crab meat usually used a two-stage process: eight to twelve minutes at 160°, followed by twenty minutes at 212°.) Workers cooled the cooked crab in chlorinated water to lessen the disintegration of meat during the shelling operation, when crab meat was removed from the shell with wringers and shakers. Finally, the meat was frozen, for Wakefield Seafoods continued to freeze its entire pack. The freezing occurred in stages, with glazing, quick-freezing, and storage in refrigerated warehouses following one another in rapid succession.[30]

Wakefield Seafoods and its competitors sought to achieve maximum efficiency at each processing step. Wakefield developed crab rollers/wringers to replace the shakers used to remove crab meat from shells. During 1961 and 1962, the company installed rollers in all its processing ships and plants to squeeze the meat out of the shells. In 1963, the company followed that innovation with a new technique for the conveyer-belt pushing of crab through

Figure 18. Processing king crabs. Author's collection.

the rollers—again, in the interest of accelerating the production process. Because of these and other technical innovations, Lowell Wakefield was able to report in 1962 that his company's "recovery is substantially better than the industry average." Although it received only 31 percent of the raw American king-crab pack, Wakefield produced 40 percent of the total processed pack.[31]

Efficiency concerns and a desire to add value continued to motivate processors in the twenty-first century. Trident Seafoods put up its king-crab pack at shore plants and processing vessels. As explained on the firm's Internet website, "In all cases, live whole king crab is butchered into sections, cleaned, cooked in fresh water, and then frozen in a super-chilled salt brine solution." The result "is a frozen, fully cooked product, which may be boxed and shipped for immediate sale around the world." However, the processed crab might also be sent to Washington State for sale or further processing. "Secondary processing begins by taking the frozen sections (essentially ½ of a whole crab consisting of three walking legs and one claw) and cutting the legs apart at the shoulder." The shoulders would be trimmed, and the legs and claws graded by size. Snow crabs, also processed at both shore plants and ships, went through many of the same steps. Like king crabs, snow crabs emerged "frozen and fully cooked" and boxed ready for shipment or additional processing. Most were marketed after only the primary processing steps were completed— "sold as sections or clusters which have been packed at the point of harvest in Alaska." A cluster consisted of "a claw, three walking legs, and a trailer leg, also known as a fifth leg, all joined at the shoulder. A cluster is essentially one half of a whole snow crab."[32]

An outside observer of the seafood-processing industry summarized technological advances made by 2008. They included, "computer-aided automation in sorting, processing, and canning." For "at-sea processors" there were "new fish-sensing technologies and advanced hauling gear" that "improved catches, increased productivity, and reduced the number of unwanted fish and bycatch (nontargeted, unwanted species)." Beyond those changes, wholesalers could "now rely on on-truck GPS navigation." Finally, "improvements in refrigeration and freezing . . . helped reduce the risk of spoilage."[33]

One example of the increased efficiencies lay in American long-line operations, such as those for Pacific cod and halibut. As fisher and writer Brad Matsen noted in 1998, "these high-endurance, efficient boats range in size from 100 to 160 feet, and all are simple statements of catching and processing efficiency." The vessels "can produce high-quality, hook-and-line fish in enough volume to justify long trips and higher initial investment than smaller longliners that ice their fish and make shorter trips." Each boat had "a quick-freezer on deck" that could "handle 10,000 pounds of finished product per day." The fish "were frozen in pans according to size and grade and then transferred to specially marked paper/polyethylene bags, each holding forty pounds." Beyond having the most advanced freezer systems, the new ships had "automated longline systems that can bait, set, and retrieve up to 20,000 hooks per twenty-four day."[34]

Nor were advancements in technological efficiencies limited to ships. In 2008, the Pacific Seafood Group opened what its officers trumpeted as a "state-of-the-art" facility in Las Vegas, with seafood trucked or flown in from the coast. It featured a large fish fillet-cutting room, a separate production room for cutting crab and other frozen products, a "modern shower-drip system" for storage of live lobsters, and a refrigerated truck docking area. The company used "advanced technology throughout the facility for longer shelf life for fresh cut from the bone fish."[35]

Crab, salmon, and bottom-fish processors stressed achieving ever-greater efficiencies in processing in their operations. In part, the seafood processors realized that they needed to use their scarce resources, raw seafood, more efficiently to conserve them; in part, the processors simply sought cost advantages in globally competitive markets. More profitable operations over the long term were their goal. There was, however, still a personal touch in the seafood industry. More was involved than the profit motive. Ron George, a processor and distributor of 600,000 pounds of king crab each year in Las Vegas, explained in mid-2009, "I don't think there's anyone in the industry that would disagree when I say I'm the one with the most passion in this business. It's my whole thing, my baby."[36]

In early 2011, Gary Noe—president of GN Seafoods, a wholesaler in Columbus, Ohio—explained how new technologies accelerated the movement of seafood from boats to consumers. Talking about swordfish caught in the Atlantic, he observed, "If it's caught that morning, it'll arrive in Boston within a few hours. From there, it will be put on a truck, sent to Columbus and make it to market the same time it goes to market in Boston." From the time swordfish were caught, they could be on restaurant plates in Columbus within twenty-four to thirty-six hours. Alaskan seafood also reached Columbus diners quickly: "If it's a West Coast product, like halibut from Alaska, it's channeled through Seattle, then to Boston, subsequently following the same route to central Ohio. . . . Alaska wild salmon arrives on Columbus Fish Market's tables via Michael's Meats 24–36 hours after it's caught." Communication via cellular phones, the Internet, and other devices, Noe thought, greatly sped the flow of fish through the seafood chain. "It's a common-sense approach to a limited resource," he concluded.[37]

The emphasis seafood companies placed on selling processed products was part of a more general trend. Processed foods—canned, frozen, or otherwise prepared—played much larger roles in the diets of Americans after World War II than in earlier times. By 1954, food processors accounted for 62 percent of all value added in the United States food sector, with farmers contributing just 21 percent, a nearly exact reversal of the ratio in 1910. The spread of new technologies, such as freezing, the growing importance of supermarkets, and the desire of working women and a smaller number of men to reduce time in the preparation of meals contributed to this trend, as did the advertising of major food processing companies such as Standard Brands, General Foods, and Kellogg. In 1953, the average American family spent 26 percent of its income on food; by 1995 the proportion was just 14 percent and in 2004, it was under 10 percent. Food processors, including those in the seafood industry, sought production efficiencies to boost their profits. "Frozen food producers installed machines," one food historian has recently written, "that took foods from a conveyer belt into a breading contraption, plopped them into hot fat to be automatically fried, drained them, and slipped them into trays for freezing." Likewise, "bakeries were 'robotized' with new precision instruments regulating dough-mixing, fermenting, proofing, and cooling." The result, he concluded, was that "small processing companies fell by the wayside, bought out or driven out by larger ones seeking diversification or economies of scale." Another scholar has similarly written that modern-day food chains "have just one single product: convenience."[38]

Processors and Catchers: Conflict and Cooperation

Increasingly efficient seafood chains were at times endangered, however, by conflicts between catchers and processors. Despite becoming partially vertically integrated, most American seafood processors long relied on independent fishers for some of the seafood they put up and distributed. Similarly, few catchers processed or marketed their own crab, salmon, or bottom fish. The salmon fishery was legendary for conflicts between catchers and processors over prices, with regional conflicts common in southeastern Alaska and in Bristol Bay. Conflicts were also common in the king-crab industry.

Wakefield Seafoods depended on independent fishers for crabs at its shore plants in the late 1950s and early 1960s, with disputes and fishers' "strikes" (refusals to deliver crabs) periodically threatening to close those plants.

Recently, agreements between processors and fishers have muted conflicts. For instance, as we saw in Chapter 4, beginning in 2005 binding arbitration between processors and fishers over prices was mandated by the NPFMC for Alaska's crab industry. Always significant, government involvement in fisheries grew in the late 1900s and early 2000s, and more and more the decisions of the members of agencies such as the Council, themselves often well-established fishers and fish processors, came to structure business relationships. "Rationalization," as Council members viewed and labeled the changes, led to relationships between fishers and processors designed to speed the flow of seafood through food chains. Strikes by fishers (at least for crabs) were not allowed. Such strikes and other disruptions were common in earlier times.

Wakefield Seafoods first felt the impact of fishers' strikes in the 1950s. In 1954, the firm installed processing machinery at Port Wakefield, not far from Kodiak. However, plans for full-scale production there came to a "screeching halt," when fishers, joined together in a cooperative marketing arrangement, refused to deliver crabs for two months, protesting a reduction in prices paid by Wakefield. A still lengthier strike took place in the following year, when 100 boat owners and captains refused to deliver to Wakefield, which once again had lowered prices paid fishers in the face of a large, unsold inventory of crab meat. Fishers who delivered crab to Port Wakefield faced "actual sabotage," as their crab pots were cut loose from their marker buoys by striking fishers. The intervention of the Federal Trade Commission ended this strike, when commissioners found the fishers in restraint of trade and ordered them to resume crab shipments to the Wakefield plants.[39]

As Wakefield Seafoods broadened its shore operations, strikes became even more burdensome. In 1960, a strike by Kodiak fishers threatened again to close down Port Wakefield, and this time company officers raised prices paid fishers. In 1967, as crab catches plummeted, another strike prompted Lowell Wakefield to aver, "There are stories of under-the-table payments to skippers. There are stories of unbusinesslike 'loans' to boat owners. . . . There are stories of fuel and other allowances." What Wakefield meant was that some processors, desperate for crabs, were doing whatever they could to persuade fishers to deliver to their plants. Strikes had a marked impact on the strategies Wakefield's officers devised for the expansion of their company. The strikes spurred them to increase production efficiencies, operate processing ships and shore plants at widely scattered locations, and obtain more reliable supplies of crabs. Owning more of their own catcher boats was deemed too expensive, but they did try to tie fishers to their plants in a variety of ways: by financing their purchases of fishing gear and supplies, for example.[40]

Conflicts between processors and fishers took place in later years. Spike Walker, the crabber turned writer, vividly described one in 1979. After observing that, "ever an independent breed, Alaskan fishermen had always shunned the idea of unions," Walker noted that, "through the years they had embraced the collective, non-union stance of fighting for what they believed was a fair-market price." Major differences separated what processors offered and what fishers were willing to accept for king crab in 1979. Fishers demanded $1.18 per pound; processors offered $0.93. Walker later remembered: "When the opening day of the Bering Sea season arrived, the entire Bering Sea fleet remained unmoved. Often heated and emotional, the meetings lasted all day, stretching into the night." For an entire week fishers held out for a higher price. Doing so was difficult. As recalled by Walker, captains complained, "We're not making any money sitting here in port! Our crews are raising hell, getting drunk and fighting." The strike was finally settled in its seventh day at the price of $1.01 per pound, although some processors later paid only $0.86, earning them the epitaph "dirty, low, bastards" from fishers.[41]

What occurred in the king-crab fishery was repeated many times in Alaska's salmon fishery. A strike in Bristol Bay in summer 1982 was typical of the many disruptions. Into the 1960s, processing companies, which then meant cannery owners, controlled most of the salmon fishing in Alaska. These were companies such as Red Salmon, New England Fish, and Whitney Fidalgo. They extended loans to fishers and supplied them with needed fuel and supplies. Matsen explained, "In many cases, the arrangement between fishermen and packers was mutually benevolent, but abuses were common and patterns of mistrust took root that remain today." To combat processing companies, independent Bristol Bay fishers formed "unions" in the late 1950s: the Alaska Independent Fishermen's Marketing Association, based in the village of Naknek on the east side of the Bay, and the Western Alaska Cooperative Marketing Association in Dillingham on the west side.[42] Anticipating a heavy run of 34 million sockeye in 1982, many fishers sought to expand their gillnetting operations, often going into debt to do so. They expected Bristol Bay to be "hopping."[43] They anticipated high prices for their catches and were dismayed when cannery owners offered much lower ones, saying that a botulism scare had partially dried up their market.[44]

When the sockeye season opened, fishers struck. They refused to put to sea, letting their boats "go dry" on the beach. Supported by their union, fishers from Naknek hoped to force the cannery operators to raise their prices for sockeye. Tense negotiations followed. In the end, the strike failed. Many independent fishers—that is, fishers not belonging to the union—caught salmon and delivered to the canneries. As time passed, so did some union fishers, for they had to pay off their loans. Then too, fishers from Dillingham accepted a lower price than the union fishers in Naknek wanted, eroding that union's power. Hurting the fishers still more, the second "run" of sockeye never materialized, costing them 13 million uncaught fish. In a political economy that permitted independent operators to compete with one another, individualistic fishers had a difficult time taking effective concerted actions, and natural events made their lives precarious.[45]

In their ties with fishers, including vertical integration, processors such as Wakefield Seafoods in the 1950s and 1960s and Trident Seafoods in the 1980s and 1990s tightened their operations. They hoped to avoid uncertainties in deliveries of seafood, and they sought to acquire scarce types of fish and crabs. In the 1950s and 1960s, Wakefield Seafoods entered into tying contracts with independent fishers, guaranteeing that the fishers would sell to company plants at preset prices. Trident Seafood did the same several decades later and had its own fleet of catcher boats. In the salmon industry, processors partially controlled fishers up to the 1950s and 1960s. Fishers experienced more independence later on, but processors still sought to ensure a steady flow of salmon to their plants in a variety of ways. They influenced fishers by extending credit to them, guaranteeing prices paid for fish, and sometimes making under-the-table payments to captains and boat owners to secure their catches. Recent developments in the commodity chains for crabs and bottom fish under the terms of new regulatory regimes are tight indeed— even, in the case of crabs, to the specification of where and how boats can deliver their catches and what prices they receive for them.

The Development of Food and Commodity Chains

Developments in commodity chains for seafood contrasted with those for cut flowers, another very perishable commodity, sold in the United States. In that industry, there developed two global commodity chains from growers to consumers, one for "abundant" flowers (such as roses, chrysanthemums, and carnations) and another for "specialty" flowers, in the late 1900s. For both types of chains, but especially for those involving rapidly changing types of specialty flowers in which flexibility was important, networks and personal connections were of prime significance. The few efforts at vertical integration—that is, combining growing and selling—in single companies failed. In the cut flower industry, large vertically integrated firms could not respond quickly enough to the rapidly changing flower markets.[46] In the seafood industry, however, processors accommodated themselves to alterations via restructurings.

An examination of linkages between harvesters and processors of Alaskan seafood shows clearly that localized food production and consumption, desired by some environmentalists, did not replace global sourcing, despite the growing cost of fuel.[47] Worldwide sourcing was the norm for seafood in the early 2000s, with American companies both importing and exporting fish and other products. There was relatively little consumption of seafood caught locally, no substantial "locavore" movement—nothing like the extensive one that which developed for farm products. (Locavores are consumers who try to eat only plants, animals, and fish sourced within about 100 miles of their homes.) The goals of locavores were to decrease the carbon footprint involved in shipping food long distances and to "eat healthy" by knowing personally the sources of their food. They often bought at farms, farmers' markets, and various types of cooperatives.

There was only a small, fledgling locavore movement for seafood. Andrew Rosenberg, professor of Natural Resources and Environment at the University of New Hampshire and former deputy director of the U.S. National Marine Fisheries Service, observed in 2009, "We can't cover the entire U.S. market with domestic [fish] landings, even including aquaculture."[48] Still, there was an effort to develop "artisanal" blast-freezing for fish. In 1998, for instance, fisher Rick Altman installed a blast-freezer on his wooden salmon troller to sell frozen salmon and ling cod off the deck of his boat at the docks at Port Townsend, on the Washington coast. Retailers, chefs, and ordinary consumers bought from him. They trusted the quality of his frozen fish because they knew him personally. One scholar observed in 2009 that "in some foodie circles, especially on the West Coast, frozen salmon with the right name attached to it had distinction. Frozen had become the new fresh." Just how far this movement is likely go remains uncertain.[49] It would appear that the recent scarcities in seafood have hurt local sourcing of seafood, as some areas have been closed to fishing, forcing retailers to range far afield in search of fish and crabs.[50]

Hygienic Safety and Quality

Processing and selling seafood involved complicated issues of hygiene, sanitation, and health safety, for improperly handled seafood can kill consumers. In the 1960s, for example, botulism in canned tuna and vacuum-packaged smoked fish led to scores of deaths, which ruined markets for months. "Eternal vigilance is needed for the proper preservation of fish," commented seafood expert Robert J. Browning in 1974. For decades, however, uniform hygienic controls did not exist. A botulism scare in winter of 1981–82, when a resident of Belgium died after eating salmon canned in Ketchikan, cut into demand for Alaska's canned salmon.[51]

Unlike the situation with regard to meat, the U.S. Food and Drug Administration (FDA) did not provide nationwide inspection and regulation of seafood. The Bureau of Commercial Fisheries (part of the Department of Commerce) recommended a common-sense set of rules for fish buyers to follow, but these were vague and open to interpretation. One stated that "Fish should have bright shiny scales," another that "Fish should have a characteristic mild, fresh odor." None of the rules had the force of law. The regulation of processing was also haphazard—even though 80 percent of U.S. and Canadian salmon was canned as late as the early 1970s, as was 99 percent of the two nations' tuna. Nor was freezing seafood regulated in a standard manner. In the early 1970s, about 300 seafood companies operated multiple freezing plants in the United States and Canada. Individual companies such as Wakefield Seafood developed their own methods. Different states regulated processing in various ways with different standards. In late 1971, the National Marine Fisheries Service (of the Department of Commerce) instituted what it called "customized inspection" of seafood processors "to provide impartial inspection and certification of processing plants and all types of processed fishery products ... plus sanitary operating requirements for the plants." However, this program was voluntary and lacked the funding needed to be effective.[52]

Not until the 1990s did national and international standards for fish processing and hygienic safety begin to become truly effective, as an increasing number of seafood companies globally began adhering to the "Hazard

Analysis and Critical Control Points" (HACCP) approach to handling food. NASA originally developed HACCP to ensure the safety of food for its astronauts. HACCP was applied to seafood in part because consumers wanted assurances of safety (and saw seafood as healthy) and in part because companies desired to expand their markets. The Trident Seafoods website praised it as "a comprehensive preventative food-safety system engineered to and utilized to protect food from actual and potential hazards." The HACCP approach was comprehensive, embracing seven major principles: identifying hazards to health in food-processing chains, developing critical control points to prevent hazards, establishing standards for each critical control point, creating monitoring procedures, establishing corrective actions, keeping records for traceability, and continuously updating the HACCP system. HACCP standards became mandatory for seafood imported into nations of the European Union in 1992. The U.S. Congress did not pass legislation requiring HACCP standards for seafood until well after most large processors had voluntarily adopted them. In 1997, the FDA began making those standards mandatory.[53]

While concerned with scientific standards designed to protect consumers, seafood quality involved much more. Processors and sellers sometimes tried to use quality standards as ways to gain competitive advantages over each other, as can be seen in the actions of executives at Wakefield Seafoods, moves that often involved them in politics. Nor were quality standards absolute. They varied from place to place and time to time, as can be seen below in how standards were developed for surimi.

Wakefield's officers had long been concerned about the quality of the Alaskan king-crab pack, for they found maintaining high quality essential in opening markets and establishing a brand name. Moreover, they discovered they could establish significant favorable price differentials between their products and those of their competitors on the basis of superior quality. Quality control and marketing went hand-in-hand.

With the tremendous growth in competition in the 1960s, Wakefield's officers moved from relying on just their own in-house quality-control measures to sponsoring mandatory legislation in Juneau. In 1965, Wakefield's officers drafted what quickly became known as the Alaska King Crab Marketing and Quality Control Bill, which called on the governor of Alaska to appoint the officers of the six king-crab processing companies as a quasi-state agency or board with broad discretionary powers both to establish quality standards for packing crab and to promote its sale throughout the United States. Expenses were to be met by a levy on the crab processors.[54]

Usually referred to simply as "the Wakefield bill," this measure exposed divisions within the king-crab industry. Wakefield's officers, joined by their counterparts in several other well-established crab-processing firms, pushed for the legislation. They hoped that the proposed board's advertising work would help them move inventories of crab that were piling up and glutting markets. It was, however, the quality-control functions of the board that they stressed most. The recent entrance into the industry of many small and often undercapitalized firms, which possessed only rudimentary quality-control programs, led the officers of the larger companies to fear the possibility of a botulism scare such as those that had disrupted markets for the Great Lakes smoked whitefish industry and the tuna fish industry. Then too, officers in the larger king-crab companies hoped that high quality-control standards would increase the costs of production of the small firms and prevent them from undercutting established retail crab prices.[55]

In their approach to quality-control legislation, Wakefield closely resembled other large twentieth-century food processors. In the late nineteenth and early twentieth centuries, large meat packers pressed for quality-control legislation from Congress as a way of boosting sales abroad, partially resulting in the passage of federal quality-control legislation in 1906. The same situation existed at the state level. Between 1909 and 1920, for example, Florida, California, Oregon, and Washington passed legislation setting quality standards for fruits and vegetables sold out of state. Most of this legislation resulted from the desires of agriculturalists to boost sales. Large growers and cooperatives (such as Sunkist in California) feared that small growers, strapped for cash and requiring immediate sales, might ruin the market for produce by shipping immature or bruised goods to the Midwest and East. Not surprisingly, the larger agriculturalists, desiring long-term rather that short-term profits, sought and usually obtained quality-control laws from their state legislators.[56]

Not everyone, however, favored king-crab quality-control legislation. Opposition came from smaller processors who, while desiring the bill's marketing provisions, objected to its quality-control requirements as likely to increase their costs of production. Several large salmon packers that had just diversified into king-crab production also opposed the measure. Owned and operated by non-Alaskans, the salmon companies had long worked against government regulation of their industry and hoped to avoid what they considered unnecessary interference with their crab operations by the legislature.[57]

The final result was passage of compromise legislation. As signed into law in 1965, the act established a six-person board of crab processors, just as executives from the large and small companies wanted, to conduct public relations, sales promotions, and advertising. The board was also charged with presenting facts to and then negotiating with local, state, and federal agencies to fix quality standards for king crab. Once the standards were promulgated, the board was empowered to close any plant violating them. These were strong powers. However, as a concession to smaller processors, the larger companies agreed to a clause declaring that none of the board's work, including its quality-control efforts, would become effective "unless and until the annual budget of those programs is assented to in writing by not less than 51 percent of the processors by number." A uniform assessment levied on the processors supported the work of the board. As might be expected, the board emphasized advertising and marketing more than quality-control work in its actual operations.[58]

Quality in processing seafood can mean very different things in different situations, as in the making and selling of surimi. Surimi is a fish paste that goes into making fish cakes and imitation crab (called "krab"). It is made from a variety of fish species, but especially from Alaskan pollock. More than biology and scientific hygiene have been involved in defining surimi's quality. Consumers in different nations have defined quality in a number of ways, as can be seen in three food chains that developed for surimi.[59]

The modern surimi industry connected Alaskan pollock to surimi products made and consumed in Japan. Initially, most of this surimi was made by Japanese firms, but by the early 2000s American companies had partially replaced them, with 100,000 mt of surimi exported from the United States to Japan each year. The most important characteristic of surimi products in Japan was their elastic, "chewy" quality. Bland, very white, and having a high gel content, Alaskan pollock was ideal for being made into fish cakes and other surimi products sold in Japan. The pollock had, at first, to be processed fresh within twelve hours of being caught and could not be frozen. This requirement mandated rapid delivery of pollock to processing vessels or use of combined catcher-processor ships. An important discovery in 1959 showed, however, that adding salts and sugars to pollock during initial processing could protect the surimi once it was frozen. By adopting these technologies, Japanese firms were able to use Alaskan pollock in a major way for surimi in the 1960s and 1970s. A grading system, as well as factory trawlers and salts and sugars, was part of this process. In this commodity chain serving the Japanese market, definitions of quality thus arose "out of the interaction between pollock biology, traditional socio-cultural expectations about surimi [especially its chewiness] and processing techniques and technologies."[60]

A second food chain sent surimi from Thai producers to Japanese markets, entailing different expectations about quality. This surimi industry began in the late 1970s. The Thai industry was started with investments by three Japanese seafood firms and grew to an industry exporting 60,000 mt of surimi to Japan annually by the late 1990s, by which time the Japanese companies had pulled back to become marketers and sources of technical assistance for Thai producers.[61] Thai firms used threadfin bream caught in the Indian Ocean to make their surimi. The bream were processed on shore, not on ships, for they could be frozen on the catcher vessels before processing, allowing them to be taken on fairly long voyages to the shore plants. However, because it had a lower gel quality (it was less chewy), Thai surimi was not suitable for traditional Japanese surimi products. Thai firms developed new types of products, especially snack foods, for which a different gel level was acceptable.[62]

A third food chain for surimi involved American processing firms making surimi, mainly imitation crab, for the United States market. Americans did not, however, easily accept surimi. In fact, an executive of Trident Seafoods explained in 2000, surimi price and quality were intertwined in a "downward spiral." Too often, American processors, he complained, added water and starches to their pollock (and Pacific whiting, also used in making surimi), until fish composed only 30 percent of the content of surimi. Unlike the Japanese, who bought high quantities of surimi as fish paste with which to make fish cakes, Americans did not accept chewy surimi products and deemed them inferior to other types of seafood.[63]

Much then was involved in the issue of seafood quality. Quality-control legislation could be intended as a competitive tool, as the 1965 Alaskan legislation demonstrated. Once again, government was involved in defining the food chain for seafood. Then, too, quality was never simply a biological absolute. One scholar has concluded about surimi, "Definitions of quality in each commodity chain are about interactions between the physical characteristics of the fish, food practices, and production strategies; different aspects of each of these become important in individual commodity chains."[64]

Retailing Seafood and Sustainability in American Markets

Thousands of retailers, mainly restaurants and grocery chains, bought sea-food from wholesalers and sold it to the American public. There were about 70,000 grocery stores, excluding convenience stores, in the United States in 2009. Like wholesaler-processors, many retailers changed their ways in light of seafood scarcities. For the most part, retailers accepted what species they could get from the processor-wholesalers. As Atlantic cod became scarce, for example, they switched to other species. In 2008 Long John Silver's, America's largest fast-food seafood chain, served Alaskan pollock and hoki/hake, another bottom fish.[65] So did Captain D's, a chain of seafood outlets in the Southeast.[66] In 2010 Wendy's advertised that the only fish it served was Alaskan cod.

Retailers sometimes took actions of their own. As over-fishing depleted the stock of swordfish, leading to the taking of small, juvenile fish, some restaurants signed onto a campaign mounted by the conservation community to "Save Baby Swordfish." In the 1990s, their managers agreed not to serve swordfish.[67] Similarly, on the West Coast, a campaign with the slogan, "Take a Pass on Chilean Sea Bass," which was being over-fished, altered many restaurant menus. In New York City some executive chefs at leading restaurants, through the groups Seafood Choices Alliance and Chefs Collaborative, agreed to serve only fish caught in sustainable manners.[68] In 2009, Wegmans Food Markets joined with sports-fishing and conservation groups to remove endangered marlin from its chain of seventy-two supermarkets in the Middle Atlantic states.[69]

A few restaurants did more. Like the Waterfront Restaurant mentioned at the beginning of this chapter, Ma Ma's Fish House, another premier restaurant on Maui, secured direct ties to desirable fish, such as the local delicacies ono and opakapapa. That eatery had its own fish boat to catch what it needed.[70] Some restaurants, such as Triples in Seattle, reserved their own cargo spaces in jet planes that flew fresh salmon south from Alaska, especially the Copper River area, daily.[71] Some upscale boutique grocers did the same. Frank Dorame, meat and seafood buyer for Jensen's Fine Foods in Palm Desert, California, made arrangements to have Copper River salmon in his store within twenty-fours of the opening of the fishing season. The cost to consumers in 2008 came to $37 per pound, which they paid "without flinching." Dorame observed, "Our customer wants what they want, when they want it."[72]

Figure 19. Ma Ma's Fish House had its own boat. Author's collection.

Most important, large global retailers flexed their muscles by purchasing only fish caught or raised in sustainable manners. By 2006, such companies as McDonald's, Unilever, the Metro Group of Germany (the world's third-largest retailer), Whole Foods Market, and Safeway were doing so. Early that year, the UK-based Compass Group, the world's largest food service group, announced a "landmark policy change," by which its American subsidiary would buy seafood only from sustainable sources. Whole Foods worked with the Monterey Bay Aquarium and the Blue Ocean Institute (Carl Safina's organization) to design a color-coded rating program measuring the environmental well-being of seafood sold in its stores. Consumers could see at a glance the impacts of their purchases. A green label indicated that the species was abundant and caught in an environmentally friendly way; yellow meant that there were concerns about a species' status or the fishing methods by which it was harvested; and red signaled over-fishing or harmful harvesting practices. Perhaps most important were steps taken by Wal-Mart, the world's largest retailer. Long criticized for stocking its stores with farmed salmon raised in unsustainable ways, Wal-Mart altered its practices.[73]

Like the other retailers mentioned above, Wal-Mart purchased fish certified by international environmental groups such as the British-based Marine

Stewardship Council (MSC) as coming only from stocks managed in sustainable ways. In 2008, Wal-Mart added wild Bristol-Bay sockeye to its array of fish caught in an approved manner. By the end of the year, Wal-Mart carried twenty-two products bearing the MSC label. The retailer won approval for its actions from Alaskan fishery groups—the Alaska Independent Fisherman's Marketing Association, the United Fishermen of Alaska, and Nunamta Alulukestai (a Native body)—and from environmental groups such as Trout Unlimited. Tim Bristol of Trout Unlimited explained the power consumers could use, saying, "You can vote with your fork."[74] In early 2009, the Food Marketing Institute, representing American food wholesalers and super-markets operating 26,000 grocery stores making three-quarters of all grocery sales in the nation, signed on to the sustainable-seafood movement.[75] In 2009–2010, Kroger and Target joined the march toward sustainability, with Kroger, for example, eliminating all farmed salmon from the seafood sections of its stores nationwide.[76]

The Marine Stewardship Council was started by Unilever and the World Wide Fund for Nature in 1996–97. According to Michael Sutton, a vice-president of the Monterey Bay Aquarium in 2009 who had worked with the World Wide Fund in the interests of sustainability in the mid-1990s, "What [Unilever] wanted was green publicity, but above all to get rid of the business risks associated with over-fishing."[77] The MSC described itself as "an independent, global, non-profit organization whose role is to recognize, via a certification program, well-managed fisheries and to harness consumer preference for seafood products bearing the MSC label of approval."[78] Probably most important in the activities of the MSC was the technical director of fisheries in the body's London headquarters. That person coordinated the reviews of individual fishery assessments, set the designs for management training, and provided advice to the organization's executive and governance bodies. In 2009, Dan Hoggarth, who had twenty years of experience in fishery management, became the new technical director. Also important were regional offices. Nancy Grace-Keller headed MCS Seattle office, providing day-to-day assistance on fishery matters about that region to the London headquarters.[79]

The environmental group Greenpeace also weighed in on sustainable retailing. In June 2008, the organization issued a report titled "Carting Away the Oceans: How Grocery Stores Are Emptying the Seas." This report lambasted twenty major American retailers, because they "ignored scientific warnings about the crisis facing global fisheries and the marine environment." However, a revised report put out in early 2009 praised four retailers—Whole Foods, Ahold USA, Target, and Harris Teeter—for strengthening their sustainable seafood purchasing practices.[80]

Important as it was, the scarcity of certain types of fish was not the only factor leading retailers to change their sourcing methods. Developments in the Chesapeake Bay crab industry during the 1990s revealed the complexity of the situation. As crab retailers expanded their operations, they needed reliable supplies of blue crabs processed according to international hygienic standards. They found that suppliers in the Chesapeake were so fragmented and so divided by state boundaries—the federal government had no nationwide hygienic standards for seafood—that suppliers could not guarantee the availability of high-quality crabs. The crabs went into crab cakes for eateries such as the growing chain of Phillips Seafood Restaurants and M & I Seafood, and for mass retailers such as Costco. By 1985, the Phillips restaurants were, for example, serving 25,000 people daily.[81]

Into the 1990s, there were plenty of crabs, but not enough processed to the standards set by the retailers. Increasingly, the retailers required that their suppliers follow HACCP procedures in preparing crabs. The retailers found blue-crab suppliers in Thailand willing, and—with lots of input from the retailers, led by Phillips Seafood—able to do so. By contrast, the state of Maryland adopted HACCP standards for its crabs only in 2003. In the early and mid-1990s, not surprisingly, American retailers switched much of their sourcing of blue crabs to Thailand, often setting up subsidiaries in that nation to catch, process, and cook the crabs, which then found markets in the United States, imported by Phillips Seafood and other firms—backward vertical integration. Between 1995 and 1999, the amount of imported blue-crab meat soared 550 percent. Probable over-fishing of the Chesapeake crabs, which became apparent between 1995 and 2000, encouraged the change, which, however, was already well underway before those years.[82]

Environmentalists sought to influence seafood companies in myriad ways beyond trying to affect retailing. The firm CleanFish, started by Tim O'Shea in 2004, sought to build brand recognition for fresh, sustainable seafood from small fishing operations around the globe. "Our goal is to create a market response to the global seafood crisis by building a network of artisanal seafood producers, both in the wild sector and aquaculture," observed O'Shea in the summer of 2008. Continuing, he noted, "We want to take them to new markets they could not reach on their own and build a branded presence." CleanFish represented twenty-four seafood producers by mid-2008, including the well-known brand of farmed salmon from Scotland called "Loch Duart." The firm's strategy was to start by selling to high-end restaurants, whose chefs were influential, and then to upscale grocery stores and high-quality chain restaurants. "I want people to think about the producer to consumer connection," said O'Shea in an interview. Not all environmentalists accepted CleanFish's basic assumptions, however. Some, for example, slammed any fish farming as inherently unsustainable.[83]

The Sea Change Investment Fund, a small San Francisco venture-capital fund formed in 2005, took a different approach. Using $20 million—half from the David & Lucille Packard Foundation, half from individual investors—Sea Change concentrated on the middle of the seafood chain, the processors and distributors. By mid-2008, Sea Change had invested in six companies. The most important three were Ecofish, a New Hampshire firm that sold sustainable fish to restaurants and offered frozen fish to consumers; Look's Gourmet Food Company of Maine, which used sustainable ingredients in its seafood chowders; and Advanced BioNutrition of Maryland, which developed protein-rich algae that could replace fish oil as a food for farm-raised fish. After just three years of existence, Sea Change had not sold any of its investments, so it was too soon to see if this approach to sustainability was profitable.[84]

Selling Seafood to American Consumers

No less than harvesting, the other links in seafood chains were affected by the scarcity of some types of fish and crabs. Processors and distributors responded by trying to tighten their grip on their sources of raw seafood. Some engaged in backward vertical integration; others devised tying contracts for harvesters. Retailers also made special agreements with fishers and changed the types of fish they served. Most notable were the efforts by large retailers such as Wal-Mart to purchase and sell only seafood that was harvested in a sustainable manner. That shift promised to alter the dynamics of the global seafood industry in important ways. As it had long been, seafood processing and sales remained complex in shape, global in scope, and susceptible to changes brought about by alterations in technologies, laws, and markets. It should be stressed that government bodies played important, sometimes even determining, roles in how food chains for seafood functioned. Thus, when the NPFMC decided to make harvesting Alaskan king crabs sustainable in

2005, it set in train motions that set prices and helped determine markets. In the actions of wholesalers and retailers, environmental and economic issues interacted in sometimes expected and sometimes unexpected ways, creating new institutions for seafood sourcing in the United States and abroad, as will be seen in the conclusion to this study.

CONCLUSION

In July 2007, David Lethin first took tourists on board his 107-foot king crabber *Aleutian Ballard*. Lethin had last fished for crabs in the Bering Sea three
years before. From the heated comfort of sheltered observation decks on his
remodeled vessel, visitors paid $189 apiece for trips to watch Lethin and his
crews haul pots of crabs from waters near Ketchikan. The venture was an
economic success. Lethin's wife remarked a year later, "This is less deadly,
and it's so much fun to share with the tourists." The *Aleutian Ballard* motored
through the offshore fishing grounds of the Metlakata community on An-
nette Island and compensated that Alaskan Native group for each tourist on
board. By summer 2008, demand was so great that Lethin was making two
trips per day.[1] Lethin was not alone, as a number of former crab fishers entered the tourism business, using their boats to take visitors on short jaunts
out to sea. Excluded from fishing by new regulatory regimes and pulled by
the lure of tourist dollars, some fishers entered a new trade. Thus did some
fishers adjust to sustainable fishing in Alaskan waters.[2]

In this conclusion to my study, I examine how global fishing practices
compared to those in Alaska; and I look at what the experiences of fishers
such as Lethin and fish processors such as Chuck Bundrant of Trident Seafoods reveal about the management of common-pool resources and, more
generally, economic globalization. I close by discussing fishing's place in
the conservation of renewable natural resources. Throughout, I argue that
governmental regulation through such agencies as the North Pacific Fishery
Management Council has largely shaped seafood chains.

Sustainable Fishing Around the Globe

The worldwide fishing situation has mirrored that in Alaskan waters: over-
fishing and the collapse of fish stocks such as tuna and red snapper encouraged

governments to limit fishing to try to achieve sustainability. The European Union (before 1992, the European Common Market) adopted a Common Fisheries Policy in the 1970s and 1980s, with many member nations setting early forms of total allowable catches and individual fishing quotas. In the 1980s and 1990s, overfishing led Iceland, New Zealand, Australia, Canada, the United Kingdom, Norway, and the Netherlands to impose harvest limits and fishing quotas on some fish stocks.[3] New Zealand led other nations in setting up no-fishing reserves, establishing its first in 1977. By 2007, it had thirty-one such reserves covering 8 percent of its coastal waters. Other major reserves existed in Australian, Hawaiian, and Californian waters. Even so, reserves covered only 0.06 percent of the world's ocean in 2007.[4]

In Europe, as in the United States, politicians were in the driver's seat. In 2003, the EU adopted an "Entry-Exit" scheme, which required that the operations of all new fishing vessels be directly offset by the withdrawal of an equivalent tonnage of fishing vessels, without any public compensation. The EU also put in place catch limits and fishing quotas for many fish species in the waters of its nations. However, the fishing outcome was not as favorable as that in Alaskan waters. A detailed report in the *Economist* in early 2009 summarized the fishing practices of EU nations: "Basic flaws in the system remain. Science is disdained. The scientists' proposals that precede the annual allocation of quotas are routinely expanded, first by the commission and then by the ministers. They often end up 50% higher than recommended, and are then usually disregarded by rapacious fishermen."[5] A failure to establish sustainable harvest limits led to continued over-fishing. In 2009, fully 88 percent of the fish stocks of the EU were being over-fished. In the North Sea, for example, 93 percent of the cod were being caught before they could breed.[6]

Failures to attain sustainable fishing outnumbered successes in the rest of the world. In 2002, China established a five-year program to scrap 7 percent of its commercial fishing fleet, and asserted that, in the first year of the plan, about 5,000 boats were withdrawn from fishing. Nonetheless, China reported about the same number of fishing vessels to the United Nations Food and Agriculture Organization in 2004 as in 2002. A UNFAO report concluded in 2008: "China's five-year programme to de-license and scrap 30,000 fishing vessels ended at the beginning of 2008. It is unclear how many vessels were scrapped under the programme. Whatever its achievements, it appears that the fleet of commercial vessels in China continues to expand."[7] According to UNFAO officials, the high seas fleets of longstanding fishing nations such as Denmark, Iceland, Japan, Norway, and Russia decreased in the early 2000s, as those nations found their ships forbidden from the exclusive economic zones of other nations. In South America, fishers from Argentina and Chile reduced the numbers of their commercial fishing vessels in the face of similar foreign restrictions. On the other hand, fishers in Indonesia and the Philippines increased the sizes of their commercial fishing fleets.[8]

Some African nations leased waters in their exclusive economic zones to fishers from the EU and elsewhere, as a way of securing badly needed revenues and foreign exchange. In doing so, they established catch limits far above what was sustainable. In the 1990s, for example, Senegal entered into arrangements with the EU that allowed—indeed, encouraged—over-fishing. The $75 million per year, a large sum for the poor nation, was eagerly sought, even if it meant putting local inshore fishers out of business. Similarly, in 2006 the EU agreed to pay Mauritania $700 million over six years for fishing rights in that nation's waters. In 2007, foreign payments for fishing rights amounted to 30 percent of that nation's annual budget, and 340 foreign ships—including Russian and Chinese as well as EU vessels—were licensed to fish in Mauritanian waters.[9] In 2009, to cite a third example, increasingly bold Somali pirates claimed that Western fishing boats had plundered their fishing grounds and destroyed their livelihoods, forcing them into piracy.[10]

Summarizing the global fishing picture, UNFAO officials concluded in 2006, "The number of fishing vessels worldwide has remained fairly constant in recent years." Those fishing vessels were more effective in catching fish than earlier ones, leading to a continuation of pressure on many fish stocks.[11] A more detailed report issued by the UNFAO two years later about fishing in the Pacific Ocean observed with dismay, "For the 181 stocks or species groups of the Pacific Ocean for which information was sufficient to evaluate the state of resources, 77 percent were determined to fall within the range of moderately-full exploited/depleted," noting that "These levels suggest little room for further expansion." Looking beyond the Pacific, the publication concluded, as had earlier reports from the organization for years, "A key fisheries management issue is the lack of progress with the reduction of fishing capacity and related harmful subsidies," despite the 2007 United Nations resolution (UNGA Resolution 67/177) condemning most such subsidies.[12]

Wherever sustainable large-scale commercial fishing has been achieved in recent times, government limitation of the number of fishers and the size of their catch has been the essential first step. That was certainly true in the United States, where business development has always been greatly influenced by government policy making.[13] Fishing became even more highly regulated than before, as fishers and processors sought economic and environmental sustainability. As much as fishers mourned the loss of their former freedoms, nearly all came to accept the regulatory state as a necessity, or at least inevitability.

Still, conflicts between regulators and fishers continued to arise. In early 2010, officials of the U.S. National Oceanic and Atmospheric Administration (NOAA), which oversaw the enforcement of the Fishery Conservation and Management Act of 1976 (as amended), shut numerous East Coast areas to fishing for many fish stocks to allow them to recover, with closures anticipated to last for as long as a decade. Some fishers protested. "At least a thousand jobs in Fort Lauderdale will be lost this year," claimed Bob Jones, director of the Southeast Fisheries Association, an organization of commercial fishers based in Tallahassee, Florida. Politicians joined the fishers. Representative Barney Frank (D-Mass.) thought that fishers should have more say in how regulations were applied: "I have a sharp disagreement with regulators who think they have to tell fishermen how important it is to have fish ten years from now. Fishermen have more of an interest and more of an understanding of keeping fish around than the people who are regulating them. It's absolutely backwards." Monica Allen, a NOAA spokesperson, countered that the closures would help fishers in the long run: "It is much more financially stable and lucrative to the fishing industries." She pointed out that the Atlantic sea scallop fishery, which had been over-fished in the early 1990s, recovered after a seven-year closure, with the value of the scallop harvest rising from $30 million in 1994 to $202 million in 2006.[14]

As in earlier times and other places, the government-mandated closure of fishing for some species in East Coast waters affected entire seafood chains. Locally caught grouper had been a staple for restaurants in Charleston, South Carolina. However, in early 2010 closures ended harvesting grouper, black sea bass, red porgy, and red snapper in American waters from Florida to North Carolina. That meant that chefs who made a point of offering fresh local seafood had to persuade their patrons to accept species such as triggerfish— which had once been considered "trash fish," but which were still plentiful and could still be caught. The closure opened opportunities as well. For instance, Mark Marhefka, who had fished South Carolina's waters for thirty years, established Abundant Seafood as a seafood distribution company, precisely to introduce chefs to new species of fish. "If I don't make Abundant Seafood work, I won't be able to survive being a commercial fisherman anymore," he observed in early 2010. Marhefka worked with the South Carolina

Aquarium's Sustainable Seafood Initiative, whose officers introduced him to chefs from restaurants such as the Boathouse, Carolina's, Red Drum and Fish, and Grady's, who were willing to pay premium prices for seafood harvested in sustainable ways. He also started a community-sponsored fishery, in which home cooks paid a share to receive two to ten pounds of fish each month.[15]

Common-Pool Resource Management

The continuing tragedy of the commons in many commercial fisheries around the world connects with similar events that took place in the nineteenth-century trans-Mississippi West. For both wild and domestic animals, a lack of clear ownership proved lethal. Unrestricted hunting brought buffalo, which no one owned, to near extinction during the 1870s and 1880s. Similarly, many cattle, which were privately owned but grazed on public lands, died during severe weather during the mid-1880s. As in fishing, a tragedy of the commons meant that when no one owned a resource, when it was common property or on common ground, it was in the interests of everyone to exploit it as quickly as possible. To have done otherwise—for instance, to have followed conservation practices—would simply have awarded advantages to competitors. However, in such situations everyone usually suffered in the end as the resource was over-used, sometimes taken to the brink of extinction.

Buffalo had long roamed across much of what is now the United States, as far east as the Carolinas and Georgia, and as far west as Oregon. They were prized by Indians and Euro-Americans for their robes and were hunted to extinction east of the Mississippi by 1833. However, there were still about thirty million buffalo west of the Mississippi in the 1850s. Those buffalo were central to the lives of many tribes on the Great Plains, who hunted them on foot and on horseback. Wastage, as defined by environmentalists today, occurred. Indians killed more buffalo than they needed for their own use, surrounding herds by fire, driving them over cliffs, and killing them on horseback. Even so, taking buffalo by Indians for their own use was not what led to their near extermination.[16]

Rather, a growing demand in eastern and midwestern cities for buffalo hides (the buffalo skin with the hair scraped off) condemned the buffalo. A cluster of technological innovations, products of the industrial revolution, was especially important. In the 1850s and 1860s, railroads entered the Great Plains, with the first transcontinental line completed in 1869. Railroads made it possible to ship buffalo hides from where the buffalo were killed to their markets. In the same period, new types of rifles, almost like small cannon, were mass produced. Finally, in 1871–72, advanced tanning methods allowed buffalo hides to be substituted for cowhides in numerous items, most important shoes and industrial belting. Industrial belting connected steam engines to individual pieces of machinery in factories. Industry itself, then, provided much of the market for the hides. Thus, industrialization linked a natural resource, the buffalo, to new production methods and to new market uses.

Between 1867 and 1884, the "Great Buffalo Hunt" took place. Commercial hide hunters moving west from the Mississippi River after the Civil War slaughtered buffalo by the millions. Since none of them had any ownership rights over the wild buffalo, none had any reason to conserve the buffalo. Moreover, the military encouraged them to kill the buffalo as a way to destroy the food supply of plains Indians. By 1874, the great Kansas-Nebraska herds were fast disappearing, and hide hunters shifted their attention south into Texas and north into the Dakotas and Montana. By 1878–79, the southern herds were virtually gone and the northern plains had come under intensified hunting pressure. By the winter of 1883, even the northern herds were eliminated. Only a few remnant bands of buffalo remained, such as one in Yellowstone National Park, created in 1872.

Cattle, domesticated animals, faced much the same fate on the Great Plains just a few years later. Ranchers grazed their cattle on the open range, on the public domain. They did not own the lands and grasses on which they kept and nourished their cattle. Consequently, they had no incentive to practice wise grazing methods. Instead, they overstocked the ranges. The result was too many cattle per acre. When bad weather hit in the mid-1880s, including an especially severe winter in 1887–88, cattle died by the thousands. Historians have estimated that perhaps three-quarters of the cattle on the northern ranges died.[17]

The western cattle industry was rejuvenated and a new bison-raising industry was created through private land ownership. From the 1880s onward, ranchers came to own lands and to rent precise parcels of the public domain for grazing purposes. As owners, they were able to limit the number of cattle per acre. The use of barbed wire to fence lands made selective breeding possible. Ranchers also provided their cattle with forage and dependable supplies of water, allowing them to weather winters in better shape than before.[18] Similarly, the commercial ranching of buffalo, which developed in the twentieth century, depended on private land ownership, fencing, and careful animal husbandry.[19] Ranches for cattle and buffalo became smaller, but much better managed.

The experiences of cattle and buffalo suggest that privatization of the commons is the best, and perhaps only, way to attain sustainability in the use of natural resources, with government usually involved in that privatization. Yet, other examples show that tradition and custom can, along with careful use of cooperative arrangements, avert tragedies on the commons. As we have seen, custom, tradition, and taboos allowed Native Americans and Alaskan Natives to manage salmon resources on the Columbia River and in southeast Alaska in sustainable ways. Then too, accepted ways of acting long protected some fisheries in New England. Only in the 1800s did those protections break down in the face of rampant industrialization and urbanization.[20]

Similarly, common land ownership among farmers has been more prevalent in some regions than might be expected, even into modern times, and that common land ownership has not led to a degradation of the productivity of the lands. For example, in early modern times about one-third of Japan's arable land was owned and worked in common in what was called a *wariichi* (common) land ownership system. This system lasted with some attenuation into the twentieth century, with no deleterious effects on agricultural productivity.[21] Similarly, people in various parts of the globe, including some living in the arid sections of the trans-Mississippi West, worked out common ways of managing water resources. The Spanish, for example, devised successful methods to handle communal water needs in what became the American Southwest.[22] These examples—and, of course, those of modern-day Alaskan and global fisheries—raise basic questions about how best to shape conservation measures to cover resources that no one group or nation completely owns or controls. How can intergroup agreements be made to work? Is government intervention needed? Again, the complexity of different situations is worthy of emphasis.

Political scientist Elinor Ostrom, who pioneered in the study of the common use of natural resources, captured that complexity: "What one can observe in the world . . . is that neither the state nor the market is uniformly successful in enabling individuals to sustain long-term, productive use of natural resource systems." "Further, communities of individuals have relied on institutions resembling neither the state nor the market to govern some resource systems with reasonable degrees of success over long periods of time." In fact, by 1989 scholars had identified 5,000 cases of successful commons property management.[23] These involved fisheries, basins of oil and natural gas worked by more than one owner, water in underground aquifers tapped by multiple users, and land worked in common. Looking at both successes and failures in the cooperative management of common pool resources, as opposed to the extremes of private ownership or government fiat, Ostrom found commonalities. Cooperative management worked best when there were clearly defined resources and resource users, when local conditions were incorporated into resource-usage provisions, when users had clear says in modifying those provisions as necessary, when monitoring usage conditions was consistent and thorough, when sanctions for violating usage provisions were graduated, when workable conflict-resolution mechanisms existed, and when larger bodies (such as governmental agencies) allowed free play of the cooperative management groups.[24]

Cooperative arrangements were most effective in long-established situations, in which custom and tradition had chances to develop into strong forces, as was the case in many Native American and Alaskan Native fisheries. Conversely, in cases where traditions were weak, tragedies of the commons resulted, unless participants were able to develop laws to prevent them. No strong traditions or laws initially governed Euro-American buffalo hunting or cattle grazing on the public domain, leading to over-use in the nineteenth century.

Similarly, open access to most American fisheries, along with government encouragement of American fishers, created tragedies of the commons in many of those fisheries, such as those for cod and blue-fin tuna in the Northwest Atlantic, and nearly created tragedies for fisheries in Pacific Northwestern and Alaskan waters. In those fisheries there were few traditions or customs of sustainable fishing among Euro-American fishers. Only when laws, based on commonly though not necessarily universally accepted ideas, and the work of governmental bodies such as the NPFMC, whose membership was made up in part of fishers and processors, closed the fisheries through the employment of total allowable catches and individual fishing quotas was sustainability achieved.

Those laws, and the NPFMC they created, embodied many of the principles Ostrom uncovered. Fisheries and fishers were clearly identifiable, especially with advances in marine science made in the 1980s and 1990s. The laws usually took into account local knowledge, as expressed by fishers at numerous public hearings. Monitoring by the coast guard and the Alaska Department of Fish and Game was generally acknowledged, despite grumblings from time to time, as fair. Perhaps most important, fishing rules were constantly reexamined and modified as a result of both scientific findings and discussions at public hearings.[25]

The fishing regulations governing Alaskan waters brought about sustainability almost despite the character of many fishers. As I observed in Chapter 4, fishers were young men and women on the make, and, much like those on the earlier frontier, they sought profits and adventure. Fishing was a way of life based, they imagined, on social and economic independence deriving from the rapid use of natural resources. While hoping to benefit from government actions, they did not want to be tied down by them. In important respects, Alaskan fishers resembled independent truckers. Valuing their independence above all else, young men turned to trucking, especially the carriage of agricultural products to market, when from the 1930s onward they could no longer prosper as independent family farmers, pushed off the land by the spread of agribusiness. Yet, there were important differences too. To try to preserve their seemingly independent way of life as kings of the open road, independent truckers joined the fight for the deregulation of the trucking industry, begun by President Jimmy Carter and his staff, and pushed by

Figure 20. A small ship on a big ocean. Author's collection.

Senator Ted Kennedy, and were successful with the passage of the Motor Carrier Act of 1980.[26] To the contrary, faced with the likely disappearance of fish and crabs, Alaskan fishers turned to the federal government for help in maintaining their businesses and lifestyles, first with the passage of the Fishery Conservation and management Act in 1976 and then through the work of the NPFMC. In short, fishers used politics to enhance their well-being through government regulation.

Can various types of user cooperatives work, with a minimum of government regulation and laws? Lowell Wakefield, the Alaskan king-crab pioneer, suggested as much in the mid-1960s, when he pondered whether government intervention was needed or whether fishers could work out some type of arrangement to limit catches on their own. Similarly, historian Anthony Scott has urged that fisher cooperatives might in some situations achieve the same results as government regulation, but with less paper work and at less cost. "Is there a reason," he has asked, "why the fishermen, working as a cooperative, cannot provide their own TAC?"[27] To date, however, few such cooperatives have existed for large commercial fisheries. Some government compulsion, whether through international or national laws and organizations, seems necessary—with, of course, fishers and seafood processors playing very active roles in the drafting of legislation and in the work of the regulatory commissions. And, to be effective, those laws and commissions have needed to be based on generally agreed upon perceptions of crises.

Fishing and Globalization

The questions raised in common-pool resource management cross regional and industry boundaries; they are worldwide in scope. As we have seen repeatedly throughout this book, modern seafood businesses exist in an industry characterized by worldwide food chains. Only a small amount of local sourcing and consumption of seafood has taken place. Nor is there likely to be much more in the future. People want to eat wild-caught fish from around the world. In 2010, the Alaskan processor SeaBear advertised its Copper River salmon as "thoroughbreds of the sea . . . widely recognized for the unmatched culinary experience they offer, as they find their way to fine restaurants and markets across the country direct from one of the most pristine, most rugged, most untouched corners of the world." SeaBear promised to airlift three pounds of frozen dinner fillets anywhere in the United States for $74.99. The company also handled Alaskan halibut, Dungeness crab, and other types of salmon.[28] The same may be said for many of the products of aquaculture. Tilapia farm-raised and frozen in China has found its largest market in the United States.

Globalization in the seafood industry has taken many forms. Most obviously, fishers harvest seafood in distant waters—sometimes in sustainable manners, but sometimes not. Fishers from EU members and other nations have recently decimated fish stocks off the coasts of African nations. On the other hand, Alaskan fishers and processors were very active in establishing exclusive economic zones that were sustainable and have benefited from them. What has mattered most has been the regulatory regimes that have governed harvesting within 200 miles of the shores. Nations may not establish catch limits that are sustainable, in decisions that are guided as much by politics as by economics. In 2009, Iceland, injured by the collapse of its financial institutions during the global economic downturn, increased the catch limits on cod in its waters by 20 percent, raising questions about the future sustainability of that fish stock.[29]

Processing and distribution, as well as harvesting, seafood have become global. As we have seen, American and Japanese firms entered into a variety of joint ventures from the 1970s. Excluded from harvesting seafood within 200 miles of American shores, Japanese processors sought and gained various types of contracts with American harvesters. More recently, outright ownership has become increasingly common. American companies own Japanese subsidiaries to get close to the large Japanese market. Trident Seafoods purchased Kako Foods to help sell salmon there. Similarly, Japanese companies have used American subsidiaries to reach the U.S. market. Through an American subsidiary, Nippon Suisan owns American suppliers Fishking, Gorton's Seafoods, Unisea, and several others. Many of the larger seafood companies in Japan, the United States, and elsewhere are multinational enterprises with operations around the globe. Consumers today are, in fact, hard-pressed to tell the sources of the seafood products they buy in supermarkets or are served in restaurants.

A related issue of economic globalization is the carbon footprint generated in getting seafood—wild or farmed—to consumers, which can be quite large. Fresh, wild Alaskan salmon from the Copper River region reaches gourmets in the lower 48 states via jet airplanes. Diners may feel good that they are eating wild-caught rather than farm-raised salmon, but they are indirectly using up lots of aviation gasoline and contributing to global warming in doing so. Shipping Copper River salmon from Cordova to Seattle by air generates fifty-seven times more CO_2 than moving the salmon by ship. Being an ecologically aware consumer in the modern world is difficult, given the global sourcing of many seafood products.[30]

It is difficult to gauge the overall impact of the global fishing industry on people around the world. There have certainly been positive impacts. The demand for seafood has created jobs that would not otherwise have existed and has led to some transfer of technologies. The desire of Japanese producers for high-quality salmon suitable for their markets altered salmon-handling practices in Alaskan waters by American catchers. Pitchforks were no longer used, for they damaged the flesh of the fish. Americans also learned some aspects of how to handle snow crabs from the Japanese. Similarly, blue-crab harvesters and processors in Southeast Asia have benefited from the demands of American markets. The insistence by U.S. firms that processors adhere to Hazard Analysis and Critical Control Points protocols raised sanitary standards there to new levels. Likewise, the demands of the American market have made farm raising tilapia in China more sustainable.

On the other hand, continued over-fishing in many seas to meet the demands of major markets such as those in Japan and the United States has sometimes cost local people jobs. Over-fishing decimated the cod fishery of the Northwest Atlantic, killing entire coastal communities. Offshore over-fishing by EU trawlers in some African waters has deprived local inshore fishers of their livelihoods. Even the move to sustainable fishing in Alaskan waters, it should be recalled, left some people, including women and Alaskan Natives, without jobs. As in so many matters of economic globalization, the results of the operations of worldwide food chains for seafood have been mixed. Consumers in wealthy nations have certainly benefited from the greater variety of seafood available, but that benefit has often come only through the incurrence of costs to others and to the environment.

The mixed consequences of the globalization of fishing and seafood chains are not surprising. Most scholars who have studied the impacts of globalization on people around the world have reached conclusions stressing both pluses and minuses. Such has especially been the case for historians who have examined how multinational enterprises have affected lives globally. No easy generalizations are possible.[31] Fishing provides, I think, ample evidence that globalization's impacts have contained both positives and negatives.

Fishing, Natural Resources, and the Environment

The goal of most international and national fishery laws, it is worth reiterating in closing, has been to make fishing profitable and sustainable. The laws and the commissions set up to administer them have very much been in the mainstream American Progressive tradition of putting nature to efficient use. The goal was not to preserve oceanic nature in a pristine state, except in the establishment of a relatively few preserves such as those around New Zealand and parts of the Hawaiian Islands. To the contrary, the UN Law of the Sea Conventions called on signatories to achieve maximum (or optimal) sustainable yields for all fisheries in their waters. If coastal nations could not do so, they were supposed to open their waters to foreign fishers who could. Most did, as was certainly the case in Alaskan waters. Only as American fishers and processors increased their capabilities were foreigners expelled.

The eight councils governing fishing in the U.S. exclusive economic zone sought optimum yields, which could take into account the impacts of fishing various species of fish on each other and the impacts of fishing on coastal communities. The basic aim remained to harvest nearly as many fish as was sustainable. For the most part, in my opinion, this approach has worked. Fisheries have become sustainable. There were social costs, however, for these regulations excluded, at least initially, many women and indigenous fishers. Environmental justice issues surfaced. Not all displaced fishers found prosperity in tourism. Over the past decade, members of government agencies such as the NPFMC have been addressing such matters, but some inequities have remained.

As fisheries grew up in the Pacific Northwest and Alaska, they came into conflict with other developing industries based on natural resources—in manners similar to conflicts that often came to pit mining, ranching, and timber interests against each other in the American West over resource usage and conservation. Hydropower, farming, and salmon companies fought about the most appropriate use of the waters of the Sacramento and Columbia Rivers, for example. In Alaska, the clear cutting of timber in the Tongass National Forest endangered the environmental health of streams upon which salmon depended. Likewise, mining enterprises sometimes threatened fisheries. Beginning in 2008, the expected development of a large gold and copper mine in southwestern Alaska, the Pebble Mine, created divisions. Opponents— mainly fishers and environmentalists, who feared that the mine's discharges might pollute salmon-rich Bristol Bay—placed a measure on the statewide ballot prohibiting such developments. In a hotly contested election, the ballot issue went down to defeat, killed by the argument that the mine would create thousands of sorely needed jobs.[32] The divisions are not yet resolved. Similarly, fishers and environmentalists sought over the years to prevent offshore oil drilling in Bristol Bay and were relieved when the administration of President Barack Obama announced in early 2009 that it would continue a moratorium begun in 1998 banning offshore drilling in that area.[33]

Most recently, seafood chains have become complicated with the entrance of large retailers as forces for sustainability. When Wal-Mart executives talk, fishers and fish processors listen. The growing insistence of such retailers that the fish they sell come from sustainable sources has had a major impact on the seafood industry. It has been greater, for example, than the similar role some American retailers have had on the tropical timber industry, with their insistence that the timber they sell come only from sustainable sources. The increasing dominance of a few large retailers, such as Wal-Mart, in retail seafood sales gives those retailers a greater voice in sustainability matters than that exercised by lumberyards in the more atomized timber-products industry.

Sustainable developments in American seafood are in line with what many scholars see as the growing importance since World War II, and especially since the 1960s, of consumerism in environmentalism. Many Americans have come to view clean air, clean water, and so on almost as birthrights like consumer goods. More than that, Americans have come to see nature itself as a consumer product to be put to good use, as in national parks for sightseeing.[34] Fisheries, too, have reflected this trend. Consumers and consumer organizations such as the Marine Stewardship Council have played growing roles in defining fishery practices and are likely to continue doing so well into the future.

There is no doubt that changes have permeated American and global fishery practices in recent decades. Especially in those I have tried to examine in detail—the salmon, crab, and bottom fish fisheries of Alaska—alterations have been dramatic. From boom-time, frontier fisheries, they matured in just a few generations, with the exact rates varying by precise region and specie. Maturity did not, however, immediately bring stability. Instead, overfishing resulted, with wild swings in catches and prices. Only when new regulatory regimes based on catch limits and quotas were put in place and enforced did over-fishing end. The often invisible work (to consumers) of fishery councils—whose existence and decisions were based on political compromises—seemed likely to promise the endurance of seafood chains into the future. As difficult as they were establish and as imperfect as they seemed to participants in their actions, the councils were probably the best options available for fishers, processors, and consumers—not to mention fish.

APPENDIX: THE TOP-TEN U.S. SEAFOOD SUPPLIERS, 1999–2006, WITH SALES

1999	2002	2006
1. StarKist $1.25 billion	ConAgra $1.2 billion	Red Chamber $1 billion
2. Sysco $1.06 billion	Red Chamber $680 million	Trident Seafoods $925 million
3. Bumble Bee $750 million	Trident Seafoods $650 million	Pacific Seafood Group $874 million
4. Trident Seafoods 600 million	StarKist $630 million	Connors Brothers $784 million
5. Fishery Prods. Ltd $493 million	Pacific Seafood $595 million	Tri-Marine International $780 million
6. Red Chamber $460 million	Nippon Suisan $575 million	Nippon Suisan $730 million
7. Pacific Seafood $425 million	Ocean Beauty $500 million	Thai Union International $711 million
8. ConAgra Seafoods $410 million	Tri-Marine $475 million	Fishery Products $664 million
9. Tri-Marine $400 million	Fishery Products $472 million	StarKist $566 million
10. Gorton's $350 million	Chicken of Sea $445 million	American Seafoods Group $540 million

Sources: *Seafood Business* 19 (February 2000): 1; 20 (February 2001): 1; 21 (May 2002): 1; 22 (May 2003): 1; 23 (May 2005): 1; 24 (May 2005): 1; 25 (May 2006): 1; 29 (May 2007): 1.

ABBREVIATIONS

EEZ: exclusive economic zone
EU: European Union
FCMA: Fishery Conservation and Management Act of 1976
FDA: United States Food and Drug Administration
grt: gross registered ton
HACCP: Hazard Analysis and Critical Control Points
ICCAT: International Commission for the Conservation of Atlantic Tunas
IFQ: individual fishing quota
IPHC: International Pacific Halibut Commission
IPQ: individual processing quota
ITQ: individual transferable quota
mmt: millions of metric tons
mt: metric tons
MSC: Marine Stewardship Council
NEFMC: New England Fishery Management Council
NPFMC: North Pacific Fishery Management Council
TAC: total allowable catch
UNFAO: United Nations Food and Agriculture Organization

NOTES

Preface

1. One of the first experiences most Americans had with frozen seafood came in 1951, when Birds Eye introduced fish sticks, sales of which reached 7 million pounds two years later. See Shane Hamilton, *Trucking Country: The Road to America's Wal-Mart Economy* (Princeton, 2008), 126.

2. I use the gender-neutral term "fishers" throughout my study, a term increasingly employed by those writing about fishing. Many women in the fishing industry, however, prefer to be called women fishermen or simply fishermen, not fishers or fisherwomen. Some women have been outspoken on the topic. In 1999, Linda Greenlaw, the captain of a sword-fishing boat based in Gloucester, Massachusetts, observed of the word fisherwoman, "I hate the term, and I can never understand why people think I would be offended to be called a *fisherman*. . . . Fisherwoman isn't even a word." Continuing, she exclaimed, "I am a woman. I am a fisherman. As I have said, I am not a fisherwoman, fisherlady, or fishergirl." See Linda Greenlaw, *The Hungry Ocean: A Swordboat Captain's Journey* (New York, 1999), 11, 51. Greenlaw's vessel, the *Hannah Boden*, was the sister ship to the *Andrea Gale* portrayed by Sebastian Junger in his *The Perfect Storm* (New York, 1997). On gender terminology, see also David F. Arnold, *Fishermen's Frontier: People and Salmon in Southeast Alaska* (Seattle, 2008), xv; Leslie Leland Fields, *The Entangling Net: Alaska's Commercial Fishing Women Tell Their Lives* (Urbana, 1997), 7, 69; and Terry Johnson, *Ocean Treasure: Commercial Fishing in Alaska* (Fairbanks, 2003), 7.

3. For details on seafood chains, see Chapters 6 and 7.

4. The 1976 legislation is also often referred to as the Magnuson-Stevens Act, after Senators Warren Magnuson and Ted Stevens, who pushed it through the Senate.

5. Among my earlier works on those relationships in the Pacific are *The Politics of Business in California, 1890–1920* (Columbus, 1977); *Pioneering a Modern Small Business: Wakefield Seafoods and the Alaskan Frontier* (Greenwich, 1979); *The Lost Dream: Businessmen and City Planning on the Pacific Coast, 1890–1920* (Columbus, 1993); *Fragile Paradise: The Impact of Tourism on Maui, 1959–2000* (Lawrence, 2001); and *Pathways to the Present: U.S. Development and Its Consequences in the Pacific* (Honolulu, 2007).

6. In the 1970s, there were over 2,000 fish species in the North Pacific, including about 80 of commercial significance. In 1977, the North Pacific produced 28 percent of

the world's catch of wild fish. In 2008, the North Pacific still accounted for about 25 percent of the globe's harvest of wild fish, despite the development of new fisheries around the world. See Edward Miles, Stephen Gibbs, David Fluharty, Christine Dawson, and David Teeter, *The Management of Marine Regions: The North Pacific* (Berkeley, 1982), 3–4, 18, 21; UNFAO, "The State of World Fisheries and Aquaculture, 2008" (Rome, 2009), 11.

Introduction

1. Spike Walker, *Working on the Edge: King Crab Fishing on Alaska's High Seas* (New York, 1991), 235–37.

2. William McCloskey, Jr., *Breakers: A Novel About the Commerical Fishermen of Alaska* (Guilford, 2004), 164.

3. Introduction to "Global Fish Crisis," *National Geographic* 211 (April 2007): 33. For similar journalistic accounts, see *Economist*, 1 December 2001, 78; 17 May 2003, 70; 3 January 2009, 3; *U.S. News & World Report*, 22 June 1992, 64–75; *Wall Street Journal*, 25 November 1997, A1; 6 November 2003, A14. Awareness of over-fishing reached even the comic pages. In April 2008, Jim Toomey's syndicated strip "Sherman's Lagoon" ran a week-long series on over-fishing.

4. UNFAO, "State of World Fisheries, 2008," 7.

5. See R. R. Churchill and A. V. Lowe, *Law of the Sea* (Manchester, 1999), 280; Charles Clover, *End of the Line: How Overfishing Is Changing the World and What We Eat* (New York, 2006), 14; Edward Miles et al., *The Management of Marine Regions: The North Pacific* (Berkeley, 1982), 48. See also UNFAO, "The State of World Fisheries and Aquaculture, 2006," www.fao.org/docrep/009/A0699e/A0699E04.htm#4.1.2, accessed 29 September 2008. For fish consumption by region, see UNFAO, "State of World Fisheries, 2008," 60, 62, 154.

6. In 2008, William Cronon, a dean of environmental history, observed that "somehow the oceans and their many gifts to humanity have almost never received the attention from historians that their intrinsic importance merits." See William Cronon, "Foreword" in Arnold, *Fishermen's Frontier*, x; "Forum: Oceans of the World," *American Historical Review* 111 (June 2006): 717–80.

7. A reference to Larry McMurtry's *Lonesome Dove* (New York, 1985), a novel depicting a nineteenth-century cattle drive in the American West.

8. On salmon, see especially Joseph E. Taylor, III, *Making Salmon: An Environmental History of the Northwest Fisheries Crisis* (Seattle, 1999); David F. Arnold, *Fishermen's Frontier: People and Salmon in Southeast Alaska* (Seattle, 2008). On the salmon canning industry, see Chris Friday, *Organizing Asian American Labor: The Pacific Coast Canned-Salmon Industry, 1870–1942* (Philadelphia, 1994). For a comprehensive approach to fishery issues, see Arthur McEvoy, *Fisherman's Problem: Ecology and Law in the California Fisheries, 1850–1980* (Cambridge, 1986). For a fuller discussion of the literature on fishing, economic globalization, and food chains, see the bibliographic essay at the end of this volume.

9. Poul Holm, Tim D. Smith, and David J. Starkey, eds., *The Exploited Seas: New Directions for Marine Environmental History* (St. John's, 2001), xiii.

10. Elinor Ostrom, *Governing the Commons: The Evolution of Institutions for Collective Action* (Cambridge, 1990), is a pioneering study of common-pool resource management. Ostrom was one of the recipients of the Nobel Prize for economics in 2009. For an encyclopedic work, see Anthony Scott, *The Evolution of Resource Property Rights* (Oxford, 2008).

11. Jagdish Bhagwati, *In Defense of Globalization* (New York, 2004), offers a solid, if at times overly optimistic, introduction to many of the issues of economic globalization.

12. Warren Belasco and Roger Horowitz, eds., *Food Chains: From Farmyard to Shopping Cart* (Philadelphia, 2008), is an excellent introduction to the history of food chains. See also Philip McMichael, ed., *The Global Restructuring of Agro-Food Systems* (Ithaca, 1994).

13. In 1999, historians Christine Meisner Rosen and Christopher C. Sellers observed, "Business history has never paid much attention to the environment" and has given "little attention to the effects of resource extraction and use on plants, animals, land, air, or water, much less entire ecosystems and climate." See Christine Meisner Rosen and Christopher C. Sellers, "The Nature of the Firm: Towards an Ecocultural History of Business," *Business History Review* 73 (Winter 1999): 577–600, esp. 577. That situation has begun to change. Articles in *Business History Review* 73 (Winter 1999) examine relationships between business and the environment, as do those in *Enterprise & Society* 8 (June 2007). See also Christine Meisner Rosen, "The Business-Environment Connection," *Environmental History* 10 (January 2005): 77–79.

Chapter 1. Global Over-Fishing and New Regulatory Regimes

1. Linda Greenlaw, *The Hungry Ocean: A Swordboat Captain's Journey* (New York, 1999), 144–45.

2. Carl Safina, "The World's Imperiled Fish," *Scientific American* 24 (November 1995): 46–53, reprinted in *Environmental Management: Readings and Case Studies*, ed. Lewis A. Owen and Tim Unwin (Oxford, 1997), 28–34, esp. 28–30. See also Carl Safina, "Where Have All the Fishes Gone?" *Issues in Science and Technology* 10 (Spring 1994): 37–43.

3. See, for example, Daniel Pauly and Reg Watson, "Systemic Distortions in World Fisheries Catch Trends," *Nature* 414 (2001): 534–36.

4. Boris Worm, Edward Barbier, Nicola Beaumont, J. Emmett Duffy, Carl Folke, Benjamin Halpern, Jeremy Jackson, Heike Lotze, Fiorenza Micheli, Stepehn Palumbi, Enric Sala, Kimberley Selkoe, John Stachowicz, and Reg Watson, "Impacts of Biodiversity Loss on Ocean Ecosystem Services," *Science* 314 (3 November 2006): 787–90.

5. Michael J. Wilberg and Thomas J. Miller, "Comment on 'Impacts of Biodiversity Loss on Ocean Ecosystem Services,'" *Science* 316 (1 June 2007): 1285b. Comments on Worm et al.'s article by three groups of critics appeared on pp. 1285a–d, as did Worm et

al.'s replies to these critics, www.sciencemag.or/cgi/content/full/sci;316/5829/1285, accessed 10 November 2007.

6. UNFAO, "State of World Fisheries, 2008," 7, 36.

7. Oceana, "Too Few Fish," www.oceana.org/north-america/media-center/press-releases/press-release/0/777, accessed 2 June 2008.

8. While fishing greatly intensified in the twentieth century, human impact on fishing is longstanding. See Torbin C. Rick and Jon M. Erlandson, eds., *Human Impacts on Ancient Marine Ecosystems: A Global Perspective* (Berkeley, 2008). Historian Glenn Grasso has shown how the commodification of Atlantic halibut led to over-fishing and the near demise of that fish stock in the Northwest Atlantic well before industrial fishing methods came into use, concluding that "Overfishing was much more common in pre-industrial fisheries than most twentieth-century fisheries scientists have imagined." Glenn M. Grasso, "What Appeared to Be Limitless Plenty: The Rise and Fall of the Nineteenth-Century Atlantic Halibut Fishery," *Environmental History* 13 (January 2008): 66–91, esp. 67.

9. Edward Miles et al., *The Management of Marine Regions: The North Pacific* (Berkeley, 1982), 28.

10. Roberts, *Unnatural History*, 184–203.

11. Gary Kroll, *America's Ocean Wilderness: A Cultural History of Twentieth-Century Exploration* (Lawrence, 2008), 7.

12. UNFAO, "State of World Fisheries, 2006," 4

13. Greenlaw, *Hungry Ocean*, 27. On many fishing vessels, digital replaced analogue sonar in the 1980s and later; see Knut Sogner, "Innovation as Adaptation: The Digital Challenge in the Norwegian Fishing Industry, 1970–1985," *Business History Review* 83 (Summer 2009): 349–67, esp. 353.

14. Suzanne Iudicello, Michael Weber, and Robert Wieland, *Fish, Markets, and Fishers: The Economics of Overfishing* (Washington, 1999), 12, 17, 20–22; Roberts, *Unnatural History*, 305–15; Colin Woodard, *Ocean's End: Travels Through Endangered Seas* (New York, 2000), 238.

15. Callom Roberts, *The Unnatural History of the Sea* (Washington, 2007), 364. Roberts was a marine biologist at England's University of York. For more detail, see D. H. Cushing, *The Provident Sea* (Cambridge, 1988), chap. 13. However, on the continued importance of small-scale, nonindustrial fishing, see John Benson, *The Penny Capitalists: A Study of Nineteenth-Century Working-Class Entrepreneurs* (New Brunswick, 1983), 10–16.

16. *Columbus Dispatch*, 20 July 2008, A5; Churchill and Lowe, *Law of the Sea*, 280; Charles Clover, *End of the Line: How Overfishing Is Changing the World and What We Eat* (New York, 2006), 14; Miles et al., *Management of Marine Regions*, 48. See also UNFAO, "State of World Fisheries, 2006."

17. UNFAO, "State of World Fisheries, 2008," 58.

18. The top ten aquaculture nations in 2004 were, in descending order, China, India, Vietnam, Thailand, Indonesia, Bangladesh, Japan, Chile, Norway, and the United States.

See UNFAO, "World Fisheries Production, by Capture and Aquaculture by Country (2004)"; UNFAO, "State of World Fisheries, 2006," 3; UNFAO, "State of World Fisheries, 2008," 17. See also Clover, *End of the Line*, 252–69; Richard Ellis, *Empty Ocean: Plundering the World's Marine Life* (Washington, 2003), 22–23. On China's efforts to make its aquaculture, especially that for tilapia, more sustainable, see "China," *Seafood Business* 27 (5 May 2008). On opportunities for historical research on aquaculture, see Darin Kinsey, "'Seeding the Water as the Earth': The Epicenter and Peripheries of a Western *Aqua*cultural Revolution," *Environmental History* 11 (July 2006): 527–66, which looks especially at developments in France. For case studies of American aquaculture, see Barbara Brennessel, *Good Tidings: The History of Shellfish Farming in the Northeast* (Lebanon, 2008); Karni R. Perez, *Fishing for Gold: The Story of Alabama's Catfish Industry* (Tuscaloosa, 2006).

19. Clyde Cussler (with Paul Kemprecos), *White Death: A Novel from the NUMA Files* (New York, 2003), 260. For a survey of developments in genetic engineering of fish, see "Superfish," *Columbus Dispatch*, 26 April 2009, G3.

20. UNFAO, "Report on World Fisheries, 2008," 6–8, 23–25, 45.

21. Miles et al., *Management of Marine Regions*, 1.

22. Anthony Scott, *The Evolution of Resource Property Rights* (Oxford, 2008), chap. 4, presents an overview of the history of national and international laws and regulation of fisheries from Roman times to the present.

23. The UN Convention for the Regulation of the Meshes of Fishing Nets and the Size Limits of Fish, also called the North Sea Convention of 1946.

24. Cushing, *Provident Sea*, 225–26.

25. Miles et al., *Management of Marine Regions*, 52–82, esp. 53, 82.

26. William McCloskey, *Highliners* (New York, 2000), 336.

27. Harry N. Scheiber, "Taking Legal Realism Offshore: The Contributions of Joseph Walter Bingham to American Jurisprudence and to the Reform of Modern Ocean Law," *Law and Society Review* 26 (Fall 2008): 649–78.

28. Churchill and Lowe, *Law of the Sea*, chaps. 1, 9.

29. Miles et al., *Management of Marine Regions*, 121.

30. Churchill and Lowe, *Law of the Sea*, 13–21.

31. *Wall Street Journal*, 18 June 1974, A1; see also McCloskey, *Highliners*, 336.

32. Churchill and Lowe, *Law of the Sea*, 15–22, 160–80, 289. See also Francis T. Christy, Jr., and Anthony Scott, *The Commonwealth in Ocean Fisheries* (Baltimore, 1965), 153–74; Rognvaldur Hannesson, *The Privatization of the Oceans* (Cambridge, 2004); J. R. V. Prescott, *Political Geography* (New York, 1972), 116–41; Scott, *Evolution*, 166.

33. American officials especially disliked a provision creating an International Seabed Authority which required that nations share technical information about deep sea mining. However, by 2009–10 they were accepting this body, and observers thought "American ratification now seems only a matter of time." See *Economist*, 3 January 2009, 3; 16 May 2009, 29–31.

34. Terry Glavin, *The Last Great Sea: A Voyage Through the Human and Natural History of the North Pacific Ocean* (Vancouver, 2000), 175–97.

35. Terry Johnson, *The Bering Sea and Aleutian Islands: Region of Wonders* (Fairbanks, 2003), 141.

36. Miles et al., *Management of Marine Regions*, 120–26, 136–38.

37. For the texts of the FCMA and its revisions, see "Magnuson-Stevens Fishery Conservation and Management Act Reauthorized," www.nmfs.noaa.gov/msa2005/index.html, accessed 16 April 2009. For valuable contemporary commentary, see William McCloskey, Jr., "Board and Seize," *New York Times Magazine*, 7 March 1976, 13–17; William McCloskey, Jr., "The 200-Mile Fishing Limit," *Oceans* (September 1976): 60–63.

38. McCloskey, *Highliners*, 336–37.

39. *Fortune*, 29 February 1979, 52.

40. Nancy Freeman, "Alaska's Sea-Going Detectives," *Alaska Magazine*, April 1976, 18. See also "Wood, Field and Stream: The Task of Implementing New Fisheries Act," *New York Times*, 28 September 1976; "Tokyo Parley Seeking New Rules on Japanese Fishing Off the U.S.," *New York Times*, 9 November 1976

41. *Time*, 5 April 1976, 71.

42. "South Pacific Tuna Act of 1987," Hearing Before National Ocean Policy Study, Senate Committee on Commerce, Science, and Transportation, 100th Cong., 2nd sess.

43. McCloskey, "The 200-Mile Limit," 61; McCloskey, "Board and Seize," 86.

44. William McCloskey, Jr., to the author, 28 April 2009.

45. University of Alaska Sea Grant Program, "200 Miles," *Alaska Seas and Coasts* 4, 1 (15 February 1976): 5.

46. Miles et al., *Management of Marine Regions*, 150.

47. *Seafood Business*, 11 June 2007, 1, www.seafoodbusiness.com, accessed 18 April 2008 The Japanese vehemently protested the proclamation of the American EEZ, estimating that 1.6 mmt of their nation's 10-mmt annual fish catch came from within that zone; see *Wall Street Journal*, 11 November 1976, 38. On the composition and working of the eight American fishery councils, see Chapter 2 of this volume.

48. On regulation and deregulation, see Mark H. Rose, Bruce E. Seely, and Paul F. Barrett, *The Best Transportation System in the World: Railroads, Trucks, Airlines, and American Public Policy in the Twentieth Century* (Philadelphia, 2010). On trucking, see Shane Hamilton, *Trucking Country: The Road America's Wal-Mart Economy* (Princeton, 2008), chap. 7.

49. For a close examination of continuing federal subsidies to business during deregulatory times, see Richard M. Abrams, *America Transformed: Sixty Years of Revolutionary Change, 1941–2001* (Cambridge, 2006), 60, 265.

50. Anthony Scott, *The Evolution of Resource Property Rights* (Oxford, 2008), 162.

51. Garrett Hardin, "The Tragedy of the Commons," *Science* 162 (13 December 1968): 1243–48, is the classic statement. For valuable discussions of the tragedy of the commons in fisheries, see Clover, *End of the Line*, 141–65; Arthur McEvoy, *Fisherman's Problem: Ecology and Law in the California Fisheries, 1850–1980* (Cambridge, 1986), 10–12; H. Scott Gordon, "The Economic Theory of a Common-Property Resource: The Fishery," *Journal of Political Economy* 62 (April 1954): 124–42.

52. Scott, *Evolution*, 159, 163.

53. Kelly Feltault, "Trading Quality, Reducing Value: Crabmeat, HACCP, and Global Seafood Trade," in *Food Chains: From Farmyard to Shopping Cart*, ed. Warren Belasco and Roger Horowitz (Philadelphia, 2008) 62–83; Becky Mansfield, "Thinking Through Scale: The Role of State Governance in Globalizing North Pacific Fisheries," *Environment and Planning* 33 (Autumn 2001): 1807–27. See also McCloskey, *Raiders*, 284.

54. Carolyn Merchant, "Shades of Darkness: Race and Environmental History," *Environmental History* 8 (July 2003): 380–94. See also Robert Bullard, *Dumping in Dixie: Race, Class and Environmental Justice* (Boulder, 1990); Luke Cole and Sheila Foster, *From the Ground Up: Environmental Racism and the Rise of the Environmental Justice Movement* (New York, 2001); Martin Melosi, "Equity, Eco-Racism, and Environmental History," *Environmental History Review* 19 (Fall 1995): 1–16; David Pellow, *Garbage Wars: The Struggle for Environmental Justice in Chicago* (Cambridge, 2002).

55. On efforts by Native Americans to regain fishing rights, see Charles Wilkinson, *Blood Struggle: The Rise of Modern Indian Nations* (New York, 2005), 150–72, 198–204, 252, 268; Roberta Ulrich, *Empty Nets: Indians, Dams, and the Columbia River* (Corvallis, 1999). On similar efforts by Maori to regain their fishing rights in New Zealand, see Ranginui Walker, *Ka Whawhai Tonu Matou: Struggle Without End* (Auckland, 2004), 273–77, 283–84, 294–99, 312, 406.

56. Scott, *Evolution*, 181.

57. Interview by the author with Catherine McCarthy and Peggy Kohler, 13 May 2009.

58. William McCloskey, *Their Fathers' Work: Casting Nets with the World's Fishermen* (New York, 1998), 52.

Chapter 2. Successes and Failures in the Regulation of American Fisheries

1. Safina earned a B.A. in environmental studies from the State University of New York at Purchase, an M.S. in ecology from Rutgers University, and honorary doctorates from Long Island University in 2003 and the State University of New York in 2005.

2. Carl Safina, *Song for the Blue Ocean: Encounters Along the World's Coasts and Beneath the Seas* (New York, 1997). Earlier books prepared the way for Safina's work. See especially James R. McGoodwin, *Crisis in the World's Fisheries: People, Problems, and Policies* (Stanford, 1990); Suzanne Iudicello, Michael Weber, and Robert Weiland, *Fish, Markets, and Fishermen: The Economics of Overfishing* (1992; Washington, 1999). More popular was Michael L. Weber and Judith A. Gradwohl, *The Wealth of Oceans* (New York, 1995), prepared as an accompaniment for a traveling Smithsonian Institution exhibit about the ocean.

3. Safina, *Song for the Blue Ocean*, xiii–xiv.

4. Ibid., 123, 126, 146.

5. Ibid., 395.

6. UNFAO, "World Fisheries Production, by Capture and Aquaculture, by Country (2004)."

7. On the history of the North Atlantic cod, see Harold Innis, *The Cod Fisheries: The History of an International Economy* (New Haven, 1940); Mark Kurlansky, *Cod: A Biography of the Fish That Changed the World* (New York, 1997).

8. Ellis, *The Empty Ocean*, 60.

9. Rudyard Kipling, *Captains Courageous: A Story of the Grand Banks* (London, 1897).

10. "Taken wet, directly from the ocean, a cod's body weight typically contains eighteen percent protein. Dried, salted cod fillets with water weight evaporated can be composed of eighty percent protein," about twice the protein content of beef. Christopher P. Magra, *The Fishermen's Course: Atlantic Commerce and Maritime Dimensions of the American Revolution* (New York, 2009), 21.

11. Quoted in Ellis, *The Empty Ocean*, 66–67.

12. Ibid., 67.

13. Ibid.; Jeffrey Bolster, "Putting the Ocean in Atlantic History Maritime Communities and Marine Ecology in the Northwest Atlantic, 1500–1800," *American Historical Review* 113 (February 2008): 41; William W. Warner, *Distant Water: The Fate of the North Atlantic Fisherman* (New York, 1983), 50 (quote), 58.

14. Grant Winthrop, "U.S. Fishermen Gear Up for a Haul," *Fortune*, 29 February 1979, 53.

15. *Seafood Business*, 11 June 2007.

16. Sean T. Cadigan and Jeffrey A. Hutchings, "Nineteenth-Century Expansion of the Newfoundland Fishery for Atlantic Cod: An Exploration of Underlying Causes," in *The Exploited Seas*, ed. Holm, Smith, and Starkey, 31–66. On the mismanagement of cod, see also Dean Bavington, *Managed Annihilation: An Unnatural History of the Newfoundland Cod Collapse* (Vancouver, 2010). On the New England Fishery Management Council, see William McCloskey, *Fish Decks: Seafarers of the North Atlantic* (New York, 1990), 277–84.

17. See NEFMC, "About the NEFMC," and "Council Members and Staff," www.nefmc.org, accessed 2 February 2010.

18. On the growth of the snow crab population, see Clover, *End of the Line*, 18–20. For an earlier fishery "regime change," as biologists call it, see Grasso, "What Appeared Limitless Plenty," 70–71.

19. On Chatham cod, see Mark Kurlansky, *The Last Fish Tale: The Fate of the Atlantic and Survival in Gloucester* (New York, 2008), 152–53, 162.

20. E. Annie Proulx, *The Shipping News* (New York, 1993), 1. Proulx never gives Quoyle a first name. Other fictional accounts set in cod-fishing towns include Michelle Chalfoun, *The Width of the Sea* (New York, 2001); Donna Morrissey, *Sylvanus Now* (New York, 2005).

21. Proulx, *Shipping News*, 64–65, 85, 199, 291.

22. Ibid., 81–82

23. Ibid., 141.

24. Ibid., 256.

25. *New York Times*, 31 May 2009, A18.

26. *Columbus Dispatch*, 23 January. 2010, A8.The fishing permits (quotas) resembled medallions purchased by taxi drivers New York City. Both were exclusive permits to conduct business.

27. Ellis, *Empty Ocean*, 69; Woodard, *Ocean's End*, 86.

28. European Commission, Brussels, 16 October 2009, carried by AP.

29. Richard Ellis, *Tuna: A Love Story* (New York, 2008), 155, 246–47, 261.

30. Stephen Sloan, *Ocean Bankruptcy: World Fisheries on the Brink of Disaster* (Guilford, 2003). In the early 1980s, Sloan was asked by senator Alfonse D'Amato (R-N.Y.) to serve on the Marine Advisory Fishery Commission, chartered by Congress to advise the National Marine Fisheries Service. He did so, becoming its chairman, and went on to become a member of the U.S. delegation to the ICCAT. He also served on the boards of the International Game Fish Association and the National Coalition for Marine Conservation and chaired the Fisheries Defense Fund. A fly fisher, Sloan set 44 world records, including one for blue-fin tuna in 1966.

31. Ibid., 1–22.

32. Ibid.

33. Ibid., 168.

34. On continuing problems for blue-fin tuna, see *Economist*, 27 January 2007, 42; 29 November 2008, 83; Fen Montaigne, "Global Fish Crisis," *National Geographic* 211 (April 2007): 42–50. On how the decline in blue-fin tuna imperiled a Japanese fishing town, see *New York Times*, 20 September 2009, 6.

35. Ellis, *Tuna*, 126.

36. Ibid., 61–63, 125; Safina, *Song for the Blue Ocean*, 13–14, 43. See also Alessandro Bonanno and Constance Douglas, *Caught in the Net: The Global Tuna Industry, Environmentalism, and the State* (Lawrence, 1996).

37. Theodore Bestor, *Tsukiji: The Fish Market at the Center of the World* (Berkeley, 2004), 309; *Columbus Dispatch*, 18 April 2009, A7. On recent ICCAT actions, see "Bluefin, Bigeye Tuna Quotas Cut," *Seafood Business*, 12 January 2009.

38. *Economist*, 21 November 2009, 82–83.

39. *Columbus Dispatch*, 13 March 2010, A14; 19 March 2010, A5, A8.

40. "Bluefin Tuna: Another Possible Gulf Casualty," *Bloomberg Businessweek*, 28 June–4 July 2010, unpaged.

41. Quoted in *Columbus Dispatch*, 28 November 2010, A13.

42. Ellis, *Tuna*, 3–20, 242–34; *Economist*, 3 January 2009, 11. In the early 2000s, efforts were also being made to farm tuna, to raise them from eggs, with some initial successes; Ellis, *Tuna*, 268–81.

43. Ibid.

44. Woodward, *Ocean's End*, chap. 4.

45. Ibid., 106, 126. For a fictional look at a dying fishing town on Texas's Gulf of Mexico, see William J. Cobb, *Goodnight, Texas* (Denver, 2006).

46. On the dead zone and shrimp, see also Jack and Anne Rudoe, *Shrimp: The Endless Quest for Pink Gold* (Upper Saddle River, 2010), 197–203. Greenpeace is an

international environmental organization formed in 1971, according to its website, by "a group of thoughtful, committed citizens" to protest nuclear testing on Alaska's Amchitka Island.

47. *Wall Street Journal*, 14 November 2009, A3. With their nation a member of the World Trade Organization, members of Congress were officially committed to increasing freedom of global trade.

48. On how some localities and states passed laws aimed at lessening fertilizer runoff, often over the opposition of lawn care companies and farmers, see *Columbus Dispatch*, 7 May 2010, A12.

49. Robert J. Browning, *Fisheries of the North Pacific: History, Species, Gear & Processes* (Anchorage, 1974), 41–42; Friday, *Organizing Asian American Labor*, 8–11. For more detail, see Gordon Dodds, *The Salmon King of Oregon: R. D. Hume and the Pacific Fisheries* (Chapel Hill, 1963).

50. Safina, *Song for the Blue Ocean*, 263. On salmon in Californian waters, see also Stephanie S. Pincetl, *Transforming California: A Political History of Land Use and Development* (Baltimore, 1999). In hydraulic mining, nozzles blasted water at hillsides. Gold was removed from the sand and gravel, and the debris swept downstream.

51. Safina, *Song for the Blue Ocean*, 263–64.

52. Ibid., 266.

53. Michael Koepf, *The Fisherman's Son* (New York, 1998), 45.

54. Ibid., 13, 99.

55. Ibid., 146.

56. Ibid., 147.

57. Ibid., 285.

58. Safina, *Song for the Blue Ocean*, 266.

59. *Economist*, 15 April 2006, 36–37.

60. *San Francisco Chronicle*, 20 February 2010, A9.

61. *San Jose Mercury News*, 17 July 2008, 1. I want to thank Martha Fulton for newspaper clippings about fishing in Californian waters.

62. *San Francisco Chronicle*, 13 September 2009, A10.

63. Ibid., 9 April 2009, A1.

64. For reports on the closures, see "Alaska Salmon Catch Expected to Drop," *Seafood Business*, 18 April 2008; *Seafood Business* 28 (May 2009): 8.

65. *San Jose Mercury News*, 17 July 2008, 1.

66. *Economist*, 24 October 2009, 27–29. State and federal officials also put in place a system to try to keep fish out of the delta pumps. See *San Francisco Chronicle*, 16 May 2009, A1.

67. *Wall Street Journal*, 7 February 2011, A3. Sardines were another California fishery that suffered from a complex combination of environmental changes and overfishing. Once the state's largest fishery, sardines precipitously declined in the 1930s, 1940s, and 1950s. See especially McEvoy, *Fisherman's Problem*; also Connie Y. Chang, *Shaping the Shoreline: Fisheries and Tourism on the Monterey Coast* (Seattle, 2008).

68. In 1972, 907 Japanese and 544 Soviet vessels worked Alaskan waters. As late as 1975, distant-water vessels, mainly Japanese and Soviet, accounted for 78 percent of the seafood harvest in the Northeast Pacific, up from just 57 percent ten years earlier. The United States and Canada accounted for only 22 percent, down from 43 percent a decade before. In 1978, foreign distant-water vessels still took the lion's share of the catch in American waters, nearly all of it bottom fish (as much as 95 percent by weight). See Brad Matsen, *Fishing Up North: Stories of Luck and Loss in Alaska's Waters* (Anchorage, 1998), 72.

69. McCloskey, *Highliners*, 4; McCloskey, *Breakers*, 126; Miles et al., *Management of Marine Regions*, 226–29, 244, 252–56, 275. On enforcement of foreign quotas by the coast guard, see Nancy Freeman, "Alaska's Sea-Going Detectives," *Alaska Magazine*, April 1976, 18–22, 57.

70. *Columbus Dispatch*, 15 August 2009, A6.

71. Miles et al., *Management of Marine Regions*, 158.

72. McCloskey, *Breakers*, 126.

73. On how the NPFMC has operated, see ibid., 63–79; and McCloskey, *Their Father's Work*, 46–48, 287–90, 316, 33–32, 344. On membership, see NPFMC, "Membership," www.fakr.noaa.gov/npfmc/membership/council/council_membership.htm, accessed 29 April 2008.

74. NPFMC, "Membership."

75. Interview by the author with Joseph Plesha, 21 September 2009.

76. McCloskey, *Raiders*, 131.

77. NPFMC, "Council Meeting FAQ," www.fakr.noaa.gov/npfmc, accessed 23 January 2008. For a look at a typical NPFMC meeting, day-by-day, see "No. Pacific Fish Council Meets," *Kodiak Daily Mirror*, 27 March 2008.

78. See NPFMC homepage, www.npfmc.com, accessed 2 April 2008.

79. For valuable commentary on the planning process, see McCloskey, "200-Mile Limit," 61.

80. Ibid.

81. Ibid. For the details on the evolving regulation of king crabbing, see Chapter 4 of this study.

82. McCloskey, *Breakers*, xv.

83. Johnson, *Ocean Treasure*, 1, 79; McCloskey, *Highliners*, 1–2; Miles et al., *Management of Marine Regions*, 4. For recent figures on the Alaskan catch, see *Economist*, 3 January 2009, 12. Earnings nearly doubled between 2002 and 2007.

84. Paula Cullenberg, ed., *Alaska's Fishing Communities: Harvesting the Future* (Fairbanks, 2007), 16–17.

85. Johnson, *Bering Sea*, 1.

86. Iudicello, Weber, and Wieland, *Fish, Markets, and Fishers*, 13, 17; Andrew Rosenberg, Jill H. Swasey, and Margaret Bowman, "Rebuilding US Fisheries: Progress and Problems," *Frontiers in Ecology and the Environment* 4 (2006): 303–8. See also UNFAO, "World Fisheries Production (2004)."

87. Care2 Petition Site, "Action Alert," www.care2.com, accessed 21 September 2008.

Chapter 3. Salmon Fishing: From Open Access to Limited Entry

1. Bert Bender, *Catching the Ebb: Drift-Fishing for a Life in Cook Inlet* (Corvallis, 2008), 6.

2. The term "salmon" is used to cover all three members of the biological family Salmonidae: trout, char, and Pacific salmon. Biologically, the "salmon" of Nova Scotia and Newfoundland are actually trout, as are other Atlantic salmon. Pacific fishers pursue five major varieties of salmon—king (Chinook), chum (dog), Coho (silver), sockeye (red), and pink (humpback)—taking them during the summer and fall. A sixth type of Pacific salmon occurs only in Japan and the nearby mainland of Asia. All Pacific salmon are anadromous: they hatch from eggs in fresh water, swim down rivers to salt water, where they mature and feed for several years, and return to fresh water to spawn and die. See McCloskey, *Highliners*, 76; and Browning, *Fisheries of the North Pacific*, 37–38.

3. Browning, *Fisheries of the North Pacific*, 37.

4. Ibid.,. 41; Samuel Elliot Morrison, "New England and the Opening of the Columbia Salmon Trade, 1830," *Oregon Historical Quarterly* 28 (1927): 111–32.

5. Friday, *Organizing Asian American Labor*, 2.

6. Browning, *Fisheries of the North Pacific*, 41–42; Friday, *Organizing Asian American Labor*, 8–11. For more detail, see Dodds, *Salmon King of Oregon*. Other firms led the way in establishing canneries on Puget Sound, with the first constructed in 1877; there were 41 by 1915. For markets, see Suzanne Friedberg, *Fresh: A Perishable History* (Cambridge, 2009), 245.

7. Report cited in Browning, *Fisheries of the North Pacific*, 42. A case was forty-eight pounds. On the operations of the canneries and the nature of their labor forces, see Friday, *Organizing Asian American Labor*, esp. 25–47. On fishing gear and catches, see also Friedberg, *Fresh*, 246.

8. Taylor, *Making Salmon*, 63–67, 140, esp. 63.

9. Ibid., 14, 23–24, 38.

10. Ibid., 3, 5.

11. The major problem was not foreign fishing. In fact, there was considerable cooperation. Set up by the United States and Canada in 1930 (and broadened in 1956), the International Pacific Salmon Fisheries Commission sought to preserve salmon runs in Canada's Fraser River system. The commission divided catches evenly between fishers of the two nations. A bilateral treaty handled salmon disputes between the United States and Canada after 1985. See Miles et al., *Management of Marine Regions*, 63–75; M. P. Sheppard and A. W. Argue, *The 1985 Pacific Salmon Treaty: Sharing Conservation Burdens and Benefits* (Vancouver, 2005); and Austin Williams, "The Pacific Salmon Treaty: A Historical Analysis and Prescription for the Future," *Journal of Environmental Law and Litigation* 22 (2007): 153–95.

12. In addition to Taylor, *Making Salmon*, see James A. Lichatowich, *Salmon Without Rivers: A History of the Pacific Salmon Crisis* (Washington, 1999); Courtland L. Smith, *Salmon Fishers of the Columbia* (Corvallis, 1979).

13. Taylor, *Making Salmon*, 68–165, 206, 212, 235, provides a close look at hatchery problems.

14. Browning, *Fisheries of the North Pacific*, 37, 40.

15. Safina, *Song for the Blue Ocean*, 123, 126, 146.

16. Browning, *Fisheries of the North Pacific*, 39.

17. Taylor, *Making Salmon*, 241.

18. *Columbus Dispatch*, 26 October 2008, A13.

19. On the origins of Native American activism in the 1950s and 1960s, see Daniel M. Cobb, *Native Activism in Cold War America: The Struggle for Sovereignty* (Lawrence, 2009).

20. Much has been written about Native American fishing rights. See Wilkinson, *Blood Struggle*, especially chapters 7 and 12. For a detailed look at Native American efforts to reclaim fishing rights on the Columbia River, see Ulrich, *Empty Nets*, which examines how Native Americans won some fishing sites on the river in compensation for others flooded by dam construction. See also Cain Allen, "Replacing Salmon: Columbia River Indian Fishing Rights and the Geography of Fisheries Mitigation," *Oregon Historical Quarterly* 104 (Summer 2003): 196–227. On developments in Canada, see Douglas C. Harris, *Landing Native Fisheries: Indian Preserves and Fishing Rights in British Columbia, 1849–1925* (Vancouver, 2009).

21. On the fish-ins, see Paul Chaat Smith and Robert Allen Warrior, *Like a Hurricane: The Indian Movement from Alcatraz to Wounded Knee* (New York, 1996), 44–46, 59–60. For more detail, see Bradley G. Shreve, "'From Time Immemorial': The Fish-in Movement and the Rise of Intertribal Activism," *Pacific Historical Review* 78 (August 2009): 403–34, esp. 406.

22. Craig Lesley, *River Song: A Novel* (New York, 1989).

23. Browning, *Fisheries of the North Pacific*, 43.

24. Richard Cooley, *Politics and Conservation: The Decline of Alaska Salmon* (New York, 1963); Anthony Netboy, *The Salmon: Their Fight for Survival* (Boston, 1974), chap. 13; and Friedberg, *Fresh*, 246–47. For a valuable contemporary work, see C. L. Andrews, "The Salmon of Alaska," *Washington Historical Quarterly* 9 (October 1918): 243–54.

25. On Hoover's actions generally, see Ellis Hawley, "Herbert Hoover, The Commerce Secretariat, and the Vision of an Associative State, 1921–1928," *Journal of American History* 61 (June 1974): 116–40. See also Ellis Hawley, "Three Facets of Hooverian Associationalism: Lumber, Aviation, and the Movies, 1921–1930," in *Regulation in Perspective: Historical Essays*, ed. Thomas K. McCraw (Cambridge, 1981), 95–123.

26. Stephen Haycox, *Frigid Embrace: Politics, Economics and Environment in Alaska* (Corvallis, 2002), 33, 46–47; Claus-M. Naske and Herman E. Slotkin, *Alaska: A History of the 49th State* (Norman, 1987), 103–5. For more detail, see Joseph E. Taylor, III, "Well-Thinking Men and Women: The Battle for the White Act and the Meaning of Conservation in the 1920s," *Pacific Historical Review* 71 (August 2002): 357–87.

27. Miles et al., *Management of Marine Regions*, 29–30.

28. Ibid., 55–63, esp. 55 (quote), 63. Scientists thought at the time that no salmon from Alaskan or Canadian streams migrated farther west than the 175th meridian, but later studies showed that in fact some did.

29. Churchill and Lowe, *Law of the Sea*, 316; Miles et al., *Management of Marine Regions*, 140–41, 170–71.

30. Matsen, *Fishing Up North*, 84–85, and McCloskey, *Their Fathers' Work*, 276–79, look at early salmon fishing on Bristol Bay.

31. McCloskey, *Highliners*, 80.

32. Ibid., 81.

33. Bill McCloskey, "Coming of Age in Alaska," *National Fisherman* (October 2000): 29–35, esp. 28.

34. Joe Upton, *Alaska Blues: A Fisherman's Journal* (Anchorage, 1977); Francis E. Caldwell, *Pacific Troller: Life on the Northwest Fishing Grounds* (Anchorage, 1978).

35. Caldwell, *Pacific Troller*, 4, 11, 85. Anyone interested in the details of trolling for salmon in the 1950s–1970s will find the photographs and diagrams in this account valuable.

36. Ibid., 41, 62, 70, 75–76, 116.

37. Ibid., 48–51.

38. Ibid., 13–14, 64.

39. Upton, *Alaska Blues*, 8, 96, 221. For the story of another gillnetter, see J. P. Tracy, *Low Man on a Gill-netter* (Anchorage, 1977). Valuable photographs, maps, and illustrations grace each account.

40. Upton, *Alaska Blues*, 44, 201, 207.

41. Ibid., 70, 136–37.

42. Ibid., 93–95.

43. Ibid., 22, 44, 60–61, 67, 88, 95, 103, 112, 119, 160.

44. Ibid., 183.

45. Ibid., 130, 216

46. McCloskey, *Highliners*, 2. On destructive logging, see especially Kathie Durbin, *Tongass: Pulp Politics and the Fight for the Alaskan Rain Forest* (Corvallis, 1999).

47. Bob Durr, *Down in Bristol Bay: High Tides, Hangovers, and Harrowing Experiences on Alaska's Last Frontier* (New York, 1999), xiii, 14, 24.

48. Ibid., 53, 92, 99, 138.

49. Ibid., 164.

50. Ibid., 72.

51. Ibid., xv, 38, 77, 147.

52. Ibid., 203.

53. The information, including all quotations, about Steve Fink's fishing experiences comes from an interview by the author with Fink on 22 June 2009.

54. McCloskey, *Highliners*, 3, 10.

55. Government bodies also limited the length of fishing boats. From the mid-1920s, federal regulations defined "Alaska limit" boats for purse seining. These vessels

came to be defined as no longer than 58 feet. Similarly, as we have seen, government officials restricted gillnetters in Bristol Bay to 32 feet.

56. Upton, *Alaska Blues*, 126.

57. Matsen, *Fishing Up North*, 27.

58. McCloskey, *Their Fathers' Work*, 265.

59. Ibid., 27–28.

60. Sig Hansen (with Mark Sundeen), *North by Northwestern: A Seafaring Family on Deadly Alaskan Waters* (New York, 2010), 16.

61. Matt Jenkins, "The Source," *Nature Conservancy* 59 (Summer 2009): 38. Since salmon fishers harvested their catches in summer and fall months, they generally avoided much accumulation of ice on their vessels. Icing, by contrast, caused tremendous problems for fishers taking crab and bottom fish, for they worked mainly in late fall, winter, and spring months.

62. Browning, *Fisheries of the North Pacific*, 44, 106; Johnson, *Ocean Treasure*, 11.

63. Arnold, *Fishermen's Frontier*, 161.

64. Iudicello, Weber, and Wieland, *Fish, Markets, and Fishermen*, 93.

65. Arnold, *Fishermen's Frontier*, 157.

66. Cullenberg, ed., *Alaska's Fishing Communities*, 31–33.

67. Iudicello, Weber, and Wieland, *Fish, Markets, and Fishermen*, 96.

68. Bender, *Catching the Ebb*, 34.

69. Ibid., 67–69.

70. Fields, *Entangling Net*, 14–27, esp. 18.

71. Ibid., 28–51, esp. 36.

72. Ibid., 52–71, esp. 54.

73. "Sarah Palin," *Seafood Business*, 3 June 2009. On set-net fishing from beaches, see Bill Carter, *Red Summer: The Danger, Madness, and Exaltation of Salmon Fishing in a Remote Alaskan Village* (New York, 2008). Carter was a set-netter for four summers in the early and mid-2000s in the village of Egegik on the Alaskan Peninsula fronting on Bristol Bay.

74. Fields, *Entangling Net*, 19. By 1986, a permit to fish for salmon in Bristol Bay might cost as much as $300,000: McCloskey, *Their Fathers' Work*, 275.

75. Arnold, *Fishermen's Frontier*, 170–72.

76. Bender, *Catching the Ebb*, 94.

77. Bestor, *Tsukiji*, 46–47; Matsen, *Fishing up North*, 88–93.

78. McCloskey, *Breakers*, 70, 260.

79. Matsen, *Fishing up North*, 46.

80. Robert J. Browning, "1976 A Good Year for Most Concerned with the Northwest Salmon Industry," *Pacific Packers Report* 72 (1977): 5.

81. Matt Jenkins, "Salmon Country," *Nature Conservancy* 59 (Summer 2009): 54. On harvest trends for 2008–2009, see also "Fisheries Had Their Challenges," *Anchorage Daily News*, 1 January 2009; *Kodiak Daily Mirror*, 11 April 2008, 1; and *Seafood Business*, 18 April 2008, 1. See also "175 Million Salmon Expected," *Anchorage Daily News*, 17 March 2009; "Alaska Salmon Harvest to Increase," *Seafood Business*, 14 April 2009.

82. *Wall Street Journal*, 4 September 1996, A1. See also Freidberg, *Fresh*, 258.

83. Johnson, *Ocean Treasure*, 11. By salmon ranching, Johnson meant raising young salmon from eggs in hatcheries, and then releasing them into the rivers running to the sea, not raising salmon in ocean pens for their entire lives. On the success of limited-entry salmon fishing in Alaska, see also Iudicello, Weber, and Wieland, *Fish, Markets, and Fishermen*, 97–98. For a more negative appraisal, especially about the harmful impact of global salmon fish farming on wild salmon sales and prices, see Arnold, *Fishermen's Frontier*, 181–85. See also Bender, *Catching the Ebb*, 24, 61, 234–35, 282. Bender sold his boat and his limited-entry permit in 1993, because he thought the prospects for salmon fishing were bleak, devastated by global competition from farmed salmon.

84. "Fishermen Close in on Predicted Catch Numbers"; "Fisheries Had Their Challenges."

85. "Dying Assets," *Economist*, 1 August 2009, 34; "Labor Difficulties Mount in Chile," *Seafood Business*, 13 February 2009; "Farmed Salmon Prices on the Rise," *Seafood Business*, 3 June 2009. On salmon aquaculture generally, see Freidberg, *Fresh*, 255–58. Genetically modified salmon raised still other issues. In fall 2010, the U.S. Food and Drug Administration opened hearings in Washington, D.C., on what would be the nation's first genetically engineered food animal, Atlantic salmon that incorporated DNA from other fish to make it grow twice as fast as its wild relatives. See *Columbus Dispatch*, 16 September 2010, A1; *Wall Street Journal*, 22 September 2010, A7.

86. *Anchorage Daily News*, 16 May 2008; *Seafood Business*, 6 June 2008; *South Florida Sun-Sentinel*, 29 May 2008.

87. Matsen, *Fishing Up North*, 157–59.

88. "Salmon Dining Aids Yup'ik Villages," *Anchorage Daily News*, 3 February 2009. See also Freidberg, *Fresh*, 236.

89. "Two More Regions Vote to Join RSDA," *Anchorage Daily News*, 27 September 2008.

90. Cullenberg, ed., *Alaska's Fishing Communities*, 59–60.

91. "Two More Regions Vote to Join RSDA."

92. On the plight of salmon in Kamchatka, see David Quammen, "Where the Salmon Rule," *National Geographic* 216 (August 2009): 28–55.

Chapter 4. King Crabbing: Catch Limits and Price Setting

1. Spike Walker, *Working on the Edge Surviving in the World's Most Dangerous Profession: King Crab Fishing on Alaska's High Seas* (New York, 1991), xvii–xxiii. For a close look at the roles the coast guard played in rescuing fishers in Alaskan waters, see Todd Lewan, *The Last Run: A True Story of Rescue and Redemption on the Alaskan Seas* (New York, 2004). For more recent first-hand accounts of the dangers of king-crab fishing, see Andy and Johnathan Hillstrand, *Time Bandit: Two Brothers, the Bering Sea, and One of the World's Deadliest Jobs* (New York, 2008); and Dan Weeks, *The Deadliest Catch* (Des Moines, 2008).

2. Patrick Dillon, *Lost at Sea: An American Tragedy* (New York, 1998).

3. Blackford, *Pioneering*, 2.

4. Unlike the smaller Dungeness crabs in the waters of the Pacific Northwest, king crabs are not true crabs, but members of the genus *Paralithodes* (crabs are members of the genus *Cancer*); they have different joint structures and fewer sets of legs than true crabs. Three major types of king crabs are harvested: red, blue, and golden. Similarly, tanner crabs (snow crabs), like king crabs, are not true crabs. They belong to the genus *Chionocectes* and, like king crabs, have different structures from true crabs. Both king crabs and tanner crabs were (are) large. In the early days of American fishing, king crabs often weighed five to ten pounds apiece and measured four to six feet across their extended legs. Tanner crabs were about half that size and weight. See Hansen, *North by Northwestern*, 163–64; McCloskey, *Highliners*, 265.

5. Blackford, *Pioneering*, 4.

6. William McCloskey to the author, 3 October 2008; McCloskey, *Highliners*, 266.

7. Blackford, *Pioneering*, 6–10.

8. Ibid.

9. Ibid., 1.

10. William H. Goetzmann, *Exploration and Empire: The Explorer and the Scientist in the Winning of the American West* (New York, 1966), esp. chap. 4.

11. For an examination of the importance of the federal government in Western American and Pacific developments, see Mansel G. Blackford, *Pathways to the Present: U.S. Development and Its Consequences in the Pacific* (Honolulu, 2007).

12. Blackford, *Pioneering*, 4–10. On the development of America's frozen-food industry, see Freidberg, *Fresh*, esp. chap. 1; Charles H. Harrison, *Growing a Global Village: Making History at Seabrook Farms* (New York, 2003); Shane Hamilton, "The Economies and Conveniences of Modern-Day Living: Frozen Foods and Mass Marketing, 1945–1965," *Business History Review* 77 (Spring 2003): 33–60. For more detail, see Chapter 7 of this study.

13. Blackford, *Pioneering*, 29–30. In the interests of transparency, I should note that my father, William Blackford, was captain of the *Deep Sea* for seven years in the 1940s and 1950s.

14. Blackford, *Pioneering*, 15.

15. Ibid., 32.

16. Ibid., 33–34.

17. Ibid.

18. Dillon, *Lost at Sea*, 7.

19. Ibid., chap. 3. On the early history of the king-crab industry, see also Sybil Beale, "The King Crab Industry of Alaska: An Economic Analysis," M.A. thesis, University of Washington, 1971.

20. McCloskey, *Highliners*, 268–69; McCloskey, *Their Fathers' Work*, 4. For a step-by-step look at catching crabs by pots in the 1990s and early 2000s, see Hansen, *North by Northwestern*, 126–35.

21. Blackford, *Pioneering*, 139–40.

22. Ibid., 141–44. To deflect criticism that it was a predatory outside interest, Wakefield Seafoods moved its headquarters to Alaska in 1960.

23. Blackford, *Pioneering*, 145–46; Johnson, *Ocean Treasure*, 10.

24. Hansen, *North by Northwestern*, 235.

25. Quoted in Blackford, *Pioneering*, 145; see also Dillon, *Lost at Sea*, 7. There were disagreements. Japanese and Soviet officials claimed that the crabs swam, were not attached to the continental shelf, and were thus fair game for any fishers. The American view prevailed. A bilateral agreement with Japan concluded in 1964 later extended significantly reduced the Japanese harvest, as did a similar agreement with the Soviet Union made in 1965 and extended in subsequent years. Quotas for foreign fishers were so low that by the early 1970s Soviets no longer fished for king crabs in waters above the U.S. continental shelf, and the Japanese sustained only a token fleet. Japanese crabbers found themselves excluded from fishing in waters above the Soviet Union's continental shelf at about the same time. See Miles et al., *Management of Marine Regions*, 53–54, 78–79, 99–100, 108.

26. Miles et al., *Management of Marine Regions*, 158.

27. Ibid., 168–69. There were two species of tanner crabs, bairdi and opilio, the former accounting for about 90 percent of the catch.

28. Ibid., 199–201.

29. Ibid., 203–5, lists Japanese joint ventures in seafood with American and British Columbia firms. See also, Dillon, *Lost at Sea*, 25.

30. McCloskey, *Highliners*, 270. See also Hansen, *North by Northwestern*, 125, 237–38.

31. Walker, *Working on the Edge*, 218.

32. Ibid.

33. Ibid., 157. On derby fishing, see also Hansen, *North by Northwestern*, 83.

34. Winthrop, "U.S. Fishermen Gear Up," 53.

35. Weeks, *Deadliest Catch*, 30.

36. Dillon, *Lost at Sea*, 42–43.

37. Walker, *Working on the Edge*, 87, 151–55.

38. Dillon, *Lost at Sea*, 7–8.

39. Walker, *Working on the Edge*, xvi.

40. Ibid., 50, 68, 116, 124, 173.

41. Ibid., 40–42, 64, 108, 165, 180, 208.

42. Andy Hillstrand and Johnathan Hillstrand, *Time Bandit: Two Brothers, the Bering Sea, and one of the World's Deadliest Jobs* (New York: Ballantine, 2008), 1, 9, 36, 52, 77, 106.

43. Weeks, *Deadliest Catch*.

44. Hansen, *North by Northwestern*, 10. Sig's father was born in Norway in 1938 and immigrated to the United States in 1958.

45. McCloskey, *Highliners*, 279.

46. For a first-hand account, see Hansen, *North by Northwestern*, 182.

47. Walker, *Working on the Edge*, 193–207.

48. Dillon, *Lost at Sea*, 15–16, 21, 27, 41–42, 78, 186–88, esp. 188.

49. On derby fishing and accidents in the king-crab industry, see Walker, *Working on the Edge*, 157, 165; Dillon, *Lost at Sea*, 7–8, 19, 60–61, 70–71, 115–17, 180.

50. Dillon, *Lost at Sea*, 9.

51. *Anchorage Daily News*, 30 March 2008.

52. Gerry Studds, a Democrat from Massachusetts, led the way for legislation in the House. Don Young of Alaska initially opposed it. On the safety legislation, see especially Dillon, *Lost at Sea*, 184–251; quote from 218–19. See also Johnson, *Ocean Treasure*, 45–46; McCloskey, *Their Fathers' Work*, 296–99; Spike Walker, *Nights of Ice: True Stories of Disaster and Survival on Alaska's High Seas* (New York, 1997), 86–87.

53. Dillon, *Lost at Sea*, 184–251; *Anchorage Daily News*, 30 March 2008. See also Hansen, *North by Northwestern*, 252–54.

54. *ABC News Online*, 25 April 2008, www.abcnews.go.com/Health/story, accessed 26 April 2008; *Anchorage Daily News*, 23 March 2008, 1, 30 March 2008, 1, and 25 April 2008, 1. See also *Kodiak Daily Mirror*, 30 March 2008, 1, and 1 April 2008, inside page. Fishing remained the nation's most dangerous occupation in 2007. Fishers suffered 112 fatal injuries per 100,000 workers, loggers 86, aircraft pilots and flight engineers 67, structural iron and steel workers 46. The average for all workers was 3.7 per 100,000. See "Fishing Is Fatal Less Frequently," *Anchorage Daily News*, 9 May 2009. On continuing problems with safety in fishing globally, see UNFAO, "State of World Fisheries, 2008," 92–93.

55. "Deadliest Catch Crew says Fishing isn't That Glamorous," *Anchorage Daily News*, 17 May 2009.

56. Hansen, *North by Northwestern*, 181.

57. *Anchorage Daily News*, 12 July 2008; and "Seeking a PFD Fishermen Will Actually wear," *Anchorage Daily News*, 10 April 2009.

58. Bill [William] McCloskey, "Coming of Age in Alaska," *National Fisherman* (October 2000), 28–31; and William McCloskey, Jr., to the author, 28 April 2009.

59. Interview by author with William McCloskey, 17 July 2009. Unless otherwise indicated, all quotations in this section are from this interview.

60. McCloskey, *Their Fathers' Work*, 8–9.

61. McCloskey, *Highliners*, 113.

62. Ibid., 113, 138–47.

63. Ibid., 166.

64. Ibid., 284.

65. McCloskey, *Breakers*, 35.

66. Ibid., 77–78.

67. McCloskey, *Raiders*.

68. Hansen, *North by Northwestern*, 251.

69. Johnson, *Bering Sea*, 169–78; Johnson, *Ocean Treasure*, 89, 100, 143–44; Nature Conservancy, *Newsletter*, Summer 2004, www.nature.org/magazine/summer2004/pribilof/features/art12831.html, accessed 11 June 2004.

70. C. Braxton Dew and Robert A. McConnaughey, "Did Trawling on the Brood Stock Contribute to the Collapse of Alaska's King Crab," *Ecological Applications* 15, 3: (2005): 919–41; Mark Zimmermann, C. Braxton Dew, and Beverly A. Malley, "History of Alaska Red King Crab, *Paralithodes camtschaticus*, Bottom Trawl Surveys, 1940–61," *Marine Fisheries Review* 71, 1 (2009): 1–22. I am indebted to C. Braxton Dew, a leading scientist for NOAA, for bringing these articles to my attention. C. Braxton Dew, email to the author, 12 June 2009.

71. C. Braxton Dew, email to the author, 11 June 2009.

72. Crab-catch figures may be found in NPFMC, "Summary of the North Pacific Fishery Management Council's Bering Sea and Aleutian Islands Crab Rationalization Program Submitted to the United States Congress, August, 2002," 2, www.fakr.noaa.gov/npfmc/current_issues/crab/BSAIcrab%20report%20to%20congress802.pdf., accessed 4 April 2008. See also Johnson, *Ocean Treasure*, 100; Matsen, *Fishing Up North*, 19; McCloskey, *Their Fathers' Work*, 349.

73. NPFMC, "Bering Sea and Aleutian Islands Crab Rationalization Program, August, 2002," 1, www.fakr.noaa.gov/npfmc/current_issues/crab/BSAIcrab, accessed 4 April 2008.

74. NPFMC to Congress, 2 August 2002, 2, www.fakr.gov/npfmc/current_issues/crab?BSAIcrab, accessed 4 April 2008.

75. *Wall Street Journal*, 1 January 2003, A11.

76. NPFMC, "Preliminary Draft of the Environmental Impact Statement for the Bering Sea and Aleutian Islands Crab Fisheries: Initial Council Review, November, 2003," 1, www.fakr.noaa.gov/npfmc/analyses/CRABEIS, accessed 23 Jan. 2008.

77. NPFMC, "Crab Rationalization Program Overview and Frequently Asked Questions, Updated June 6, 2007," www.fakr.noaa.gov/sustainablefisheries/crab/rat/progfaq.htm, accessed 2 April 2008.

78. Ibid. Imports affected prices. In 2008, Russia exported 31.4 million pounds of king crabs and 9.7 million pounds of snow crabs to the U.S. market. Canada exported 764,000 pounds of king crabs and 82.4 million pounds of snow crabs, China 1.7 million pounds of king crabs and 2.1 million pounds of snow crabs, and Norway and Argentina each 530,000 pounds of king crabs—all to the American market. See "King, Snow Crab," *Seafood Business*, 16 October 2009.

79. NPFMC, "Crab Rationalization, 2007."

80. "State Reveals Data on Fishing Trends," *Anchorage Daily News*, 6 December 2008; Hillstrand and Hillstrand, *Time Bandit*, 149–50. See also "Feds Consider Cuts in Snow Crab Harvest," *Anchorage Daily News*, 6 June 2009.

81. "King, Snow Crab."

82. NPFMC, "18–Month Review Bering Sea and Aleutian Islands Crab Management," 41, www.fakr.noaa.gov/npfmc/current_issues/crab/18MonthRev.pdf, accessed 4 April 2008.

83. *Seafood Business*, 11 June 2007, 1.

84. Cullenberg, ed., *Alaska's Fishing Communities*, 40–41.

85. Ibid., 44.

86. *Kodiak Daily Mirror*, 11 April 2008, inside page. Additional discussions may be found in *Kodiak Daily Mirror*, 28 March 2008, inside page.

87. "Fisheries Had Their Challenges," *Anchorage Daily News*, 3 January 2009.

88. McCloskey, *Their Fathers' Work*, 316.

89. Hillstrands, *Time Bandit*, 149–50.

90. Hansen, *North by Northwestern*, 254.

91. NPFMC, "Draft Report to Council Crab Advisory Committee, February, 2008," 7, 9, www.fakr.noaa.gov/npfmc/current_issue/crab/CrabCommittee_rept_108.pdf, accessed 30 March 2008. See also NPFMC, "Public Draft Review: Regulatory Impact Review and Initial Regulatory Flexibility Analysis of the Provisions of Modifying the Arbitration System, April, 2008," www.fakr.noaa.gov/npfmc/current_issues/cra, accessed 30 March 2008.

Chapter 5. Bottom Fishing: Quotas and Sustainability

1. Later, fishers used computerized fish finders that detected bubbles of air fish hold in their gills. Fishers were able to differentiate among cod, pollock, and other bottom fish with these devices. See Hansen, *North by Northwestern*, 160.

2. Miles et al., *Management of Marine Regions*, 5–6.

3. McCloskey, *Highliners*, 195.

4. Hansen, *North by Northwestern*, 98.

5. McCloskey, *Highliners*, 195, 210, 219–23.

6. Upton, *Alaska Blues*, 133.

7. Ibid., 196. Between 1926 and 1935, Canadians harvested 17 percent of the catch, Americans 83 percent; the distribution was 37 and 63 percent between 1946 and 1955; and 51 and 49 percent between 1966 and 1975. On the history of the IPHC, see Miles et al., *Management of Marine Regions*, 63–75, esp. 66.

8. Miles et al., *Management of Marine Regions*, 166; Cushing, *Provident Sea*, 291. The regulatory system changed, partially in response to Soviet and Japanese intrusions. The treaty creating the IPHC was renegotiated after 1976 to bring it into agreement with the FMCA. The IPHC continued under a new protocol agreed to by the United States and Canada in 1979. Thereafter, the IPHC and NPFMC worked to regulate halibut catches.

9. Freeman, "Alaska's Sea-Going Detectives," 31.

10. McCloskey, *Raiders*, 74, 90, 189; see also Dillon, *Lost at Sea*, 27.

11. Quoted in Winthrop, "U.S. Fishermen Gear Up," 54.

12. Matsen, *Fishing up North*, 212–14.

13. Browning, *Fisheries of the North Pacific*, 95.

14. Cushing, *Provident Sea*, 49. See also Gus Dagg, "Codfishing in the Bering Sea," *Alaska: The Magazine of Life on the Last Frontier*, September 1975.

15. "American Fishermen's Alaskan Woes," *Columbus Citizen Journal*, 18 May 1979.

16. Browning, *Fisheries of the North Pacific*, 95–96. Of the two spellings, pollack is the older.

17. McCloskey, *Breakers*, 68.

18. For details on catches of bottom fish in Alaskan waters by foreign fishers, see Miles et al., *Management of Marine Regions*, 229, 234, 259, 242–24, 251–56.

19. McCloskey, *Breakers*, 114–20. See also Hansen, *North by Northwestern*, 217.

20. McCloskey, *Breakers*, 114.

21. Ibid., 177–249, esp. 196.

22. Ibid., 146. For details on fishing methods, see especially Matsen, *Fishing up North*, particularly chaps. 9, 10.

23. Matsen, *Fishing up North*, 76–77.

24. Ibid.

25. Becky Mansfield, "Property Regime or Development Policy? Explaining Growth in the U.S. Pacific Groundfish Fishery," *Professional Geographer* 53, 3 (2001): 384–97. See also Miles et al., *Management of Marine Regions*, 177.

26. Mansfield, "Property Regime."

27. Ibid.

28. Ibid., 384.

29. NPFMC, "Summary of the Bering Sea and Aleutian Islands Groundfish Fishery Management Plan, March 31, 1997," www.fakr.noaa.gov/npfmc/fmp/bsai/BSAIFMP?bsfmp97.htm; NPFMC, "Summary of the Gulf of Alaska Groundfish Fishery Management Plan, August 2001," www.fakr.noaa.gov/npfmc/fmp/goa/GOASummary.pdf. See also NPFMC, "Groundfish of the Bering Sea and Aleutian Islands Area; Species Profiles 2001," www.fakr.noaa.gov/npfmc/summary_reports/species2001.pdf; NPFMC, "Groundfish of the Gulf of Alaska: A Species Profile," June 1, 1998," www.fakr.noaa.gov/npfmc/fmp/goa/GOAProfile.pdf; all accessed 8 April 2008. For comments on proposed changes to bottom-fish management in Alaska, see *Kodiak Daily Mirror*, 10 April 2008, inside page; see Churchill and Lowe, *Law of the Sea*, 295; Miles et al., *Management of Marine Regions*, chaps. 3–4; also *Seafood Business*, 15 June 2005, unpaged.

30. "Pacific Halibut," *Seafood Business*, 16 October 2009. In contrast, Canada limited the number of halibut-catching licenses to about 430 and early established a system based on ITQs. See Matsen, *Fishing up North*, 219–21.

31. Ibid.

32. *Columbus Dispatch*, 24 April 2010, A10, reprints the story from the *Seattle Times*.

33. Mansfield, "Thinking," 1815–17.

34. Mansfield, "Thinking," 1808. On the early history of the pollock industry, see also J. Anthony Koslow, "Anatomy of a Modern Fishery: The Bering Sea Pollock Fishery," *Marine Technology Society Journal* 10 (January 1976): 28–34.

35. Ibid.; Johnson, *Ocean Treasure*, 140; Mansfield, "Thinking Through Scale," 1823.

36. "Fish Council Rids Trawl Fleet of Unused License," *Kodiak Daily Mirror*, 10 April 2008.

37. Mansfield, "Thinking," 1817. On early bottom-fish joint ventures, see also Miles et al., *Management of Marine Regions*, 202–8.

38. Mansfield, "Thinking," 1819–20.

39. "Catching the Quota, March 16–21, 2004," *National Fisherman*, www.national fisherman.com, accessed 12 February 2008.

40. "Easter Sunday, March 27 Through March 29, 2005," *National Fisherman*.

41. "April 5 and 6, 2005," *National Fisherman*.

42. The information about Derek Lawson derives from an interview with him by the author on 5 August 2009. All quotations are from the interview.

43. The *Anchorage Daily News* and *Kodiak Daily Mirror* covered this disaster extensively. See especially "Rescuers Tell of Perilous Conditions," *Anchorage Daily News*, 26 March 2008; "Coast Guard Honors Crewman in Alaska Ranger Rescue," *Kodiak Daily Mirror*, 15 May 2008.

44. "Four Rescued After 15 Hours in Raft" and "Rescuer Fought Wild Water," *Anchorage Daily News*, 23, 25 October 2008.

45. "Katmai Survivors Recall Desperate Struggle," *Anchorage Daily News*, 28 October 2008.

46. Becky Mansfield, "Property, Markets, and Dispossession: The Western Alaska Community Development Quota as Neoliberalism, Social Justice, Both, and Neither," *Antipode* 39, 3 (June 2007): 479–99.

47. "Flatout Facts About Halibut," pamphlet (Fairbanks, n.d.).

48. Scott, *Evolution*, 173.

49. NPFMC, "Community Development (CDQ) Program," 1, www.fakr.noaa.gov/cdq/default.htm, accessed 8 April 2008. See also NPFMC, "Gulf of Alaska Rationalization Community Provisions, Revised as of June 5, 2005," www.fakr.noaa.gov/npfmc/current_issues?groundfish/GOACommProv605.pdf, accessed 4 April 2008.

50. Cullenberg, ed., *Alaska's Fishing Communities*, 63; "Firms That Fish Western Alaska Village Quotas Seek Tax Relief," *Anchorage Daily News*, 4 February 2009; Johnson, *Ocean Treasure*, 80.

51. Ibid.

52. "Platinum to Get Fish Processing Plant," *Anchorage Daily News*, 31 May 2009.

53. Cullenberg, ed., *Alaska's Fishing Communities*, 27, 47–49, 54.

54. "State House Passes Cod Resolution," *Anchorage Daily News*, 23 March 2009.

55. "Dutch Harbor Tops US Fishing Ports," *Anchorage Daily News*, 19 July 2008. Dutch Harbor remained the nation's leading seafood port in 2008; see "Dutch Harbor Top Port," *Anchorage Daily News*, 25 July 2009.

56. "Fisher Poets Ready to Read," *Kodiak Daily Mirror*, 12 March 2009.

57. This section is based on an interview conducted by the author with Catherine McCarthy and Margaret Kohler, 13 May 2009. McCarthy is Catherine's current married name; Kohler is Margaret's later married name. All quotations are from that interview.

58. "Long Criticized, Bottom Trawling Off Limits in Parts of the Bering Sea," *Anchorage Daily News*, 25 August 2008.

59. "Two Fleets Battle over Allocation of Halibut Catch" and "Plan to Split Catch Approved," *Anchorage Daily News*, 3, 5 October 2008. On conflicts between sports and commercial fishers, see also "Lawmakers Reject Palin Nominee for Fish Board," *Kodiak Daily Mirror*, 16 April 2009.

60. "Greenpeace Puts Pollock Fishery in Its Cross Hairs," *Anchorage Daily News*, 2 December 2008; *Economist*, 3 January 2009, 13. On the other hand, sablefish landings and quotas remained stable at about 29 million pounds annually. See "Sablefish Harvest Steady," *Seafood Business*, 12 January 2009.

61. "Feds Advise Slashing Pollock Catch by 18.5%," *Anchorage Daily News*, 13 December 2008.

62. "Feds Advise Slashing Pollock Catch"; "Alaska Pollock Quota Cut 18.5 Percent," *Seafood Business*, 12 January 2009.

63. Plesha interview.

64. UNFAO, "World Fisheries, 2008," 87.

65. "Council Outlaws Arctic Fisheries," *Anchorage Daily News*, 7 February 2009; "Arctic Fisheries Plan Approved," *Seafood Business*, 16 October 2009.

66. "Council Outlaws Arctic Fisheries."

67. James R. Skillen, *The Nation's Largest Landlord: The Bureau of Land Management in the American West* (Lawrence, 2009).

68. Plesha interview.

69. Clover, *End of the Line*, 280–96. On the work of the MSC, see *Economist*, 8 October 2005, 66; MCS, homepage, www.msc.org, accessed on 28 April 2008; MSC, "Certified Fisheries," www.mcs.org/html/content_484.htm, accessed 28 April 2008. See also Laine Welch, "Fisheries Say Long and Costly Eco-Label Worth the Effort," *Alaska Journal of Commerce*, 5 May 2005; *Seafood Business* 12 June 2007, unpaged.

70. *Seafood Business*, 15 June 2007.

71. *Kodiak Daily Mirror*, 7 July 2008, 1; "Alaska Pollock Quota Cut."

72. Margaret Bauman, "From Foreign Boats to Farmed Fish, Seafood Industry Weathers the Storm," *Alaska Journal of Commerce*, 24 June 2007.

73. "Overall, Fishing in'08 a Plus," *Anchorage Daily News*, 27 December 2008.

74. "Fisheries Had Their Challenges," *Anchorage Daily News*, 3 January 2009.

75. "Seafood Industry Takes Big Hits from Fuel Costs," *Anchorage Daily News*, 13 September 2008; "Fisheries Had Their Challenges."

76. Laine Welch, "Prices May Not Follow Economic Trends," *Anchorage Daily News*, 28 February 2009.

Chapter 6. The Companies: Controlling Food Chains

1. Peter Redmayne, "Frank Dulcich, President Pacific Seafood Group, Interview," *Seafood Business* 22 (October 2003): 86.

2. In this chapter, I am concerned mainly with America's leading processing firms, especially how and why they changed their operations and structures. However, it is worth reiterating that executives from some of these, such as Trident Seafoods, strongly supported sustainable limits on fishing. Arguing that only through total allowable catches could fishing methods be made sustainable, and worried about the future of seafood stocks, they helped sparkplug the movement toward sustainable fishing. As we have seen in previous chapters, company executives were voting members of the NPFMC and were influential in decisions that body reached.

3. Historical literature is growing but still sparse on the development of food chains—linkages of people, companies, technologies, and sciences connecting farms and boats to consumers—in the United States and throughout the world. See especially Warren Belasco and Roger Horowitz, eds., *Food Chains: From Farmyard to Shopping Cart* (Philadelphia, 2009).

4. "Seafood Processing and Distribution," 1, *Hoover's Industry Profiles*, www.premium.hoovers.com, accessed 16 March 2009.

5. The best estimates suggest that food industries employed 40 percent of the world's workers. See Warren Belasco, *Food: The Key Concepts* (New York, 2008), 20, 56.

6. On the development of cold chains, see Freidberg, *Fresh*, esp. chaps. 2, 3.

7. Scholars are just beginning to understand the impacts environmental issues, broadly conceived, have had on corporate growth. See Christine Meisner Rosen, "The Role of Pollution Regulation and Litigation in the Development of the U.S. Meatpacking Industry, 1865–1880," *Enterprise & Society* 8 (June 2007): 297–347. On how the environment affected companies drilling for oil in the Gulf of Mexico, see Tyler Priest, "Extraction Not Creation: The History of Offshore Petroleum in the Gulf of Mexico," ibid., 227–67.

8. It is only for those seven years that comprehensive comparative company data are currently available, collected and reported by the industry trade journal *Seafood Business*. See *Seafood Business* 19 (February 2000): 1; 26 (July 2007): 1; also 28 (May 2009): 18. It is not possible, given the sources available from the privately held processors, to tell exactly the proportion of sales made in the United States and abroad. Moreover, several top companies reported no sales information for 2007, 2008, or 2009. In 2007, the top twenty-five suppliers that did issue public reports made sales of $11.6 billion; their sales in 2008 totaled $11.5 billion, and in 2009, $11.4 billion. See "In Seafood We Trust," *Seafood Business*, 1 May 2010.

9. "Buying Quality Fish from China," *Seafood Business*, 5 May 2008.

10. Bestor, *Tsukiji*, 202, 203; Hoover's Online, "Maruha Nichiro Holdings, Inc.," 1, www.biz.yahoo.com, accessed 16 March 2009. Bestor lists the sales in yen for the six largest Japanese seafood companies in 1990, 1995, and 2000, 2003.

11. On Nippon Suisan, see "Investor Relations, Balance Sheet, 2006," www.nissui.co.jp/english, accessed 26 July 2007; also Hoover's Online, "Nippon Suisan Kaisha, Ltd.," 1, www.biz.yahoo.com, accessed 16 March 2009.

12. See Hoover's Online, "Kyokuyo Co. Ltd," 1, www.biz.yahoo.com, accessed 16 March 2009.

13. *Seafood Business* 19 (Feb. 2000): 1; 20 (Feb. 2001): 1; 21 (May 2002): 1; 22 (May 2003): 1; 23 (May 2005), 1; 24 (May 2005), 1; 25 (May 2006), 1. For 2006 sales, see *Seafood Business* 29 (May 2007): 1.

14. On StarKist's sales, see "Charlie Gets the Hook," www.forbes.com, accessed 7 July 2008.

15. On Unilever's earlier vertical integration backward into seafood, see Geoffrey Jones, *Renewing Unilever: Transformation and Tradition* (Oxford, 2005), 64–66.

16. Joe Plesha, "Trident Seafoods to Acquire ConAgra Surimi," *Chef2Chef*, 14 March 2006, unpaged, www.chef2chef.net, accessed 23 July 2007; *Seafood Business* 24 (April 2006): 1–2.

17. More was involved in ConAgra's exit from seafood than inability to deal with the over-fishing crisis. ConAgra's officers explained that the company was "refocus[ing] its portfolio of brands and businesses to produce strong long-term results. . . . Meat, produce, and cheese businesses such as Butterball, Armour, Echrich, Swissrose, and Louis Kemp [Seafoods]" were all being sold. See ConAgra, "Company Timeline," www.conagrafoodscompany.com/corporate/aboutus/company_history_timeline.jsp, accessed 26 September 2008.

18. *Seafood Business* 24 (May 2005), 1; 25 (May 2006), 1.

19. Ibid., 22 (October 2003): 86.

20. "Seafood Processing and Distribution," 1.

21. Thomas Peters and Robert Waterman, Jr., *In Search of Excellence: Lessons from America's Best-Run Companies* (New York, 1982), 292, coined this phrase.

22. Alfred D. Chandler, Jr., *The Visible Hand: The Managerial Revolution in American Business* (Cambridge, 1977).

23. Welch, "A Look."

24. "The Red Chamber Co.," www.redchamber.com; "Red Chamber Company Profile," www.premium.hoovers.com; and "Red Chamber Co.," www.forbes.com; all accessed 23 July 2007. See also Premium Hoovers "Red Chamber Company," 1–2, www.premium.hoovers.com, accessed 16 March 2009. In 2008, Tampa Bay Fisheries, a subsidiary of Red Chamber, was the sixteenth-largest processor for the American market, with sales of $305 million. See *Seafood Business* 28 (May 2009): 19.

25. Plesha interview. Plesha joined Trident Seafoods in 1988, becoming the firm's general counsel in 2008 and its chief legal officer a year later. See also Stephanie E. Ponder, "Success at Sea," *Costco Connection* 26 (Feb. 2011): 26–28.

26. Ibid.; "Trident Seafoods," www.tridentseafoods.com, accessed 23 July 2007. See also Hansen, *North by Northwestern*, 176, 246, 249–50.

27. Plesha interview.

28. At this time, Trident also invested a lot in marketing, trying to get branded seafood products into retail stores. See Plesha interview.

29. Cullenberg, ed., *Alaska's Fishing Communities,* 40; *Seafood Business* 20 (Jan. 2001): 1; 23 (June 2004): 6; 25 (April 2006): 1; Plesha interview; and Joseph Plesha email to the author, 15 September 2009. See also "Trident-Ocean Beauty Deal Off the Table," *Seafood Business,* 12 June 2007; "Icicle, Trident Partner with Salmon Farms," *Seafood Business,* 24 April 2007.

30. *Seafood Business,* 5 May 2008.

31. *Seafood Business* 28 (May 2009): 6.

32. Ibid., 18–22.

33. Ibid. Disaster struck one of the company's operations in summer 2008, when a fire destroyed Trident's large salmon-processing plant at Chignik Bay in the Aleutians about 450 miles southwest of Anchorage. Some 250 workers had to be evacuated, and a floating processor was sent in to temporarily handle some of the salmon the plant had put up. "Fish Plant Goes Up in Flames," *Anchorage Daily News,* 22 July 2008.

34. Plesha interview.

35. McCloskey, *Their Fathers' Work,* 282–84, 316–17, 332, esp. 283. In 2009, Trident's vessels included three specialized pollock catcher/processors and four or five ships that processed salmon and crab, as well as general-purpose fish-harvesting vessels for pollock, cod, and crabs. Plesha to author, 15 Sept. 2009. See also *Seafood Business* 28 (May 2009): 20.

36. NPFMC, "Home Page," www.npfmc.com/NPFMC.htm., accessed 2 April 2008.

37. *Seafood Business* 22 (Aug. 2003): 6.

38. *Seattle Times,* 16 July 2005.

39. *Seafood Business* 25 (September 2006): 4. See also *Seafood Business,* 4 May 2008; Ponder, "Success at Sea," 26.

40. "Trident Seafoods," www.tridentseafoods.com, accessed 16 March 2009.

41. Ibid.

42. "Pacific Seafood" contains a timeline of the company's history, www.pacseafood.com, accessed 23 July 2007.

43. *Seafood Business* 22 (October 2003): 86.

44. Ibid. See also Dian Cox, "Pacific Seafood Becomes Big Fish," *Portland Business Journal,* 3 February 1997, unpaged, www.bizjournals.com/portland/stories, accessed 23 July 2007.

45. For the details of Pacific Seafood's expansion, see "Pacific Seafoods," and "Pacific Seafoods Becomes a Big Fish." It is unclear how the expansion was financed, although Frank Dulcich, Jr., emphasized in several interviews at the time the need to maintain good relationships with bankers. See also Wendy Culverwell, "No Fish Tale," *Portland Business Journal,* 19 September 2008, reprinted www.pacseafood.com, accessed 16 March 2009.

46. *Seafood Business* 22 (October 2003): 86. On the recent status of Pacific Seafood Group, see also "Pacific Seafood," *Corporate Spotlight,* August 2005, 1, www.american executive.com/spotlights/sl.

47. Culverwell, "No Fish Tale."

48. Premium Hoovers, "Pacific Seafood Group," 1.

49. "Icicle, Trident Partner with Salmon Farms," *Seafood Business*, 24 April 2007.

50. See press releases on Pacific Seafood's website, www.pacseafood.com, accessed 16 March 2009. See also John Fiorillo, "Pacific Seafood Hunting for More Aquaculture Acquisitions," *IntraFish*, 20 November 2008, www.pacsefood.co, accessed 16 March 2009.

51. *Seafood Business*, 29 May, 5 May, 1 May 2009.

52. Ibid.

53. Ibid.

54. Ibid., 29 May 2007, 1.

55. Laine Welch, "A Look at the Top Seafood Firms Show Promising Future," *Alaska Journal*, 1 July 2007.

56. *Seafood Business*, 5 May 2008.

Chapter 7. Reaching Consumers: From Processing to Retailing

1. "The Waterfront Restaurant," www.waterfrontrestaurant.net/index.htm, accessed 7 March 2008.

2. The greatest profits were often made in processing, distributing, and selling fish, not in catching it. For instance, in the early 2000s fishers received 10 percent of consumers' dollars spent on salmon, tender operators 3 percent, headers and gutters (workers on the slime or processing line) 4 percent, processors 16 percent, shippers 3 percent, cold storage operators 3 percent, traders 4 percent, distributors 17 percent, filleters 17 percent, and retail stores 23 percent. See Johnson, *Ocean Treasure*, 119.

3. Freidberg, *Fresh*, 237.

4. McCloskey, *Breakers*, 39, 42–43.

5. Friday, *Organizing Asian American Labor*, 84–85.

6. McCloskey, *Highliners*, 236–37.

7. Johnson, *Ocean Treasure*, 116.

8. McCloskey, *Raiders*, 22.

9. Bender, *Catching the Ebb*, 87.

10. McCloskey, *Highliners*, 41–42, 238

11. Koepf, *Fisherman's Son*, 97–98.

12. Trident Seafoods, "Frequently Asked Questions," www.tridentseafoods.com/join_our_team/faqs.php, accessed 13 Feb. 2009.

13. Johnson, *Ocean Treasure*, 166.

14. Bender, *Catching the Ebb*, 61, 94.

15. UNFAO, "State of World Fisheries, 2008," 42–43.

16. Freidland, *Fresh*, 249.

17. Ibid., 249–53.

18. Hamilton, *Trucking Country*, 125.

19. Freidland, *Fresh*, 44–45, 249–53. Freon was synthesized in 1930.

20. Hamilton, *Trucking Country*, 118–28, esp. 125.

21. Johnson, *Ocean Treasure*, 118, 126; Browning, *Fisheries of the North Pacific*, 268.

22. "Keeping It Cold," *Seafood Business*, 9 April 2010.

23. Johnson, *Ocean Treasure*, 118, 126; "Seafood a Priority for Some Airlines," *Seafood Business*, 11 August 2009. Alaskan Airlines carried about 15 million pounds of seafood annually.

24. McCloskey, *Highliners*, 28.

25. Johnson, *Ocean Treasure*, 122–23.

26. Ibid.

27. Blackford, *Pioneering*, 25–26.

28. Ibid., 61; McCloskey, *Highliners*, 30–31, 268; McCloskey, *Breakers*, 132.

29. McCloskey, *Breakers*, 199.

30. Blackford, *Pioneering*, 61–62.

31. Ibid.

32. Trident Seafoods, "Shellfish," www.tridentseafoods.com/company/processing_shillfish.php, accessed 13 February 2009.

33. "Seafood Processing and Distribution," 1.

34. Matsen, *Fishing Up North*, 181, 187.

35. "Pacific Seafood Opens State-of-the-Art Processing Facility in Las Vegas," Press Release, Pacific Seafood Group, 22 September 2008, www.pacseafood.com/PressArticles, accessed 16 March 2009.

36. "Unlikely Middle Man Provides Connection for King Crab," *Anchorage Daily News*, 18 July 2009.

37. Jon Theiss, "Follow the Fish," *CityScene*, January/February 2011, 12–14.

38. Belasco, *Food*, 55, 58; Harvey Levenstein, *Paradox of Plenty: A Social History of Eating in Modern America* (New York, 1993), 101, 108. See also Shane Hamilton, "Introduction," *Business History Review* 83 (Summer 2009): 234.

39. Blackford, *Pioneering*, 43, 66–68.

40. Ibid., 69–70, 111–13. See also Hansen, *North by Northwestern*, 45–46. Sig Hansen's father was captain of the *Foremost*, owned by Wakefield Seafoods.

41. Walker, *Working on the Edge*, 144–45, 156–58.

42. Matsen, *Fishing Up North*, 89.

43. McCloskey, *Breakers*, 222.

44. Ibid., 251–53

45. Ibid. For relationships between salmon canneries and fishers, see also Bender, *Catching the Ebb*, 87–88.

46. Catherin Ziegler, *Favored Flowers: Culture and Economy in a Global System* (Durham, 2007).

47. For a discussion of the recent development of localized food chains and environmentalism, see Michael Pollan, *Omnivore's Dilemma: A Natural History of Four Meals* (New York, 2006), chap. 13.

48. "Scientists Look to Catch-Share System to End Overfishing," *Seafood Business*, 9 September 2009,

49. Freidberg, *Fresh*, 9–10, 261–62, 277–83, esp. 262. On the failure of Alaskan fishers to sell locally, see "Fishermen Show Little Interest in Dockside Sales," *Anchorage Daily News*, 9 August 2008.

50. "In Florida, the Seafood Business Becomes Less Local," *New York Times*, 30 March 2010.

51. Browning, *Fisheries of the North Pacific*, 265–72, esp. 265–66, 272; McCloskey, *Breakers*, 236, 238.

52. Ibid.

53. Kelly Feltault, "Trading Quality, Producing Value: Crabmeat, HACCP, and Global Seafood Trade," in Belasco and Horowitz, eds., *Food Chains*, 62–83. For more detail, see A. M. Pearson and T. R. Dutson, eds., *HACCP in Meat, Poultry, and Fish Processing* (London, 1996). On Trident Seafoods and HACCP, see Trident Seafoods, "Quality Assurance," www.tridentseafoods.com/company/haccp.php, accessed 13 February 2009. In 2009, FDA officials started working with those at the National Oceanic and Atmospheric Agency to further improve seafood safety in the United States. See "NOAA, FDA Partner on Safety," *Seafood Business*, 17 December 2009.

54. Blackford, *Pioneering*, 132.

55. Ibid., 133.

56. Mansel G. Blackford, *The Politics of Business in California, 1890–1920* (Columbus, 1977), 21–29.

57. Blackford, *Pioneering*, 133–34.

58. Ibid., 135–36. Lowell Wakefield also actively sought quality-control legislation from Congress in the mid- and late 1960s, to no avail. Many smaller seafood companies opposed any such legislation then as too costly.

59. Becky Mansfield, "Fish, Factory Trawlers, and Imitation Crab: The Nature of Quality in the Seafood Industry," *Journal of Rural Studies* 19 (2003): 9–21, esp. 10–11.

60. Ibid., 13–15.

61. Ibid., 15.

62. Ibid., 16–17.

63. Ibid, 18–19.

64. Ibid., 19.

65. "About Us," www.ljsilvers.com, accessed 7 March 2008. The company had 1,200 outlets worldwide.

66. *Seafood Business*, 15 June 2007. There were 500 outlets.

67. Sloan, *Ocean Bankruptcy*, 106.

68. Clover, *End of the Line*, 188–97.

69. "Wegmans Says 'No' to Billfish," *Seafood Business*, 7 July 2009.

70. *Maui News*, 19 March 2007, A3; 21 March 2007, A3.

71. Matsen, *Fishing up North*, 158–59.

72. "Competition Crunch," *Seafood Business*, 6 June 2008.

73. "Alaska Salmon Will Hit Wal-Mart Freezers," *Anchorage Daily News*, 23 November 2009; *Seafood Business*, 15 June 2007; "Whole Foods to Post Seafood Environmental Ratings," *Tulsa World*, 14 September 2010.

74. Ibid.

75. "Retailers Laud FDI policy," *Seafood Business*, 14 April 2009.

76. *Columbus Dispatch*, 27 January 2010, A11; "Kroger Taps WWF for Sustainability," *Seafood Business*, 17 December 2009.

77. "Buyer-NGO Partnerships Propel Sustainable Seafood Movement," *Seafood Business*, 9 November 2009.

78. On the origins of the MSC, see Churchill and Lowe, *Law of the Sea,* 323. The MSC was not the only such body. For a list of organizations certifying seafood as being caught in sustainable ways, see UNFAO, "State of World Fisheries, 2008," 96–100. In 2008–2010, there was some effort to establish a global organization that would certify aquaculture fisheries as sustainable. See ibid., 101; "NGOs Oppose Aquaculture Stewardship Council," *Seafood Business*, 7 July 2009; "WWF, GlobalGAP to form Aquaculture Council," *Seafood Business* 11 August 2009.

79. "People in the News," *Seafood Business*, 28 January 2008.

80. "Greenpeace Re-Releases Retail Report," *Seafood Business*, 12 January 2009.

81. Feltault, "Trading Quality, Producing Value."

82. Ibid.

83. *San Francisco Chronicle*, 10 August 2008, D1, D6.

84. Ibid.

Conclusion

1. "Crabber Profits from Curious Tourists," *Anchorage Daily News*, 22 June 2008.

2. Another example of fishing becoming tourism occurred at Ward Cove on Alaska's Kenai Peninsula. The Columbia Wards Fisheries salmon-canning plant there closed in 1998, but was reborn in the early 2000s as a tourist lodge and shops. See Bender, *Catching the Ebb*, 24–25.

3. Scott, *Evolution*, 166–67, 172–74. On Iceland's success in achieving sustainable fishing, see *Anchorage Daily News*, 3 January 2009, 15–16.

4. Hannesson, *Privatization of the Oceans*, 85–162; Iudicello, Weber, and Wieland, *Fish, Markets, and Fishermen*, 89–159. On New Zealand's recent success, see Kennedy Warne, "Blue Haven," *National Geographic* 211 (April 2007): 70–81. For a summary of the literature on reserves, see Roberts, *Unnatural History*, 350–77. For a case study on a fishing reserve, see Peter Borrelli, *Stellwagen: The Making and Unmaking of a National Marine Sanctuary* (Hanover, 2009), which examines a reserve in Massachusetts Bay between 1992 and 2008.

5. *Economist*, 3 January 2009, 16.

6. *Economist*, 25 April 2009, 58; *Wall Street Journal*, 26 May 2009, A13.

7. UNFAO, "State of World Fisheries, 2006," 22; "State of World Fisheries, 2008,"

30. On fisheries in Indian waters, see Rohan Dominic Mathews, "Indian Fisheries: A Historical Alternative," Centre for Civil Society, New Delhi, 2005, Social Science Research Network Working Paper, http://papers.ssrn.com/sol3/papers.cfm?abstract_id=861825, accessed 21 June 2011. In 2001, India had a fishing fleet of 280,491 vessels, of which 181,284 were traditional, 44,578 were motorized traditional craft, and 53,684 were mechanized vessels. Some 6 million Indians were employed in fishing. Rohan proposed a two-tier system of regulation, with individual transferable quotas for modern trawlers and some sort of community-based management system for more traditional vessels.

8. UNFAO, "State of World Fisheries, 2008," 30.

9. On Senegal's experience, see Clover, *The End of the Line*, 46–51. On over-fishing in western African waters, see *New York Times*, "Empty Seas," 14, 15 January 2008; *Wall Street Journal*, 18 July 2007, A1, A13.

10. *Columbus Dispatch*, 1 November 2009, A9.

11. UNFAO, "State of World Fisheries, 2006," 22.

12. UNFAO, "State of World Fisheries, 2008," 9, 135.

13. In an article about twentieth-century transportation developments in the United States, historian Mark Rose has astutely written, "In a polity ostensibly committed to entrepreneurship, fluid markets, sharp competition, and the inherent right of managers to guide their firms, lawmakers had created a vast, complex, and formidable regulatory regime." Much the same might be said about the seafood industry, particularly after 1976. Mark Rose, "The Political Economy of American Transportation," *Enterprise & Society* 10 (March 2009): 90–97, esp. 95.

14. *Columbus Dispatch*, 25 February 2010, A7; Barney Frank, "Press Release," 24 February 2010, www.house.gov/frank/pressreleases/2010/02024-10-fishermen, accessed 25 February.

15. "Catch Me if You Can," *New York Times*, 27 January 2010.

16. Andrew C. Isenberg, *The Destruction of the Bison: An Environmental History, 1750–1920* (Cambridge, 2000). See also Wayne Gard, *The Great Buffalo Hunt* (Lincoln, 1959).

17. Classic works on the cattle industry include Lewis Atherton, *The Cattle Kings* (Lincoln, 1972); Edward E. Dale, *Cow Country* (Norman, 1942); Ernest S. Osgood, *The Day of the Cattleman* (Minneapolis, 1929).

18. Paul Starrs, *Let the Cowboy Ride: Cattle Ranching in the American West* (Baltimore, 1998).

19. Dan O'Brien, *Buffalo for the Broken Heart: Restoring Life to a Black Hills Ranch* (New York, 2001).

20. Judd, *Common Lands, Common People*.

21. Philip C. Brown, *Cultivating Commons: Joint Ownership of Arable Land in Early Modern Japan* (Honolulu, 2011).

22. Donald Pisani, *Water, Land, and Law in the West: The Limits of Public Policy, 1850–1920* (Lawrence, 1996).

23. Ostrom, *Governing the Commons*, xv, 1. For another pioneering work, see Panel on Common Property Resource Management, National Research Council, *Proceedings of the Conference on Common Property Resource Management, Washington, D.C., 21–26 April 1985* (Washington, D.C., 1986).

24. Ostrom, *Governing*, 90–91.

25. TACs and ITQs have not always led to sustainability in fisheries worldwide. Edward Garrity, a faculty member in business management at Canisius College, observed, "Fisheries management is a very complex decision making area because it involves consideration of variables from biology, ecology, economics, organization or institutional design, politics and human decision making behavior, among others." He noted that a 2008 study showed that "a recent survey revealed that in 20 stocks managed by ITQ systems, 12 of the 20 stocks showed improvements in stock biomass but 8 of the 20 stocks continued to decline after ITQ implementation." The setting of too-high ITQs and a failure to adequately enforce ITQs may have been the reason some ITQ regimes did not lead to sustainable fishing. Edward Garrity, "Implementing Effective Quota Management for Sustainable ITQ Fisheries," esp. p. 1. I am indebted to Garrity for sharing his paper with me.

26. Hamilton, *Trucking Country*, esp. chap. 7. The economic independence was often only imaginary, as fishers and independent truckers were often deeply indebted to financial institutions. The Teamsters Union and major common-carrier trucking firms opposed the deregulation of trucking, fearing competition from independents and loss of jobs.

27. Scott, *Evolution of Resource Property Rights*, 185.

28. SeaBear, "Fresh and Wild" catalog, 2010, 2.

29. "All Eyes on Iceland," *Seafood Business*, 11 August 2009.

30. "Salmon Caught in Carbon Net," *Seattle Weekly*, 14 May 2008.

31. Business historian Geoffrey Jones, a leading scholar of multinationals, observed in 2007, "The business history literature provides a caution against easy generalizations, either positive or negative, about the role and impact of global firms." He argued, "In providing empirical evidence on the complexity of historical outcomes, business history enables debates about globalization to be conducted at a more informed and nuanced level." Geoffrey Jones, "Globalization," in *The Oxford Handbook of Business History*, ed. Geoffrey Jones and Jonathan Zeitlan (New York, 2007), 141–68, esp. 161.

32. "Court OKs Initiative for Ballot," *Anchorage Daily News*, 4 July 2008; "State Confident Fish Are Protected," *Anchorage Daily News*, 15 July 2008; "Both Sides of Pebble Fight Throw Money to Lure Voters," *Anchorage Daily News*, 24 July 2008; "Measure 4 Failing by Large Margin," *Anchorage Daily News*, 27 August 2008; "Will Environmental Regulations Protect World's Largest Salmon Run if Pebble Mine Develops Near Bay?" *Kodiak Daily Mirror*, 17 August 2008; "Coalition Sues to Block Pebble Mine Permits," *Anchorage Daily News*, 29 July 2009.

33. On the history of conflicts between oil men and fishers in Alaska, see Mansel S. Blackford, *Pathways to the Present: U.S. Development and Its Consequences in the Pacific*

(Honolulu, 2007), 114–21. On recent developments, see "Politicians, Oil Reps, Environmentalists Play Tug-of-War over Development," *Kodiak Daily Mirror*, 16 April 2008. However, a proposal by the U.S. Minerals Management Service to open the North Aleutian Basin to oil and gas leasing in 2011 caused considerable controversy. See "Borough Hesitates Backing Bristol Bay Petroleum Lease," *Anchorage Daily News*, 17 June 2009.

34. Samuel P. Hays, *Beauty, Health, and Permanence: Environmental Politics in the United States, 1955–1985* (Cambridge, 1987).

BIBLIOGRAPHIC ESSAY

This study draws on a wide range of primary and secondary sources, as indicated in the notes for each chapter. In this bibliographic essay, I highlight those sources which have been most valuable to me and which might lead readers into additional avenues of thought. Much remains to be done on the topics of fishers, over-fishing, and seafood chains.

Recent studies about oceanic history have helped inform my work. See especially W. Jeffrey Bolster, "Opportunities in Marine Environmental History," *Environmental History* 11 (July 2006): 567–97; W. Jeffrey Bolster, "Putting the Ocean in Atlantic History: Maritime Communities and Marine Ecology in the Northwest Atlantic, 1500–1800," *American Historical Review* 113 (February 2008): 19–47; Rainier Buschmann, *Oceans in World History* (New York, 2007); "Forum: Oceans of the World," *American Historical Review* 111 (June 2006): 717–80; and Helen M. Rozwadowski, "Forum: Ocean's Depths," *Environmental History* 15 (July 2010): 520–25. See also Karen Wigen, Jeremy Bentham, and Renate Bridenthal, eds., *Seascapes, Littoral Cultures, and Trans-Oceanic Exchanges* (Honolulu, 2007). Those interested in connections among changes in fishing technologies, marine science, and the law of the sea will find R. R. Churchill, *The Law of the Sea* (Manchester, 1999); and D. H. Cushing, *The Provident Sea* (Cambridge, 1988), valuable.

Numerous semipopular accounts about global over-fishing exist. I found especially valuable Carl Safina, *Song for the Blue Ocean: Encounters Along the World's Coasts and Beneath the Seas* (New York, 1997); and Charles Clover, *The End of the Line: How Over-Fishing Is Changing the World and What We Eat* (New York, 2006). There are also many scientific reports on the topic. The two most important are Carl Safina, "The World's Imperiled Fish," *Scientific American* 24 (November 1995): 46–53, reprinted in Lewis A. Owen and Tim Unwin, eds., *Environmental Management: Readings and Case Studies* (Oxford, 1997), 28–34; and Boris Worm et al., "Impacts of Biodiversity Loss on Ocean Ecosystem Services," *Science* 314 (November 3, 2006): 787–90.

Reports compiled by the UNFAO are also valuable. William B. McCloskey, Jr., *Their Fathers' Work: Casting Nets with the World's Fishermen* (New York, 1998), looks at fishing worldwide from the point-of-view of a practitioner.

While attracting considerable notice, none of these works caught national attention the way Rachel Carson's *Silent Spring* did in 1962. None led to popular outrage against unsustainable fishing practices or sparked a widespread movement to conserve fish. Fish lacked the appeal of birds, whose eggs were destroyed by DDT. More "cuddly" and more intelligent than fish, oceanic mammals such as whales, even killer whales (orca), have garnered human sympathy, as seen in the movie *Free Willy*, and have received more international protection than fish. Douglas Abrams, *Eye of the Whale* (New York, 2009), a fictional eco-thriller, features communications between humans and whales, but not fish, and asks of humankind, "Can we survive as a species?"

One group of researchers, composed of scientists and humanists, has provided some historical background on fisheries, members of the History of Marine Animal Populations (HMAP) project. These scholars have prepared a "Census of Marine Life" in "a research program designed to assess and explain the diversity, distribution and abundance of marine life in the oceans." Based in universities in Denmark, the United States, and Great Britain since 2001, members of this group have examined global fishing via case studies. See H-MAP, "History of Marine Animal Populations," at http://akira.ruc.dk/~marboe/hmap/hmappros.html, accessed 16 November 2006. Some scholars have criticized this group. Historian Lance Van Sittert has concluded, "HMAP's primary focus on quantification and building a historical data base has tended to restrict 'context' to the verification of historical time series and rendered the humanists the data serfs of 'scientist' model lords." See Lance Van Sittert, "The Other Seven Tenths," *Environmental History* 10 (January 2005): 106–9, especially 107.

For encyclopedic accounts on the development of fishing in the waters of the Pacific Northwest and Alaska, consult Robert J. Browning, *Fisheries of the North Pacific: History, Species, Gear & Processes* (Anchorage, 1974); and Terry Johnson, *Ocean Treasure: Commercial Fishing in Alaska* (Fairbanks, 2003). The many reports of the North Pacific Fishery Management Council are of great value for anyone seeking an understanding of the recent rationalization of fishing in Alaska. Newspapers, especially the *Anchorage Daily News* and *Kodiak Daily Mirror*, are useful sources of information about recent fishing trends in Alaskan waters.

Specific works deal with fishing for salmon and sardines. On salmon, see especially Joseph E. Taylor, III, *Making Salmon: An Environmental History of the Northwest Fisheries Crisis* (Seattle, 1999); and David F. Arnold, *Fishermen's Frontier: People and Salmon in Southeast Alaska* (Seattle, 2008). On the salmon-canning industry, see Chris Friday, *Organizing Asian American Labor: The Pacific Coast Canned-Salmon Industry, 1870–1942* (Philadelphia, 1994). For a pathbreaking, comprehensive approach to fishery issues, see Arthur McEvoy, *Fisherman's Problem: Ecology and Law in the California Fisheries, 1850–1980* (Cambridge, 1986). Useful first-hand accounts of fishing for salmon include Bert Bender, *Catching the Ebb: Drift-fishing for a Life in Cook Inlet* (Corvallis, 2008); Francis E. Caldwell, *Pacific Troller: Life on the Northwest Fishing Grounds* (Anchorage, 1978); Bill Carter, *Red Summer: The Danger, Madness, and Exaltation of Salmon Fishing in a Remote Alaskan Village* (New York, 2008); Bob Durr, *Down in Bristol Bay: High Tides, Hangovers, and Harrowing Experiences on Alaska's Last Frontier* (New York, 1999); and Joe Upton, *Alaska Blues: A Fisherman's Journal* (Anchorage, 1977).

My *Pioneering a Modern Small Business: Wakefield Seafoods and the Alaskan Frontier* (Greenwich, 1979) provides an introduction to the history of Alaska's king-crab fishery. Valuable first-hand accounts include Spike Walker, *Working on the Edge* (New York, 1991); Andy and Johnathan Hillstrand, *Time Bandit: Two Brothers, the Bering Sea, and One of the World's Deadliest Jobs* (New York, 2008); and Sig Hansen (with Mark Sundeen), *North by Northwestern: A Seafaring Family on Deadly Alaskan Waters* (New York, 2010). Dan Weeks, *Deadliest Catch* (Des Moines, 2008), reprints interviews with crabbers. Becky Mansfield's articles dealing with whiting and pollock are good places to start in trying to understand the modern-day bottom-fish industries of the Pacific Coast and Alaska.

Fictional accounts are valuable. On the decline of the Atlantic fisheries, see E. Annie Proulx, *The Shipping News* (New York, 1994), a Pulitzer Prize winner. Michelle Chalfoun, *The Width of the Sea* (New York, 2001), and Donna Morrissey, *Sylvanus Now* (New York, 2005), are also set in cod-fishing communities, in modern-day New England and Newfoundland. On salmon fishing in California's waters, see Michael Koepf, *The Fisherman's Son* (New York, 1998). On Alaskan fishing, see McCloskey's trilogy: *Highliners: A Novel* (New York, 1979), *Breakers: A Novel About the Commercial Fishermen of Alaska* (Guilford, 2000), and *Raiders: A Novel* (Guilford, 2004). For a look at a dying fishing town on the Texas Gulf of Mexico, see William J. Cobb, *Goodnight, Texas* (Denver, 2006).

My volume is partially informed by the literature on economic globalization. Those writings include Jagdish Bhagwati, *In Defense of Globalization* (New York, 2004), an optimistic account; Michael Goldman, *Imperial Nature* (New Haven, 2005), which makes connections between global and local environmental and economic changes; A. G. Hopkins, ed., *Globalization in World History* (New York, 2002), a collection of essays spanning millennia; Thomas Friedman, *The Lexus and the Olive Tree* (New York, 2000), a journalistic account, which I think is more valuable than his later ones; Joseph Stiglitz, *Globalization and Its Discontents* (New Haven, 2005); and Martin Wolf, *Why Globalization Works* (New York, 2003).

Similarly, recent works on the history of food chains have influenced my approach. Warren Belasco and Roger Horowitz, eds., *Food Chains: From Farmyard to Shopping Cart* (Philadelphia, 2008), serves as an excellent introduction. See also Susanne Freidberg, *Fresh: A Perishable History* (Cambridge, 2009); and Philip McMichael, ed., *The Global Restructuring of Agro-Food Systems* (Ithaca, 1994). On specific food chains, see Douglas Sackman, *Orange Empire: California and the Fruits of Eden* (Berkeley, 2005), and John Souri, *Banana Cultures: Agriculture, Consumption, and Environmental Change in Honduras and the United States* (Austin, 2005). More generally on food trends in the United States, see Harvey Levenstein, *Paradox of Plenty: A Social History of Eating in Modern America* (New York, 1993); Warren Belasco, *Food: The Key Concepts* (New York, 2008); and Michael Pollan, *The Omnivore's Dilemma: A Natural History of Four Meals* (New York, 2007). The summer 2009 *Business History Review* is devoted to articles on the history of food; and the April 2009 *Environmental History* contains a forum on food.

Works valuable for comparative purposes, studies dealing with natural-resource issues include Samuel P. Hayes, *Conservation and the Gospel of Efficiency: The Progressive Conservation Movement, 1890–1920* (New York, 1969), and J. R. McNeill, *Something New Under the Sun: An Environmental History of the Twentieth-Century World* (New York, 2000). Anthony Scott, *The Evolution of Resource Property Rights* (Oxford, 2008); Elinor Ostrom, *Governing the Commons: The Evolution of Institutions for Collective Action* (Cambridge, 1990); and Herbert Reid and Betsy Taylor, *Recovering the Commons: Democracy, Place, and Global Justice* (Urbana, 2010), look at matters surrounding common-pool resource management. Theodore Bestor, *Tsukiji: The Fish Market at the Center of the World* (Berkeley, 2004), examines important aspects of fisheries developments in Japan.

Finally, I would like to also thank the people who took the time to talk with me in oral-history interviews: Steve Fink, Margaret Kohler, Derek Lawson, Catherine McCarthy, Michael McCarthy, William McCloskey, Jr., and Joseph Plesha. I conducted the interviews under Institutional Review Board protocols established by The Ohio State University, with the protocol number 2009E0270.

INDEX

Italicized page numbers indicate maps and illustrations.

Commercial Fishing Industry Vessel Safety
Act of 1988, 109, 239n52

commodity chains, 188–89. *See also* food
chains; seafood chains

Common Fisheries Policy (European Union),
202

common-pool resource management, 6, 102,
120, 201, 205–10; Alaskan waters and, 6,
208–9. *See also* tragedy of the commons

Community Development Quotas. *See* CDQs

community quota system, 139–41

ConAgra Foods, 5, 160–62, 164, 217, 246n17.
See also processor-supplier companies

Connors Brothers Income Fund, 168–69, 217

conservation: farming fish and, 198–99;
FCMA and, 3–4, 25; global political economies and, 7, 223n13; king crabbing recovery and, 118–19, 148; North Pacific and,
69; NPFMC critiques and, 51; over-fishing
versus fishers' support for, 11; regulatory
regimes and, 24–25; retailing to consumers
and, 197, 214; United Nations and, 3–4, 39,
69. *See also* habitat degradation; natural
phenomena effects; *specific environmental
groups*

continental shelves: Alaskan waters and, 53,
100; dimensions of, 53; 200-mile limit and,
x, 3, 19–20, 69, 226n47; 200-mile limit including fisheries over, 20, 100–101, 238n25

cooperatives, 101–2, 120, 210. *See also*
common-pool resource management

Cronon, William, 222n6

Cussler, Clyde, 16

Deadliest Catch (television program), 106–7.
See also king crabbing

dead zone, Gulf of Mexico, 41, 42, 104. *See
also* shrimp and shrimpers in Gulf of
Mexico

Del Monte, 160

derby fishing (Olympic fishing): overview
and definition of, 25–26; halibut fishing
and, 126, 132–33; king crabbing and, 105;
safety issues and, 26, 80, 112–13, 235n61;
salmon fishing and, 79–80, *80*, 86, 88,
112–13, 116, 126; technological innovations and, 26; tragedy of the commons
and, 25–26

deregulation policies, 24, 82, 209–10, 253n26.
See also United States regulations

Dew, C. Braxton, 116

diets and lifestyles. *See* lifestyles and diets

Dulcich, Frank, Jr., 155–56, 161, 167, 247n45.
See also Pacific Seafood Group

Dulcich, Frank, Sr., 167

Durr, Bob, 75–76

Eaton, Bart, 22, 49, 120, 163, *163*. *See also*
Trident Seafoods

economic and social costs of sustainable fishing: overview, xii, 6; for Alaskan Natives,
83, 85, 88–90, 139, 140, 212; bottom fishing and, 139–42; cod fishing in North Atlantic and, 150; king crabbing and, 119–20;
salmon fishing in Alaskan waters and, 83,
85, 88–90; women and, 6, 60, 85, 90, 212

economics of fishing: overview, 7–8; assistance from institutions, 95, 103, 131,
253n26; bottom fish and, 131, 133; business development and, 6, 203–5, 252n13;
business historians' perspectives and, 7–8,
223n13; economic sustainability concerns
and, 150; farming fish and, 87; FCMA and,
22–23; fisheries, 7–8; halibut fishing and,
133; king crabbing and, 95, 97, 103, 105–6;
North Pacific and, 48–49; sablefish and, 83.
See also global political economies; markets and marketing

EEZs (exclusive economic zones), 20–21, 25,
33, 203, 211

Ellis, Richard, 38

employment opportunities, 16–17, 25–26,
76–77, 93, 135–39. *See also* canned-salmon
industry; lived experiences for laborers;
processing seafood; retailing to consumers

entrepreneurs. *See* business leaders

environmental activism, 145–48. *See also
specific groups*

environmentalism. *See* conservation

environmental justice movement, 26–27,
64–67, 213

Environmental Protection Agency, 25

escapement periods, 79, 81. *See also* salmon
fishing in Alaskan waters

EU (European Union), 202–3, 211–12

exclusive economic zones (EEZs), 20–21, 25,
33, 203, 211

factory trawlers, 24, 30–32, *31*. *See also*
trawlers

International North Pacific Fisheries Com-
  mission. *See* INPFC
International Pacific Halibut Commission.
  See IPHC
International Pacific Salmon Fisheries Com-
  mission, 18, 232n11
international regulatory regimes, 19–21. *See
  also specific regimes*
International Seabed Authority, 225n33
IPHC (International Pacific Halibut Com-
  mission), 18, 124–25, 241n8
IPQs (individual processing quotas), 118
ITQs (individual transferable quotas), 25–27,
  253n25

Japan, 12–13, 18, 48; ad hoc regulatory agreements with, 18, 100, 238n25; continental
  shelf 200-mile limit and, 69, 226n47,
  238n25; global seafood sales and, 159,
  245n10; halibut fishing in Northeast Pacific and, 124–25, 241n8; joint ventures
  with, 85–86, 103–5, 114–15, 125, 129,
  130, 134, 159–60; king crabbing and, 100,
  102, 238n25; limited-entry fishing and,
  18–19, 69, 226n47, 238n25; limited-entry
  fishing in North Pacific and, 125; NPFMC
  limited-entry fishing and, 48; over-fishing
  blue-fin tuna and, 38, 39, 40; quality and
  hygienic safety and, 86; salmon fishing in
  Alaskan waters and, 69, 87; statistics for
  catches and, 18, 47, 48, 87, 231n68. *See also*
  foreign fishers; *specific companies*
joint ventures: with Canada, 124–25, 241n7;
  for halibut fishing, 124–25, 241n7; with
  Japanese processors, 85–86, 103–5, 114–
  15, 125, 129, *130*, 134, 159–60; for king
  crabbing, 103–4, 114–15; for maximum
  sustainable yields, 124–25, 241n7; NPFMC
  debates and, 129; for pollock fishing, 129,
  130, 133–34; for salmon fishing in Alaskan
  waters, 85–86, 103–5
Jones, Geoffrey, 253n31

king crabbing: overview and history of, *2*,
  90–93, *94*, 99, 121, 237n4; Alaskan Natives
  and, 93; Alaska statehood effects and, 100;
  arbitration organizations and, 118, 186;
  business leaders and, 95; collapse of, 99,
  115–16, 148; continental shelf 200-mile
  limit including fisheries and, 100–101,

238n25; cooperatives and, 102, 120; derby
  fishing and, 105; economic and social costs
  of sustainable fishing and, 119–20; economics of fishing and, 95, 97, 103, 105–6;
  fast-freezing process and, 95–96, 180–81,
  183; FCMA and, x, 102, 116; fisher-
  processor relations and, 185–87, 186–87;
  foreign fishers and, 102–3; gear conflicts
  and, 99–100; global political economies
  and, 102–3; inequities and, 92, 118; Japan
  and, 100, 102, 238n25; joint ventures and,
  103–4, 114–15; Kodiak, Alaska and, 93, *94*,
  100, 114, 120; limited-entry fishing and,
  20; lived experiences for fishers and, 95,
  96–97, *101*, 104–11, 113–15, 120; marketing and sales and, 97–99, 118, 187, 240n78;
  NPFM and, 92, 102–3; open-access fishing
  and, 90, 119, 121; over-fishing and, 1, 99;
  price fixing and, 118; processing seafood
  and, 180–84, *182*; processor-trawlers and,
  95–96, *97*, 180; purse-seining and, 109,
  113; quality and hygienic safety and, 191–
  92; quota system and, 100, 117–20, 160,
  186; rationalization plan and, 117–20,
  148, 160, 186; regulatory regimes and, 20,
  100–102, 110–11; safety issues and, 91, 97,
  105–11, 235n61, 239nn52,54; statistics for
  catches and, 99, 100, 116, 150; sustainable
  fishing and, 52, 115–19, 148; technological innovations and, 95–96, *96*, 104, 109;
  trawling and, 95–96, *96*, 97, 99, 116;
  under-utilized fisheries access for foreign
  fishers and, 102; women and, 92. *See also*
  snow crabs (tanner crabs)
Kipling, Rudyard, 30
Klamath River salmon runs, 45, 67. *See also*
  California waters
Kodiak, Alaska: bottom fishing and, 124, 127,
  136, 141–42; canned-salmon industry and,
  67; community quota system and, 141;
  derby fishing and, 113; fisher-company
  relations, 186; king crabbing and, 93, *94*,
  100, 114, 120; lived experiences for fishers
  and, 79; map, *50*; quota system, 83; regulatory regimes, 100; salmon fisheries, 109,
  112; sustainable fishing, 149
Koepf, Michael, *The Fisherman's Son*, 44–46,
  175
Kohler, Margaret, 123, 142–44, 243n57
Krenz, Chris, 145–47

ACKNOWLEDGMENTS

Few studies in history are truly individual efforts, for nearly all build in part upon the works of earlier scholars. Most historians also depend on the suggestions of others to help them define and clarify their thoughts. I certainly do. I would like to thank William Childs, William B. McCloskey, Jr., and Tom Weeks for their comments on earlier drafts of this work. I would like to thank as well Mark Rose, who took the lead for the editors of the book series in which this volume appears, and Robert Lockhart, Senior History Editor for the University of Pennsylvania Press, for their many insights and suggestions. Arthur McEvoy, the outside reader for the Press, also deserves my thanks for his comments. I remain, of course, solely responsible for any errors of fact or interpretations which this work may contain.

I presented parts of this information in seminars at the Eleutherian-Mills Hagley Foundation and the Harvard Business School in the fall of 2008 and would like to thank the participants of those seminars for their thoughts. Some of the themes developed in this book were foreshadowed in Chapter 4 of my *Pathways to the Present: U.S. Development and Its Consequences in the Pacific*; in my "Business Historians and the Global Over Fishing Crisis: Opportunities for Research," which I presented at the 2008 meeting of the Business History Conference, and in two published articles: "A Tale of Two Fisheries: Fishing and Over Fishing in American Waters," *Origins* 11 (September 2008): 1–5, www.ehistory.edu/osu/origins, and "Fishers, Fishing, and Over Fishing: American Experiences in Global Perspective, 1976–2006," *Business History Review* (Summer 2009): 239–66.

As always, I am indebted to my colleagues in the Department of History at The Ohio State University for creating a stimulating atmosphere in which to work. On this project, I am especially grateful to Philip Brown for discussions about the history of the management of common-pool resources. Finally, I would like to thank the College of the Arts and Humanities at The Ohio State University for released time from teaching and service in 2009 to conduct research on this project.

LITERATURE & WRITING WORKSHOP

EXPLORING
LYRIC
POETRY

SCHOLASTIC INC.

ISBN 0-590-49304-3

CONTENTS

4

NATURE

Illustrated by
Ellen Joy Sasaki

In Quiet Night
Myra Cohn Livingston

In quiet night
the horns honking up from the street
make mad voices
to other horns, tires shriek
to other tires, brakes shriek
to other brakes.

Somewhere, there is a night of trees,
of great, bulging bullfrogs croaking
in ponds. Screech owls cry to a forest
of birds
      shrieking.

Horns, in quiet night, honk up songs
no frog, no bird, has ever sung.

April Rain Song
Langston Hughes

Let the rain kiss you.
Let the rain beat upon your head with silver liquid drops.
Let the rain sing you a lullaby.

The rain makes still pools on the sidewalk.
The rain makes running pools in the gutter.
The rain plays a little sleep-song on our roof at night—

And I love the rain.

April

Sara Teasdale

The roofs are shining from the rain,
    The sparrows twitter as they fly,
And with a windy April grace
    The little clouds go by.

Yet the backyards are bare and brown
    With only one unchanging tree—
I could not be so sure of Spring
    Save that it sings in me.

The Sea
James Reeves

The sea is a hungry dog,
Giant and grey.
He rolls on the beach all day.
With his clashing teeth and shaggy jaws
Hour upon hour he gnaws
The rumbling, tumbling stones,
And 'Bones, bones, bones, bones!'
The giant sea-dog moans,
Licking his greasy paws.

And when the night wind roars
And the moon rocks in the stormy cloud,
He bounds to his feet and snuffs and sniffs,
Shaking his wet sides over the cliffs,
And howls and hollos long and loud.

But on quiet days in May or June,
When even the grasses on the dune
Play no more their reedy tune,
With his head between his paws
He lies on the sandy shores,
So quiet, so quiet, he scarcely snores.

The Fall Of Plum Blossoms
Rankō

I came to look, and lo!
The plum tree petals scatter down,
A fall of purest snow.

Theme In Yellow

Carl Sandburg

I spot the hills
With yellow balls in autumn.
I light the prairie cornfields
Orange and tawny gold clusters
And I am called pumpkins.
On the last of October
When dusk is fallen
Children join hands
And circle round me
Singing ghost songs
And love to the harvest moon;
I am a jack-o'-lantern
With terrible teeth
And the children know
I am fooling.

The River Is A Piece Of Sky

John Ciardi

From the top of a bridge
The river below
Is a piece of sky—
    Until you throw
    a penny in
    Or a cockleshell
    Or a pebble or two
    Or a bicycle bell
    Or a cobblestone
    Or a fat man's cane—
And then you can see
It's a river again.

The difference you'll see
When you drop your penny:
The river has splashes,
The sky hasn't any.

The Hurricane

Pales Matos
Translated by Alida Malkus

When the hurricane unfolds
Its fierce accordion of winds,
On the tip of its toes,
Agile dancer, it sweeps whirling
Over the carpeted surface of the sea
With the scattered branches of the palm.

Silver

Walter de la Mare

Slowly, silently, now the moon
Walks the night in her silver shoon;
This way, and that, she peers, and sees
Silver fruit upon silver trees;
One by one the casements catch
Her beams beneath the silvery thatch;
Couched in his kennel, like a log,
With paws of silver sleeps the dog;
From their shadowy cote the white breasts peep
Of doves in a silver-feathered sleep;
A harvest mouse goes scampering by,
With silver claw, and silver eye;
And moveless fish in the water gleam,
By silver reeds in a silver stream.

The Rum Tum Tugger

T. S. *Eliot*

The Rum Tum Tugger is a Curious Cat:
If you offer him pheasant he would rather have grouse.
If you put him in a house he would much prefer a flat,
If you put him in a flat then he'd rather have a house.
If you set him on a mouse then he only wants a rat,   ~,.
If you set him on a rat then he'd rather chase a mouse.
Yes the Rum Tum Tugger is a Curious Cat—
   And there isn't any call for me to shout it:
      For he will do
      As he do do
         And there's no doing anything about it!

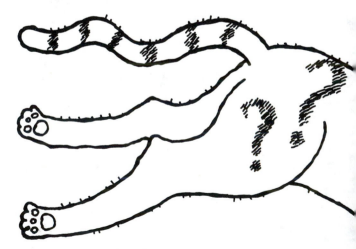

NATURE

The Rum Tum Tugger is a terrible bore:
When you let him in, then he wants to be out;
He's always on the wrong side of every door,
As soon as he's at home, then he'd like to get about.
He likes to lie in the bureau drawer,
But he makes such a fuss if he can't get out.
Yes the Rum Tum Tugger is a Curious Cat—
   And it isn't any use for you to doubt it:
      For he will do
      As he do do
         And there's no doing anything about it!

The Rum Tum Tugger is a curious beast:
His disobliging ways are a matter of habit.
If you offer him fish then he always wants a feast;
When there isn't any fish then he won't eat rabbit.
If you offer him cream then he sniffs and sneers,
For he only likes what he finds for himself;
So you'll catch him in it right up to the ears,
If you put it away on the larder shelf.
The Rum Tum Tugger is artful and knowing,
The Rum Tum Tugger doesn't care for a cuddle;
But he'll leap on your lap in the middle of your sewing,
For there's nothing he enjoys like a horrible muddle.
Yes the Rum Tum Tugger is a Curious Cat—
　　And there isn't any need for me to spout it:
　　　　For he will do
　　　　As he do do
　　　　　　And there's no doing anything about it!

NATURE

The Grass
Emily Dickinson

The grass so little has to do,—
  A sphere of simple green,
With only butterflies to brood,
  And bees to entertain,

And stir all day to pretty tunes
  The breezes fetch along,
And hold the sunshine in its lap
  And bow to everything;

And thread the dews all night, like pearls,
  And make itself so fine,—
A duchess were too common
  For such a noticing.

And even when it dies, to pass
  In odours so divine,
As lowly spices gone to sleep,
  Or amulets of pine.

And then to dwell in sovereign barns,
  And dream the days away,—
The grass so little has to do,
  I wish I were the hay!

The Grass On The Mountain

From the Paiute American Indian
Transcribed by Mary Austin

Oh, long long
The snow has possessed the mountains.

The deer have come down and the big-horn,
They have followed the Sun to the south
To feed on the mesquite pods and the bunch grass.
Loud are the thunderdrums
In the tents of the mountains.
Oh, long long
Have we eaten chia seeds
And dried deer's flesh of the summer killing.
We are wearied of our huts
And the smoky smell of our garments.

We are sick with desire of the sun
And the grass on the mountain.